LEICESTERSHIRE
FIELDWORKERS
Bringing archaeology to life

The Medieval Earthworks of Rutland

by Robert F. Hartley

Foreword by
Tim Clough

Editing and layout by Kathleen Elkin
on behalf of Leicestershire Fieldworkers

Monograph No 5

2023

ISBN 978-0-9548200-4-6

Published by Leicestershire Fieldworkers, Leicester 2023

Printing by 4Word, Bristol

Cover design and illustration and Psalter figures by Maureen Hallahan

The front and rear cover illustrations are based on an original plan of the manor of Lyndon in the county of Rutland reproduced in his book *Geodaetes Practicus* of 1664 by Vincent Wing, astrologer, astronomer and professional land surveyor. The full plan from the book is on page vii courtesy of and copyright The Science Museum Group.
The medieval figure on the front page design, on the rear cover and in the text are based on those in the margins in the Rutland Psalter now in the British Library, London. It is the earliest surviving example of an English Psalter and dates to around 1260 (BL Add MS 62925).

Leicestershire Fieldworkers

Leicestershire Fieldworkers is an active county archaeology society that supports individuals and local groups in Leicestershire and Rutland to investigate the remains of past human activity by practical investigation, research and small-scale excavation. It provides a forum for interested individuals to come together to hear the results of the latest research both locally and nationally and provides assistance to professional archaeologists in the field and by reporting fieldwork results to the Heritage and Environment Record (HER).

CONTENTS

Frontispiece - Plan of the Manor of Lyndon by Vincent Wing	vii
Introduction and acknowledgements - Kathleen Elkin	ix
Dedication of this volume to Anthony Squires (1940 - 1921)	xi
Foreword - Tim Clough, Honorary Editor, Rutland Local Record and History Society	xiii
Robert F Hartley - About the author	xv
Introduction to Medieval Rutland - Robert F Hartley	xvii
Gazetteer	1 - 88
The Landscape Maps	89 - 106
References	107
Abbreviations	109

Gazetteer index

Site names listed in the gazetteer are indexed together with locations whose name differs from their civil parish name. DMV = Deserted medieval village.

Alstoe DMV 12
Ashwell 1
Ayston 2
Barleythorpe Ponds 58
Barn Hill, Hambleton 35
Barnsdale Deer Park 30
Barrow 3
Barrowden 4
Beaumont Chase 5
Belmesthorpe DMV 65
Belton-in-Rutland 6
Bisbrooke 6
Braunston 6
Brooke 7
Burley-on-the-Hill 12
Caldecott 12
Catmose Water Mill 59
Clipsham 14
Cottesmore 18
Edith Weston 20
Egleton 21
Empingham 22
Essendine 25
Exton 26
Flitteris Park 59
Fregthorpe DMV 36
Geeston 36
Glaston 31

Great Casterton 31
Greetham 32
Gunthorpe 32
Hambleton 34
Hardwick DMV 24
Horn 35
Horn Water Mill 30
Ingthorpe DMV 80
Ketton 36
Kilthorpe Grange 41
Langham 42
Leighfield 42
Little Casterton 44
Luffenham, North & South 46
Lyddington 48
Lyndon 50
Market Overton 53
Martinsthorpe 53
Morcott 55
Morcott Spinney 46
Normanton 55
North Luffenham 46
Oakham & Barleythorpe 56
Pickworth 60
Pilton 63
Preston 65
Ryhall 65
Sculthorpe DMV 46
Seaton 67
Snelston 12
South Luffenham 48
St Mary's Well 59
Stoke Dry 70
Stocken Hall DMV 71
Stocken Park 72
Stretton 70
Teigh 74
Thistleton 76
Thorpe By Water 76
Tickencote 76
Tinwell 80
Tixover 81
Tolethorpe Hall 44
Top Pickworth DMV 62
Uppingham 82
Wardley 82
Wenton DMV 18
Whissendine 83
Whitwell 87
Wing 88
Woodhead Castle 31

Landscape Maps Overview 89

Map 1 Whissendine 90
Map 2 Ashwell, Market Overton 91
Map 3 Cottesmore, Thistleton 92
Map 4 Clipsham 93
Map 5 Pickworth 94
Map 6 Essendine, Rythall 95
Map 7 Braunston, Langham 96
Map 8 Oakham, Hambleton 97
Map 9 Exton, Whitwell 98
Map 10 Empingham, Tickencote 99
Map 11 Ryhall, Tinwell, Casterton 100
Map 12 Leighfield, Ridlington, Belton 101
Map 13 Uppingham 102
Map 14 Seaton, Morcott, Luffenham 103
Map 15 Tixover, Ketton 104
Map 16 Caldecott, Lyddington 105
Map 17 Thorpe by Water 106

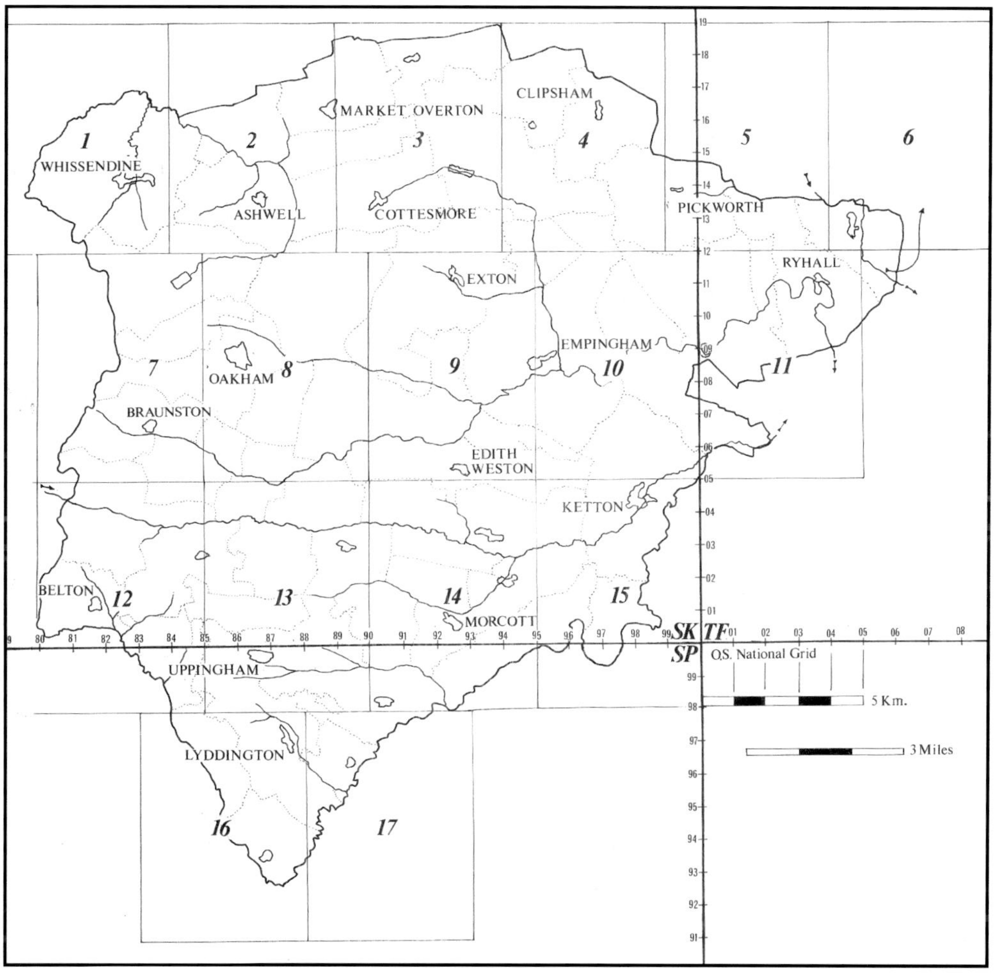

Vincent Wing

Vincent Wing was born at North Luffenham, Rutland, in 1619, the eldest of four sons of Vincent Wing, farmer and astronomer. Wing was not university educated but acquired a working knowledge of Latin, Greek and mathematics. He became a land surveyor and invented or developed the use of the forty-link two-pole chain for measuring tracts of land in rods and poles, a method explained in his books (source: en.wikipedia/wiki/Vincent_Wing). Wing was the author of several works; his *Harmonicon Coeleste*: *or The Coelestiall Harmony of the Visible World:...*, was published in 1651: *Astronomia Britannica*, his chief and most useful work, appeared in 1652. His *Astronomical Almanac*, which was in the press at the time of his death in 1668, contains a mass of information on astrology, astronomy, and mathematics, and his *Almanacs* continued to be published at intervals until 1805 (VCHR 2, 196).

The Wing family had a long association with the Barker family of North and South Luffenham and in 1662 Abel and Thomas Barker of Hambleton bought the Lyndon estate for £9400 (Waites 1999, 8, also see Gazetteer entry for Lyndon). Vincent Wing was probably commissioned to provide a plan of the manor when the land was purchased and used a portion of the plan in his 1664 book *Geodaetes Practicus, Or, The Art of Surveying*, for illustrative purposes. Further information on Wing and astrology can be found in Vincent Wing and Political Astrology (Capp 2010, 386).

Vincent Wing died in 1668 and was buried at North Luffenham. Tycho Wing, the philosopher and astronomer, whose portrait is in the Hall of the Stationers' Company, was descended from Moses Wing, the younger brother of Vincent (VCHR 2, 196).

Vincent Wing 1619 - 1668
astrologer, astronomer & professional land surveyor
A plan of Lyndon, County of Rutland

'Part of the Mannor of L(yndon) in the County of Rutland' by Vincent Wing of North Luffenham, astronomer, astrologer and professional surveyor. From *'Geodaetes Practicus, or, The Art of Surveying Surveyed and laid out in a more Accurate, Plain and Expeditious Plat, then hath hitherto been Performed : Being a WORKE very usefull for Surveyors, Architects, Engineers, Masons, Carpenters, Joyners, Brick-layers, Glasiers, Painters, &c. and generally for all them that are Ingeniously affected with such kinde of Learning. By Vincent Wing, London. Printed by Wil. Leybourn, for George Sawbridge, at the Signe of the Bible upon Ludgate-hill, 1664'.*

Note: This map does not appear in all extant copies of Geodaetes Practicus. North is to the right of the plan. A rotated version with north at the top is on page 51 for comparison with the survey of Lyndon.

INTRODUCTION AND ACKNOWLEDGEMENTS

Kathleen Elkin

In 1979 I and others from our archaeology course at the University of Leicester were sent for a week at Easter to learn landscape surveying with the Leicestershire Archaeological Survey Team comprising Peter Liddle and Robert 'Fred' Hartley. It was my first introduction to the medieval earthwork remains in the Leicestershire countryside and I had, of course, no idea that 40+ years later I would still be in the county and publishing plans in Fred Hartley's Medieval Earthworks series. Many of the surveys were done pre-1995 but in this volume on Rutland they have been updated and added to recently and the text revised. The original books were produced to provide a baseline for earthwork survival in the fields, allowing these sites to be managed through the planning process and then for work with the Countryside Stewardship scheme with which Fred was also involved.

The importance of these surveys cannot be understated. When thinking about this Introduction I asked Richard Clark, Principal Archaeologist with the Planning Service at Leicestershire County Council, what the influence of these surveys has been for Leicestershire and Rutland. He replied:

I am more than happy to confirm that Fred's work - most especially his medieval earthworks series - contributes significantly to the work of the section here, they are a regular resource and point of reference, and sit next to me as I type! Interestingly, in respect of his field work, given the elapse of time between the surveys (sometimes undertaken more than 25 years ago), and the present day, we have on a number of occasions had reason to revisit the earthworks, applying modern digital survey techniques to the recording process. In many cases the results show an on-going process of erosion particularly of those sites lacking statutory protection or designation (e.g. Scheduled Monuments or Registered Parks), most commonly within the agricultural environment, where the mechanisms of the planning process can't readily be applied.

In that context Fred's work stands as a hugely valuable point-in-time reference to the former and current earthwork landscapes of the county, a comment on the positive and negative effects of change in the agricultural environment, most especially a feature of the post-war period. In other circumstances where earthworks survive in, or close to the condition Fred recorded them, a regular feature of note is how accurate his survey has been (every bit as good as modern survey techniques), and furthermore how helpful the interpretation and knowledge he brought/ brings to each site is in informing current management. I would also note, alongside the moats, shrunken and deserted village earthworks, the country house gardens and parks, that Fred has also recorded the ordinary landscapes of medieval and early post-medieval industry and agriculture, the latter the 'Champion' landscapes of the Midland Open field system studied by Howard Gray and most recently David Hall. If anything this confirms Fred's credentials as a landscape archaeologist, a labour beyond anything I could contemplate, and represents an outstanding example of the integrated relationship of settlement and landscape, and the communities who lived and worked there (Gray 1915, Hall 2014) (Richard Clark, pers comm).

The Earthworks series began publication in 1983 with Rutland (Hartley 1983) and continued soon after with North-West Leicestershire in 1984, North-East Leicestershire (Melton District) in 1987 and Central Leicestershire (Charnwood, Leicester City, Oadby and Wigston, and Blaby) in 1989. All of these volumes were originally published by Leicestershire Museums, Arts and Records Service. Departmental and council reorganisations in both county and city then meant there was then a gap of nearly 20 years until Leicestershire Fieldworkers underwrote the cost of the next publication. The Earthworks of South-West Leicestershire (Hinckley and Bosworth) was edited and put together by me and published by the Fieldworkers in 2008 (Hartley 2008), and was the first digital version, previous volumes having been produced by the offset litho process at County Hall. Three areas then remained unpublished: Market

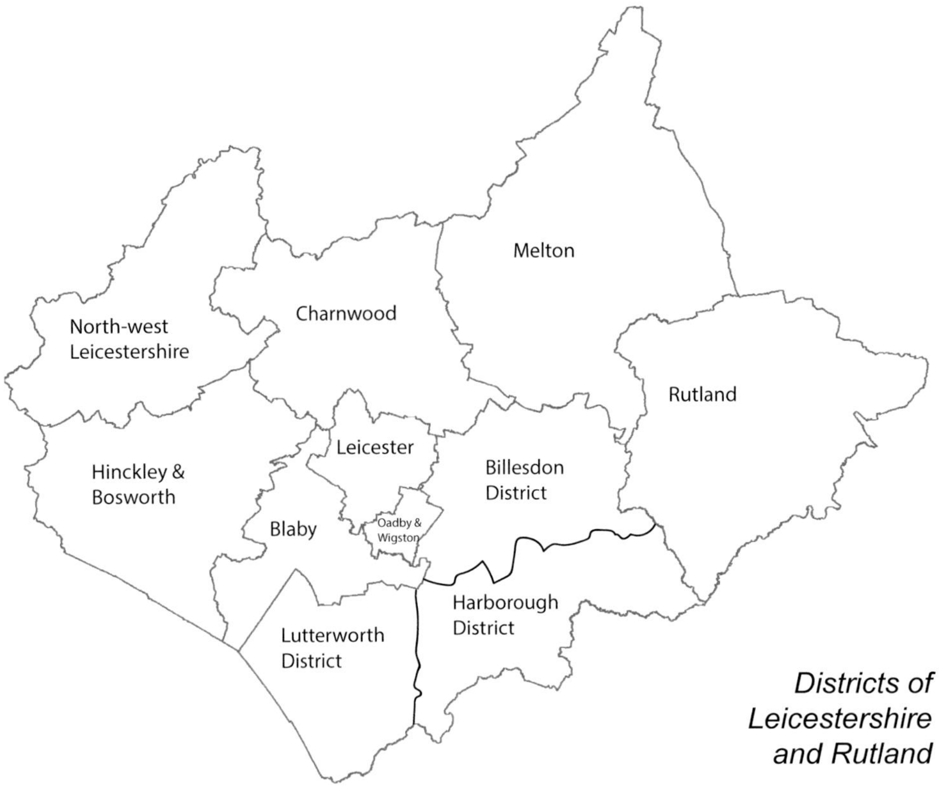

Districts of Leicestershire and Rutland

Harborough, Lutterworth and Billesdon. After publishing the papers from the Fieldworkers 'Medieval Leicestershire' conference in 2015 and as both Fred and I were by then retired from the County Council it seemed apposite that these three promised books should be undertaken. These were combined into one volume as the Medieval Earthworks of South and South-east Leicestershire, published in 2018. I thought that this series was finished, though there had been hints from Fred that he was thinking of a revised version of the Rutland book from 1983. I didn't entirely take this seriously, but it transpired that I was wrong when Peter Liddle and Fred both contacted me to ask if I would do the layout and editing for a revised Rutland volume. It seemed that during the Covid pandemic of 2020-21 Fred went back out into the field to revise and add plans to his original publication. This volume is the result and is a much expanded version with additional plans and much rewritten text.

Acknowledgements

The author would like to thank Tim Clough for writing the Foreword; the late Bob Rutland, Peter Liddle, Anne Graf, Richard Knox and Richard Clark from the County's archaeological staff, and the work of amateur fieldworkers, especially Mick Harding and the late Arthur Hurst. Thanks are due to Leicestershire Fieldworkers for taking on the cost and publication of this volume and Kathy Elkin for layout and editing of the original manuscript and digitised drawings.

The editor would like to thank Maureen Hallahan for cover design and additional artwork from the Rutland Psalter, Karolina Koziel from the Science Museum Group for her persevering efforts to get a photograph of the Vincent Wing map of Lyndon, Adam Goodwin and staff at Leicestershire, Leicester and Rutland Record Office for assistance with access to the map archive, Tim Clough for additional text checking and adding his knowledge of Rutland and to John Roost and staff of 4Word, Bristol, for final layout checks and printing.

DEDICATION OF THIS VOLUME TO ANTHONY SQUIRES 1940 - 2021

Peter Liddle - Some Memories

Peter Liddle, Chair of Leicestershire Fieldworkers, writes: Anthony Squires, a member of the Fieldworkers committee for many years, died in 2021 after a long illness borne with great good humour. Tony was born in Loughborough, taught in schools around the County and in Africa and, from his interest in natural history (he was a proud member of the Loughborough Naturalists' Club) became a gifted landscape historian, specialising in ancient woodland, deer parks and gardens. He was the author of numerous articles and books including on The Greys of Groby, Bradgate Park, Donington Park and (with Prof Len Cantor) the Medieval Parks and Gardens of Leicestershire and Rutland. He, with Ernie Miller, helped organise many of our summer trips, often leading us through the landscape, sharing his great knowledge.

What's what at Whatborough Hill in east Leicestershire. Tony Squires (left), the late Elaine Jones, leader of the Rutland Fieldwork Group, (middle) and Peter Liddle, Chair of Leicestershire Fieldworkers (right) looking at Robert F Hartley's plan of the earthworks on Whatborough Hill, East Leicestershire.

Fred Hartley has contributed these memories of Tony

At the end of his book *Leicester Forest,* Percy Russell evoked the value of the old hunting chase as a place where there was the chance of "passing beyond the bustle of the streets and of walking in peace beneath the trees" (Fox & Russell 1948, 120). I have sometimes thought that this may have inspired the young Anthony Squires, together with his involvement in the remarkable group of like-minded souls in the Loughborough Naturalists' Club.

I probably first met Tony at a meeting of the Fieldworkers at Jewry Wall Museum in 1979. He was a very regular supporter of all our events. As I began to make survey records of earthwork features Tony arranged visits to various parts of the county where he was already beginning to interpret and write up the history of woodlands and deer parks. I remember sunny days at Staunton Harold and Bagworth Moats. A day of incessant torrential rain at Ashby Old Parks left us looking like drowned rats but failed to discourage us.

Following my move to run Harborough Museum in 1995 we saw less of each other, but it was good to catch up again during 2012-2014 when we had some splendid days discovering previously hidden earthwork features in one of his favourite places - Bradgate Park. During 2020, by which time he was far from well, he was helping me by providing information about Rutland, where again were some of his favourite pieces of old woodland landscape.

I last saw Tony at the launch for the Harborough Earthworks book in 2018. He seemed genuinely surprised and honoured to be invited. Such was his modesty, I don't think he realised the extent of the quiet influence he had exerted in encouraging us all to value the natural world, and the evidence of human history that surround our towns, in the "peace beneath the trees."

Leicestershire Archaeological & Historical Society / Aubrey Stevenson, Hon. Librarian

Tony was one of the stalwarts - and one of the characters - of the local history and archaeology scene. As a naturalist and landscape historian, he had a particular interest and expertise in the history, heritage, nature and countryside of Leicestershire, and was recognised as an authority on medieval woodland, deer parks and gardens. Tony was a regular contributor to the *Leicestershire Historian,* most recently in 2020 with an article written with Chris Peat, 'Market Bosworth in Domesday Book: a cautionary approach' (Squires & Peat, 2020, 32). He contributed articles to the LAHS Transactions as well as other journals, and the Society's 'Leicester Abbey' volume (2006). References to his publications can be found on the Society's indexes on their website, in the catalogue of Leicestershire Libraries, and by googling 'Anthony Squires'. His publications are too numerous to list here but many can be found in the Society's library at the Guildhall.

Ernie Miller, Leicestershire Fieldworkers honorary member

I first met Tony at Jewry Wall. We both took the University of Leicester Certificate in Archaeology with Tony Brown in 1977 and were on the first Leicestershire Museums Archaeological Fieldwork Group Committee made up from people associated with the museum. I was Treasurer. Terry Pierce from the museum used to run summer excursions and when he stopped, we decided to continue. Tony mostly came up with the places to visit as he was so knowledgeable, and I did the driving. Except on one occasion, when we went to Shropshire and Wroxeter, all our trips were in Leicestershire and Rutland. They usually had a theme such as 'Abbeys and Priories'. We had to agree access to the site and ensure that the coach could get near, not easy with narrow lanes and low clearance. We always made sure to sample the lunches for the pub visit! I remember particularly that we managed to organise a visit for the group to Ratby Burroughs earthwork as we wrote a guide together to Ratby church and then gave the landowner's son one hundred free copies. He couldn't say 'no' after that as he owed us you see. On the day Tony retired my wife Sheila and I were sitting in the garden and Tony appeared and threw his hands up "goodbye to the lot of them!" - he was really pleased to have finished teaching. He was a great fan of Tommy Cooper, the comedian, and would mimic him and tell his jokes. He was also on the Committee of Loughborough Naturalists Club and his first writing was a contributory chapter to 'Charnwood Forest: A Changing Landscape' (Crocker 1981). Flora and fauna were his interests which led on particularly to the development of parks in the landscape.

Kathy Elkin remembers

I got to know Anthony 'Tony' Squires when I joined the committee of the Fieldworkers. Tony and Ernie Miller reconnoitred the Fieldworkers annual trip, working out the timings of the day. Tony's knowledge of Leicestershire proved invaluable and he often addressed the group at the places we were visiting. It was his retiring manner that meant I took some time to realise that he was, in fact, a prolific author with wide-ranging historical and landscape interests as well as having a science and natural history background. He was known for his work on ancient forests and medieval parks (in conjunction with Leonard Cantor) as well as his books on Donington Park and the Hastings family, Lady Jane Grey and Bradgate Park, and a book on the Grey family. In his last years he published on parks in Rutland and in detail on Leighfield Forest (Squires 1992, 2003, 2014), before turning his attention to Market Bosworth and its boundaries (Squires & Peat 2020). We became friends and I went occasionally to tea, where he would tell me very precisely what he did, and did not, want me to do when editing his paper for the Medieval Leicestershire book (Squires 2015). His research was extremely detailed and thorough and he would show me something he was working on and then say "But, my dear, I'm not going to show you the rest", at which I could only nod and say 'ok' politely without having any clue as to why that should be. Our last meeting, on one of his 'good' days, was over coffee and his favourite chocolate eclairs at his local café, and he was, as ever, full of detail about the history of the streets of Cosby that we walked through to get there. He is much missed.

FOREWORD
by Tim Clough,
Honorary Editor, Rutland Local History & Record Society
former Curator of Rutland County Museum

When I was appointed Keeper of the Rutland County Museum and took up the post on All Fools' Day 1974 – the day that England's smallest county lost its independence, even if not permanently – little did I think that I would still be living there half a century later, and still involved with its intriguing past. Still less did I think that I would have the privilege of being invited to write a Foreword to the revised edition of a seminal work on such an important aspect of Rutland's landscape archaeology as its medieval earthworks, or that it would have been written by someone who had been a colleague in the county's museum service for much of that extended period.

Although my appointment was in some ways like being thrown in at the deep end – I was an archaeologist, not a social historian – it did have some advantages. For a start, the museum service's HQ in Leicester's New Walk was some 20 miles away, which facilitated a certain degree of autonomy; but equally important was access to the expertise of a multi-disciplinary curatorial resource, fellow professionals, many of whom had a great interest in Rutland and what it could offer, especially in the natural sciences, archaeology, history and archives. For some of them, the opportunity to undertake fieldwork in the county could be seized upon with alacrity. For the rest, I rather think that they may have been somewhat green-eyed as they visualised one of their number, a certain Fred Hartley, spending his days at local taxpayers' expense just wandering about the fields of Rutland (providing it wasn't raining) and jotting down his observations on bits of paper.

But, dear reader, we know better than that. Our author has ably set out for us in this work the context in which he was inspired and enabled to undertake this survey of the fields and earthworks of Rutland, and we know that the first edition of *The Medieval Earthworks of Rutland* (Hartley 1983) was an extraordinary testament to the archaeological value of his 'wanderings'. Of course, the relatively compact size of Rutland meant that surveying the evidence of its medieval landscape was a project which could realistically be completed within a reasonable time-frame, tied in with other evidence such as enclosure maps, estate records and the post-war RAF aerial photographs, and published in an accessible format. Equally, it wasn't undertaken entirely alone, and Fred gives credit where it was due to those of his colleagues who were involved in one way or another, including the late Tony Squires, to whose memory this revised work is dedicated and whose research into Rutland's woodland history also has such lasting value.

However, that first edition appeared forty years ago, in 1983. Although it successfully documented the state of the landscape at the time and pointed to changes which had taken place in preceding decades, clearly the continuing scale and pace of landscape change which has taken place since then – more aggressive agricultural practices, extensive building and infrastructure projects, the construction of Rutland Water – meant that it represented a picture frozen in time. Meanwhile Fred's continuing fieldwork across the whole of adjoining Leicestershire had achieved complete coverage of that county's archaeological landscape, and thus it seemed both logical and beneficial to revisit the Rutland volume and bring it up to date in a revised edition. In one way it is sad now to see that so many landscape features recorded in the original edition have been lost: we can find in these pages details of sites which have vanished or been ploughed out at places like Brooke, built over as at Whissendine, or submerged as at Nether Hambleton. The important thing, though, is that the record has been made, both on the ground and from the air, the latter including Fred's own co-operation with Jim Pickering whose aerial photography added so much to our knowledge of, mostly, earlier periods than covered here. Archaeologists and historians will be forever grateful that this has been done.

There is something else that we can remember when we put this work into context, namely that researchers and scholars and antiquarians have been interested in our historical landscapes and the monuments that populate them for generations. We can go back in time hand in hand with them to identify the remains of medieval deer parks, village roads and houses, castles and defended manors, and religious sites. We can link them with people and events of the past – the desertion of the hamlet of Nether Hambleton almost certainly due to the impact of the Black Death, the failure of other settlements due to changes in farming practice, even the difficulties brought upon ordinary people by the unscrupulous abuse of power by the likes of Peter de Neville, the infamous thirteenth century Warden of the Forest of Rutland.

We should also browse the writings of antiquarians such as William Stukeley who was resident in Stamford from 1730 to 1747. Although his interests were particularly in Roman Britain as well as places like Stonehenge and Avebury, he was also intrigued by sites and monuments of the early and later medieval period, to the extent that he undertook excursions in the vicinity of Stamford, amongst them to places where earthworks survive until the present day. It is illuminating to place the maps and plans presented in this volume alongside Stukeley's descriptions of his visits to Ryhall with its lost manor house and its associations with St Tibba, Tolethorpe with its manor house and chalybeate spring, Great Casterton with the 'antient' ruins of Woodhead lying a little to the north, and Essendine castle 'intirely ruin'd', not to mention the site of the battle of Losecoat Field fought in 1470 (Honeybone & Honeybone 2022). Such accounts complement what we see on the ground today and may perhaps lead us to look further into archival sources which may illuminate the history of these places beyond what our antiquarians – William Stukeley, James Wright (1684), Thomas Blore (1811) – can tell us. If we persist, we can even begin to populate those fields and their strips and to visualise those village and manor sites with smoke rising from their houses and noisy with the shouts of villagers, the cries of children and the sounds of animals; sometimes we shall actually have the names of some of the occupiers. That is beyond the reach and purpose of this volume: but it is a logical corollary and a demonstration of where field archaeology and historical research, with persistence and not a little good fortune, can begin to merge. That is something which could not be envisaged without the fruits of Fred's 'wanderings' across the fields of Rutland over the past forty years, and we are indebted to him for it.

ROBERT F. HARTLEY - ABOUT THE AUTHOR

Robert F Hartley (Fred) was born in Glossop, Derbyshire but grew up in Stalybridge and went to Stockport Grammar School. He remembers the diesel trains freezing up in the winter of 1967 and the service reverting to steam for the duration which probably started his love of trains and industrial heritage. Taking an historically-focused Combined Studies degree at Leicester University Fred then worked for a year at Newarke Houses Museum which included cataloguing the collections for Bob Rutland. He was an archaeology site assistant for Patrick Clay at the Sproxton Barrow site and followed this up by post-excavation experience at Humberstone Store, Leicester. When a vacancy came up under the job creation programme in 1979 which had to be filled quickly Fred was in the right place at the right time to become Assistant Archaeological Survey Officer working for Peter Liddle at Jewry Wall Museum.

Although Peter and Fred worked together on some of the earthwork surveys their duties soon diverged with Peter concentrating on fieldwalking and identification and Fred specialising in earthwork survey and aerial photography (the latter with Jim Pickering). Most of the earthworks surveys were carried out alone which he now finds preferable as it allows him to work quickly carrying a mental 'map' of the shape of the field as he surveys it.

In the early 1990s Fred gained his Diploma in Museum Studies and became a very busy Curator at Harborough Museum before local government reorganisation in 1997 brought him back to County Hall as a Curator splitting up the collections of the County and City. He thus found that the card indexing done all those years ago at Newarke Houses was incredibly useful! After taking on the Curatorship of Snibston Museum for a short time in 2001 Fred became Curator for the Social History collections of the County Museum Service until 2012, when he officially retired although he continued to assist with collections research until 2014. Now fully retired he has found time to join local history and gardening societies in Nottinghamshire as well as go back to Rutland to revise the plans for this new edition of Rutland's earthworks. Fred has a special interest in the history of coalmining - publishing a paper on this in the Leicestershire Fieldworkers 'Medieval Leicestershire' book, (Hartley 2015), and has published research on the life of George Stephenson. His last published paper is in the Journal of the Railway and Canal Historical Society about the S. W. A. Newton Collection of photographs that record the building of the Great Central Railway (preserved at the Record Office for Leicestershire, Leicester and Rutland).

INTRODUCTION TO MEDIEVAL RUTLAND
Robert F Hartley

This volume is a much revised survey of earthwork evidence of medieval and post-medieval landscape features in the county of Rutland. The original book was issued by the Leicestershire Museums, Art Galleries and Records Service in 1983 in their Archaeological Report Series, this being the seventh to be produced. It was the first in a series of publications on this aspect of the landscape history of the counties of Leicestershire and Rutland. Most of the original survey work was carried out between 1979 and 1995, when the author was a member of the Leicestershire Museums Archaeological Survey Team. At that time Rutland and the City of Leicester were included in Leicestershire for administrative purposes, but they were given unitary status in 1997. Additional survey work for this revised volume was carried out during 2020-2021 with some finishing work completed in 2022.

Earthworks are archaeological features in which evidence of past human activity can be seen as mounds and hollows in areas which have subsequently been abandoned or, more usually, used as pasture land. Throughout much of lowland England the commonest earthworks are those of the middle and late medieval period (*c.*900 - 1600 AD) because in the later part of this period there was a considerable change from the cultivation of cereal crops to the grazing of sheep and cattle. The new pasture fields preserved evidence of the former plough-ridges, and the fall in population led to the abandonment of areas where houses had previously existed.

One of the most important areas of England for the survival of such evidence is neighbouring east Leicestershire, where the wholesale change from plough land to grazing land saw numerous villages become depopulated. Dozens of these sites survive, and the evidence has been presented in previous publications in this series.

Only the western edge of Rutland has, or had, evidence in such abundance. Much of the county's farmland is ploughed each year to grow cereal crops, and has been used in this way for most of the last two millennia, but even so there are still quite a number of places where earthwork evidence has been recorded, and in some cases still survives. The purpose of this publication is to provide as complete a record of this evidence as is possible, making use of site surveys and vertical aerial photographs including those taken in the mid 20th century by the RAF. Many are on-line, or are being digitised and can be found at https://historicengland.org.uk/images-books/archive/collections/aerial-photos/.

The Area of Rutland

Rutland is England's smallest historic county and is currently a unitary authority. It has proved to have an enduring sense of self-identity, despite the fact that it did not exist as a county either at the time of the Domesday Survey in 1086, or indeed in the 1980s when much of the fieldwork described here took place. In 1086 the north-western area was administered as a detached part of Nottinghamshire, and the south-east was in Northamptonshire. It became identified as a separate county in the 12th century, but most historians seem to conclude that a distinct territory of Rutland existed before the Norman Conquest in 1066 (Phythian-Adams, 1980, 5-12).

Between 1973 and 1997 it was administered by a District Council as part of Leicestershire, and it was during these years that I and my colleagues on the museums staff of Leicestershire County Council worked in Rutland monitoring planning applications, recording sites, and encouraging the creation of local groups of amateur archaeologists. We compiled information for the Heritage and Environment Record (HER) database. Initially this was based at the Jewry Wall Museum in Leicester but was transferred in 1997 to County Hall at Glenfield.

The Need to Record Information

There is no doubt that much of the motivation to study and revive Rutland's past has come from a sense of loss, actual and perceived, a feeling that the pace of change in modern life was destroying many things that form the local heritage. When W. G. Hoskins wrote a guidebook to the county in the 1950s he was able to say that "no other county in England surpasses Rutland for unspoiled, quiet charm" (Pevsner & Williamson 2003, 433). In fact there had already been twentieth century intrusions. In the 1930s large areas around Pilton in the south of the county, and around Market Overton, Cottesmore and Burley in the north, had been quarried for ironstone. This process accelerated in the 1960s when one of the world's largest dragline excavating machines dug away most of the historic landscape around Exton Park. During the Second World War three large areas were levelled for airfields at Woolfox Lodge, North Luffenham and Cottesmore, with RAF Cottesmore continuing development as a base for jet fighter planes until closure in 2011.

In the 1970s another threat emerged, when England's smallest county became the construction site for England's largest man-made lake. More than 11 square kilometres of land were taken, including the hamlet of Nether Hambleton. There was no official provision for archaeological recording or preservation at the time, and the "rescue digs" which took place largely relied on the efforts of unpaid volunteers.

In recent years, almost unnoticed, the Ketton cement works quarries have gradually destroyed an area of landscape approximately half the size of Rutland Water. There has also been unremitting pressure for housing development. Rutland is seen as a desirable place to live, with easy access to the A1 motorway and the East Coast Main Line railway. The planning regulations encourage "infill" rather than expansion of settlements, and many of the areas available within villages are the same sites which contain earthwork evidence. In addition, during the last twenty-five years, with the construction of a bypass, the built-up area of Oakham has quadrupled in size.

In the background behind all these processes of landscape change was the greatest of them all - the steady spread of mechanised arable farming. When the first edition of this book was being prepared in the early 1980s I spent much time in the record office in Leicester plotting the evidence of medieval field systems from sets of vertical aerial photographs taken by the RAF., mainly in 1945-47. They showed a landscape of which roughly half still had visible evidence of medieval earthworks, mainly field systems. By the 1980s this was a landscape which had largely vanished, except for some parishes such as Whissendine and Braunston along the Leicestershire border.

There was nevertheless still much to find and record, as had been made clear by the work of Anthony Brown, then the extra-mural tutor in Archaeology at the University of Leicester. Working with students he prepared an invaluable little typed and duplicated publication - *Archaeological Sites and Finds in Rutland - A Preliminary List (*Brown 1975). In collaboration with Christopher Davies of the Royal Commission on Historic Monuments he also arranged training courses at Knuston Hall in Northamptonshire where it was possible to learn the skills of recording and interpreting medieval earthworks.

The Initial Programme of Survey Work

In the 1970s there was a growing feeling that archaeological evidence threatened by development should be properly recorded, and archaeological staffing was added either to planning departments or museum services of most county councils. Peter Liddle, Martyn Winter and Lyn Barrow were appointed to form the Survey Team for Leicestershire and Rutland. In 1979, Martyn resigned to take a post elsewhere and I was appointed in his place as Assistant Archaeological Survey Officer.

I began to survey earthwork sites in February of the following year, using a very simple technique called a "crosshead survey", learned on the courses at Knuston Hall. This involved setting out ranging poles at regular intervals to form a "base line" across each field of earthwork remains. I then measured out at right-angles and 45 degrees, recording the top and bottom of any slope I crossed, and indicating this slope by means of triangular marks called "hachures". The resulting plan, made on paper using pencil, would be redrawn in ink on drawing film back at the Jewry Wall Museum in Leicester.

I made Rutland my priority almost from the start, carrying out most of the surveys in 1981-2. I was at work continuously in Rutland during the last two weeks of May and the first two weeks of June 1981. Ned Heywood and Annie Rainsbury kindly arranged for me to use their spare room so I did not need to travel back and forth from Leicester each day.

Air photo of Brooke, Rutland, looking east over the village with the earthworks of 'Town Park' in the right foreground and much evidence of the ridge and furrow field system. The photo was taken by the author on December 9th 1986, since when almost all these earthworks in this fascinating landscape have been levelled and ploughed, apart from the garden terraces of the lost Brooke House, on the site of Brooke Priory in the left foreground.
(R. F. Hartley and S. Thursfield [pilot]. © R. F. Hartley).

The first edition of "The Medieval Earthworks of Rutland" came out as No. 7 of the Leicestershire Museums, Art Galleries and Records Service series of Archaeological Reports (Hartley 1983). In retrospect it would have been better if more time had been spent on the publication process, but although some sites had still not been surveyed, and the reproduction of some of the plans was not perfect, it has formed a useful reference work.

Subsequently I continued to survey sites in other areas of Leicestershire, but opportunities also came along to record additional sites in Rutland which for one reason or another had not been included in the book. In addition, a large and previously private archive of documents from Exton Hall was deposited with the Leicestershire Record Office, where it can be accessed for research but not currently reproduced. This collection has greatly increased the available information on the landscape history of central Rutland. In 2006 the Rutland Local History & Record Society published Ian Ryder's book *Common Right and Private Interest: Rutland's Common Fields and their Enclosure*, (Ryder 2006) which is an excellent comprehensive history of Rutland's open fields.

During the 1980s the Leicestershire Museums Service went on publish the results of my survey work in North-west, North-east and Central Leicestershire, (Hartley 1987, 1987, 1989) but changing work commitments took me away from archaeology for much of the 1990s.

The hachured survey gradually began to seem a rather primitive means of recording information, but the computer-based technical recording methods which have emerged over the past three decades have not entirely supplanted it. During the early 2000s, colleagues working within the planning department of Leicestershire County Council and in the University of Leicester Archaeological Unit (ULAS) continued to tell me that they still referred to my surveys and found them useful for interpreting sites. As much of the survey work for the remaining parts of the county had already been done, it seemed worthwhile to complete the series of publications. Eventually, in 2008, with considerable assistance from Kathy Elkin and the financial support of the Leicestershire Fieldworkers we were able to publish *The Medieval Earthworks of South-West Leicestershire*, (Hinckley & Market Bosworth) now out of print (Hartley 2008). After another interval, during which I took early retirement, the final three areas appeared in 2018 as one volume *The Medieval Earthworks of South and South-East Leicestershire*, (Lutterworth, Market Harborough & Billesdon), also published by the Leicestershire Fieldworkers (Hartley 2018).

By this time the style and content of the reports had been greatly improved. In particular I had realised that I could in many cases give a much more extended interpretation of the earthwork remains than I had done in the early volumes.

The first volume, on Rutland, stood out in particular as having the potential to be improved, so I began to draw up additional plans, and from 2011 to begin making occasional site visits to places which seemed to have the potential to reveal more information. Most of the plans were redrawn and new text written during the summers of 2020 and 2021.

Scope of this Volume

This edition follows the format of the original, with missing sites added, and with plans extended in many cases to improve the completeness and the interpretation of the evidence. It is still purely a study of earthwork evidence. I have not removed any sites because they no longer exist as such, or attempted to update information on what still survives, beyond noting some of the major losses, such as the extensive area of earthworks which used to extend between the villages of Brooke and Braunston, and of Nether Hambleton now beneath Rutland Water.

The Survey

There are two types of survey reproduced here. At the back is a set of maps of the whole area with earthwork features sketched out (initially at a scale of 1:10560) from vertical air photographs, mainly RAF photographs taken in the mid-late 1940s or in the 1920s, before the large scale conversion of pasture to ploughland in the second half of the 20th century.

In the gazetteer are more detailed surveys, done initially at a scale of 1:1000, by measurement in the field using measuring tapes and a crosshead. Additional information, for example ridge and furrow, or features no longer in existence, have been plotted from aerial photographs. The original field surveys are kept by the Historic Environment Record Centre (formerly the Sites & Monuments Record) at County Hall, Glenfield, Leicestershire. Information has also been added based on recent site visits, recording features visible from roads and public footpaths.

The Map Base

All of the plans are drawn up on a base of the Ordnance Survey First Series 25 inch large-scale maps, surveyed in the mid-1880s.

The Parishes

The parishes are the Civil Parishes defined on theOrdnance Survey First Series maps in about 1885. These largely follow the medieval boundaries, and in most cases within Rutland the same boundaries have been maintained to the present day.

Types of Earthwork

This survey is concerned with earthwork features created in the landscape between late Anglo-Saxon times and the 18th century. Most of them are elements of the Medieval arable farming landscape which was converted to pasture land (and enclosed with hedges) as part of a slow and patchwork process between the 14th and 19th centuries. Because the former arable fields, villages and other features were simply allowed to grass over, a huge amount of evidence remained visible as undulations or earthworks. This was particularly the case up to the 1960s, and it is fortunate that we have the RAF vertical air photographs to record the appearance of these features in the first half of the twentieth century and particularly in the 1940s and 1950s. Many of these photographs are now online at the Historic England website https://historicengland.org.uk/images-books/archive/collections/aerial-photos/ and are therefore not included in the this book.

1. Open-field Earthworks

The area was intensively cultivated during the Medieval period, with no major woodlands or open wastes. Most of the population lived in compact "nucleated" villages, surrounded by the arable fields which provided most of their food. Usually a village had three large "open fields", divided into roughly rectangular blocks called furlongs, each of which was further subdivided into cultivation strips or "lands". The strips are generally 7 to 9 metres in width depending on soil surface geology (Ryder 2006, 75) with the soil mounded up to form long, narrow ridges. A huge amount of physical work, ploughing and digging year after year, must have gone into creating them, and the pattern of them survived long enough over the great majority of this area to be recorded as "ridge and furrow" on aerial photographs. The exact process of ridge and furrow creation is still a subject for debate.

Each furlong had a name, and in the case of some villages there are detailed maps made before the system was dismantled. Where we have both maps and surviving medieval documents it is possible to find out a great deal about the ownership and management of the farming landscape. The best maps within Rutland are probably those of Cottesmore and Barrow. Several villages in the Welland Valley were enclosed at a late date, in the 19th century, and maps with records of the open field survive for Pilton, Barrowden and North Luffenham. Nor have I attempted to include the findings from the numerous small excavations which have taken place over the past 30 years. Anyone seeking further information is recommended to visit the "Heritage Gateway" website (https://www.heritagegateway.org.uk/gateway/) and contact the Heritage and Environment Record Centre at County Hall, Glenfield, Leicester (https://www.leicestershire.gov.uk/leisure-and-community/history-and-heritage/historic-environment-record). More information may be found in the reports of fieldwork and research in the annual editions of *Rutland Record* and in the *Transactions of the Leicestershire Archaeological and Historical Society*.

Because medieval fields were farmed in common, with villagers being allocated different strips each year, the boundaries of the strips and the furlongs would have been carefully marked with posts or stones.

Ian Ryder's 2006 study cited above on the open fields of Rutland, *Common Right and Private Interest: Rutland's Common Fields and their Enclosure* describes how the open field system worked and the reasons for it, illustrated with documents and plans and concludes with a comprehensive Rutland settlement gazetteer with details of open fields. For those who wish to read further this publication is now available as a pdf download from the website of the RLHRS (https://www.rutlandhistory.org/occasionalpublications.htm). A very detailed study of measurements of medieval fields, ridge and furrow is discussed in Anthony Brown's paper *Ridge and Furrow in Southern Leicestershire* (Brown 2015, 143-159).

2. Settlement Earthworks

The abandonment of the open-field system of cultivation was accompanied by a reduction in the population and a process of migration within village sites or between villages. As a result most villages locally have some evidence of areas where houses, outbuildings and their related small fields have been abandoned. In some cases there may now only be a single farm, and the sites have been described as "Deserted Villages" though they may also be hamlets rather than villages. The process of desertion is much debated and probably differs from settlement to settlement and area to area in England. For a discussion about this see Richard Jones *Contrasting patterns of village and hamlet desertion in England* (Jones 2010, 8-27).

3. Watermills

Watermills existed before the Norman conquest and continued in use in many cases into the early 20th century. Related earthworks include dams for the millpond, supply channels (leets or lades) and tailrace channels. Watermills were developed and repaired over many years, and the surviving surface evidence is more likely to be post-Medieval rather than earlier.

4. Windmills

Windmills were introduced to this area during the Medieval period. Often they were built on existing or newly-constructed earth mounds to gain extra height, and in many cases these mounds survive as earthworks. Further information is available at the website of the Mills Archive at https://new.millsarchive.org/ and there is a catalogue at https://catalogue.millsarchive.org/ covering both water and windmills.

5. Castles

The various medieval castles of Rutland have been discussed by Creighton (1999 & 2000). The Normans built castles in the period after 1066 to subjugate the local English population. The most prominent feature was usually a conical mound or "motte". For a gazetteer of castle sites in the county see Richard Knox *The medieval fortified sites of Leicestershire and Rutland* (Knox 2015).

6. Medieval Parks

The word 'park' is from the old French 'parc' and means an enclosure. These were usually wooded to provide cover for fallow deer and were often sited on the edge of the manor outside the cultivated land and used for hunting. They were often elliptical to make them easier to construct and were enclosed by ditch and bank with a wooden pale on top Most were built between 1150 and 1350 and in Rutland thirteen are known, with Exton the earliest in 1175. After the Black Death many were abandoned or repurposed for pasture and agriculture. In the fifteenth century parks again became fashionable for the wealthy but were much larger and often took up arable land which could not be farmed due to shortage of labour. These larger parks were not enclosed by high banks but probably by hedges or fences (Cantor & Squires, 1997).

7. Manorial Sites

Most villages had one or more large houses for the lords of the manors. In many cases there will still be a "Manor Farm" on the site. Manorial sites often had fishponds, enclosures, and gardens, as well as substantial buildings, and in many cases these features, having gone out of use, can still be identified as earthworks. In the 15th and 16th centuries particularly there was a fashion for surrounding manor houses and some other buildings with water-filled "moats", generally rectangular in plan.

8. Monastic Sites

Until their suppression by Henry VIII in the 1530s, there were monastic houses of varying size and wealth in most parts of England and several occur in Rutland.

9. Ponds

Within the Rutland landscape, which has only small rivers and no natural lakes, ponds have long been created for fish rearing and to provide water for livestock. Ponds, whether full or drained, quite often survive as features forming part of a manorial site, park or garden.

10. Formal Gardens and Amenity Parks

During the 16th century the suppression of the monastic houses, and the gradual enclosure of the open-fields, provided opportunities for wealthy and powerful men to create mansion houses, surrounded by gardens and parks. Sometimes they would build their mansion on a new site, but more often they enlarged an existing manor house, clearing away the cottages of the poorer villagers to create space and privacy for the exclusive use of their family.

Around the house would be levelled parterres with ornate flower beds, raised terraces to walk along and view the gardens, and ornamental fishponds and moats. Avenues of trees were laid out, radiating from the mansion towards the horizon, and plantations of trees were created to add variety to the view. The creation of these formal gardens involved much movement of earth, and earthwork evidence now often survives, long after the flowers and trees have gone.

11. Negative Evidence

Despite the extent and diversity of the recorded earthwork evidence, there are many areas which appear never to have had earthwork features. These are mainly the low-lying areas alongside streams, which were used a hay meadows in summer and pasture land after the hay crop had been taken. Some of the more remote upland areas seem also to have a long history as pasture land, and perhaps in early medieval times as woodland.

12. Access and Further Information

The sites described in this volume are on private land, and while many are crossed by rights of way, they should not be explored further without first seeking the permission of the land owner. Anyone interested in further research should in the first instance contact the Heritage and Environment Records service at Leicestershire County Council.

Robert F Hartley
The Green
Elston
Newark
Nottinghamshire

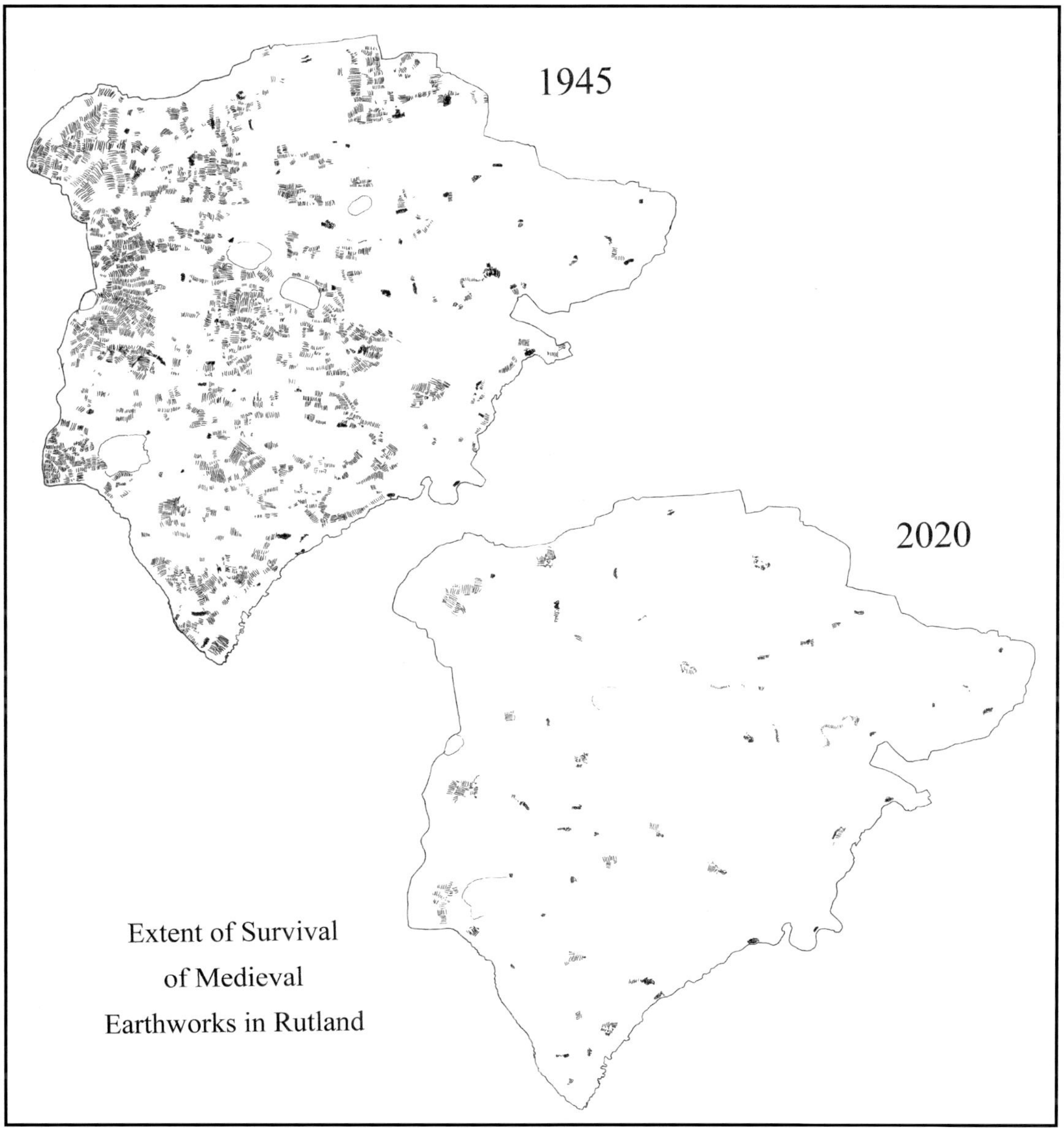

Extent of Survival of Medieval Earthworks in Rutland

GAZETTEER AND SITE SURVEYS

ASHWELL

The parish was enclosed in *c*.600. Ryder (2006, 62) considered there might have been three fields, West, Middle and East.

Village Earthworks, Fishponds and Water Mill Site (figs 1, 2) ***SK865139/862138***

Ashwell village lies on either side of a small stream flowing from the south, which joins another stream from the west near to the Old Hall. Just upstream of the confluence of the streams is a rectangular depression (a), perhaps originally a moat, surrounding a platform (b). There are two more platforms adjacent (c, d), the whole seeming likely to be part of the site of a medieval manor house and its gardens.

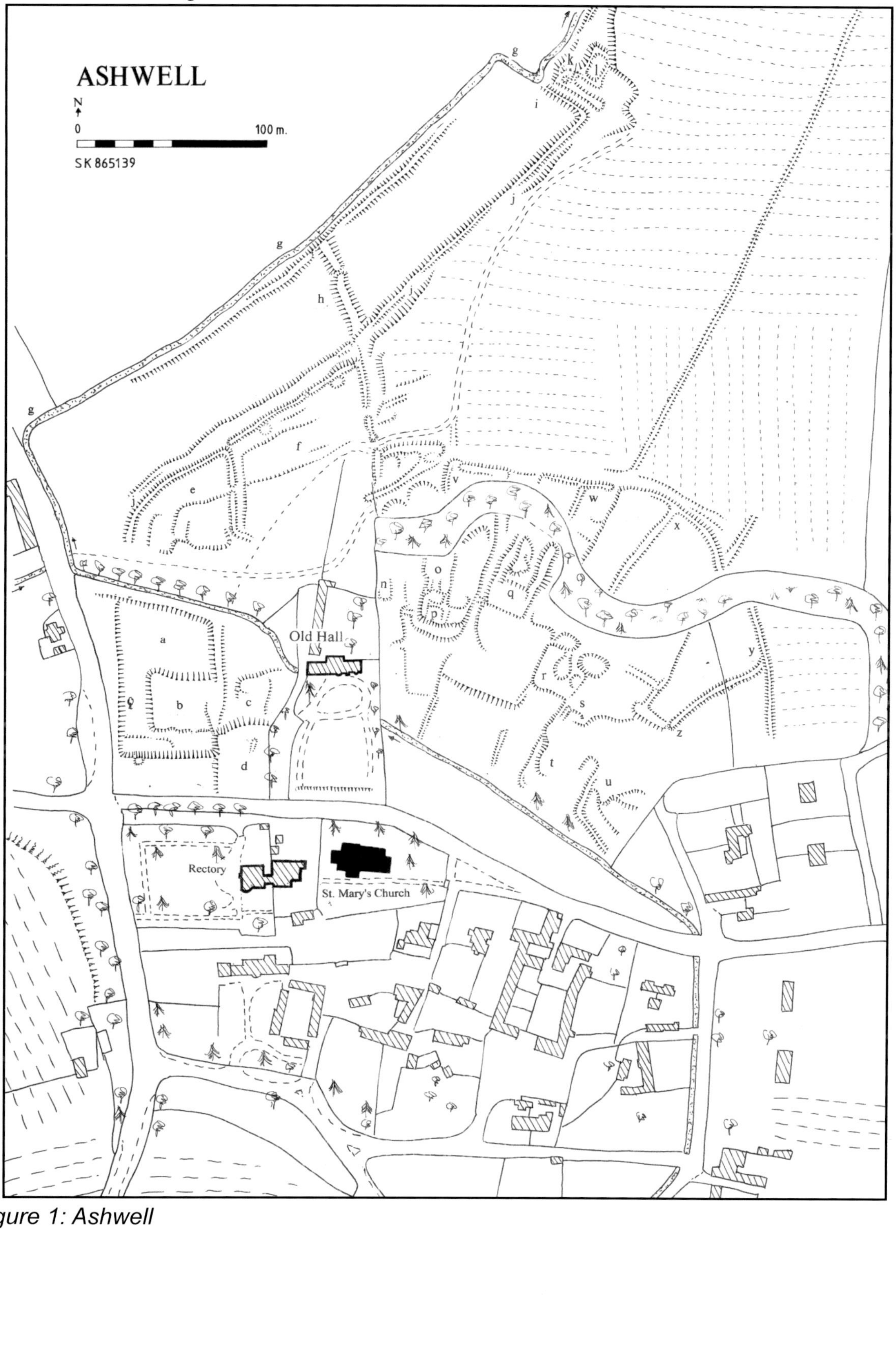

Figure 1: Ashwell

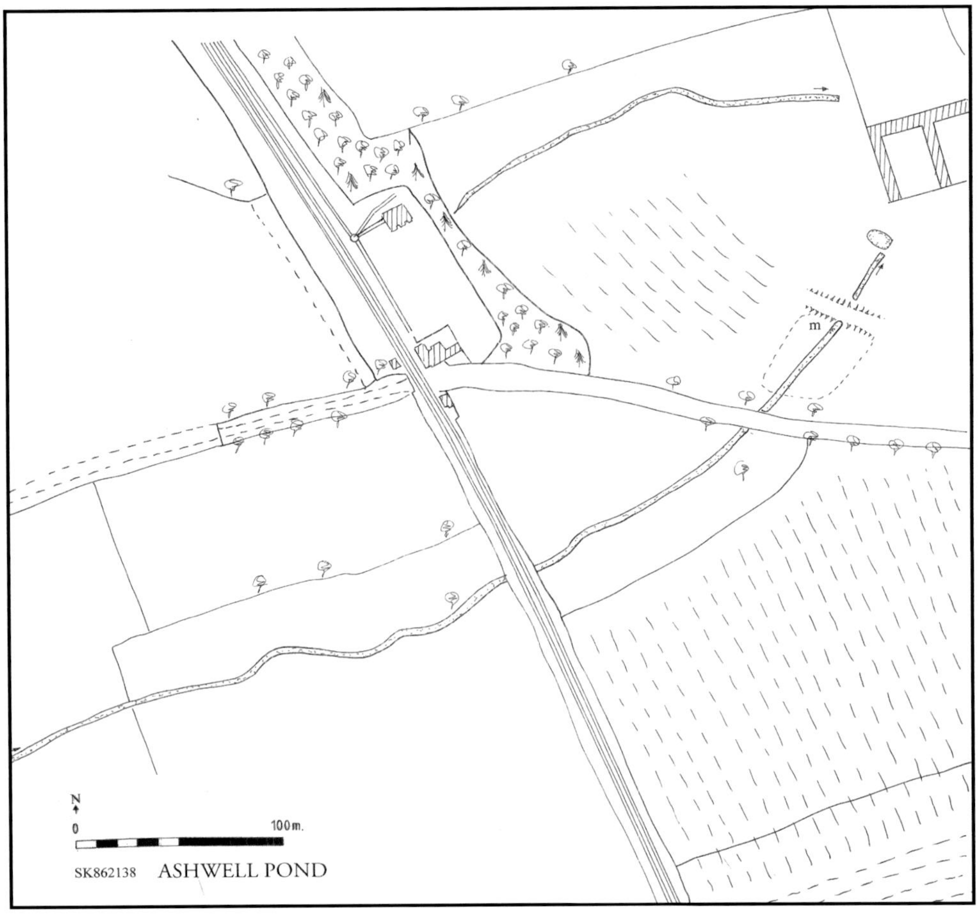

Figure 2: Ashwell Pond

To the north, across the stream, are more earthworks indicating the site of two enclosed areas (e, f) which were probably also part of the manorial gardens. Further north again the shallow valley extends downhill to the north-east. The course of the stream has been diverted into a bypass channel (g, g, g). Remains of two dams (h, i) indicate the former location of fishponds which the bypass channel went round. There may have been another bypass channel (j, j) on the south side of the fishponds. Below the second dam (i) are earthworks indicating the former existence of buildings (k, l) which are surely the site of a watermill. There are remains of another small pond (m) further to the west (fig 2 above) near Manor Farm. This may be recent as it is not marked on the 1885 First Edition Ordnance Survey 1:2500 map.
East of the Old Hall an area of the medieval village has gone out of use at some point and been incorporated into parkland. There are platforms where buildings may have stood (n, o, p, q, r, s, t, u), surrounded by the pattern of old closes which were walled but are now indicated by low stony banks (v, w, x, y, z).

AYSTON

The village fields were enclosed in *c*.635. A map drawn up at the time shows three open fields, East, West and Dam (Ryder 2006, 62, ref to Northamptonshire Record Office 2991/11).

Village and Garden Earthworks (fig 3) **SK860012**

The northern end of Ayston village used to have several cottages and enclosures in an area which later became parkland for Ayston Hall. An estate map of 1635-7 shows buildings (a, b, c) which have since been cleared away, and there are earthwork platforms perhaps indicating the sites of additional buildings (d, e). Probable village earthworks extend to the north of Ayston Hall, but the most obvious features here are two ponds, one circular (f) and one elongated (g) which were probably features of the hall gardens in the 18th century.

Pond Dam (fig 4) **SK871007**

At an isolated location about a mile east of the village are the remains of a substantial dam with evidence of stone facings. The dam would have been about 60m long, retaining a large body of

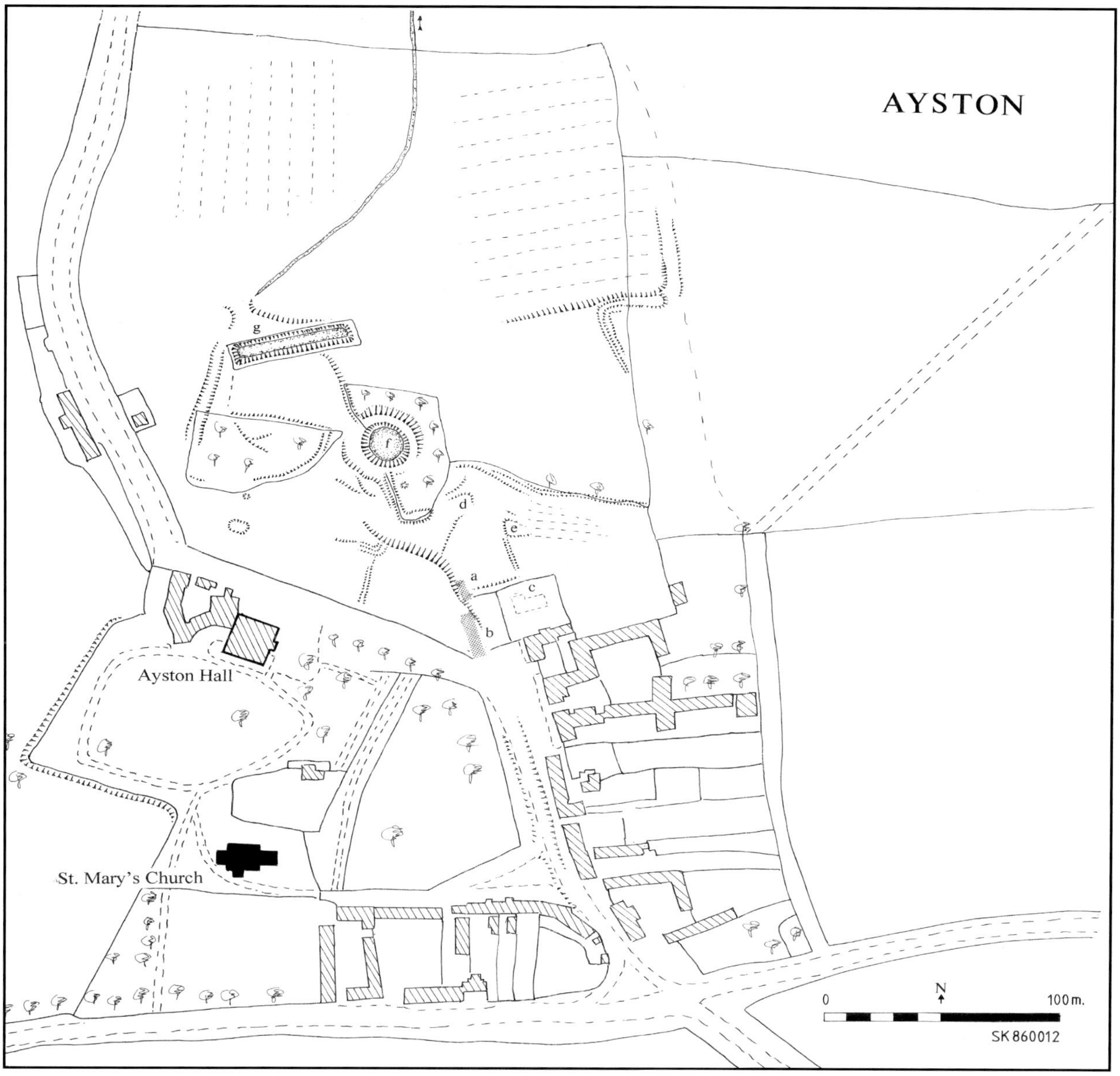

Figure 3: Ayston

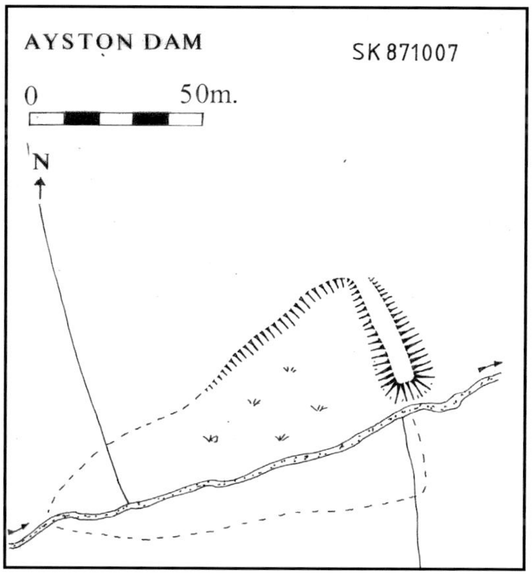

Figure 4: Ayston Dam

water. It seems likely to have been the site of a water mill, but the pool would have also been a valuable source of fish. Its use must predate the 1630s as the surrounding open field was named "Dam Field" on a map of 1635-7, although there is no indication of a pond existing at that time (*op cit*).

BARROW

Barrow is a hamlet in the parish of Cottesmore. The low-lying western part of the parish was enclosed in the early 17th century (see figure 18, 19), the remainder under an Act of 1800.

Village Earthworks (fig 5 overleaf)

SK889152 - SK890154

The small village of Barrow is on a limestone ridge, and a short way down the slope the original western boundary of the settlement is marked by a bank (a, a, a) and several small ponds on the spring line (b, c, d, e). The lane along the south end of the village (f) used to extend west into the fields, where the hollow way still exists (g). There are several possible building

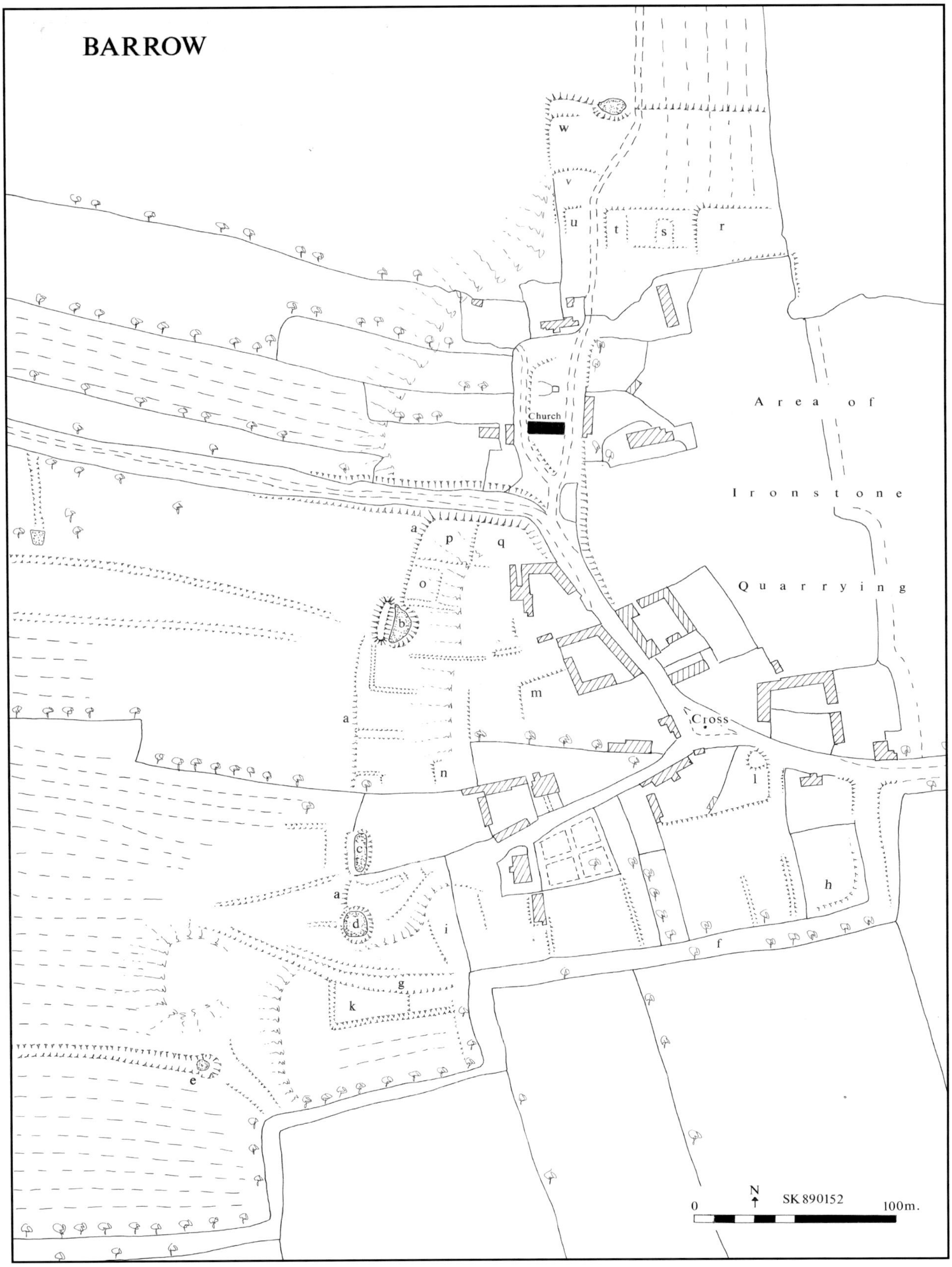

Figure 5: Barrow

platforms along this lane (h, i, j, k), and also just south of the Cross (l) and west of it (m, n, o, p, q). The village chapel, consecrated in 1831, was on the site of an earlier one, destroyed by 1660 (VCHR 2, 126). The village used to extend further to the north, with earthwork platforms indicating the former existence of buildings (r, s, t, u, v, and w). The earthworks noted above have been plotted from RAF vertical photo CPE/UK/1932 4139 and from site visits in 1988 and 2019.

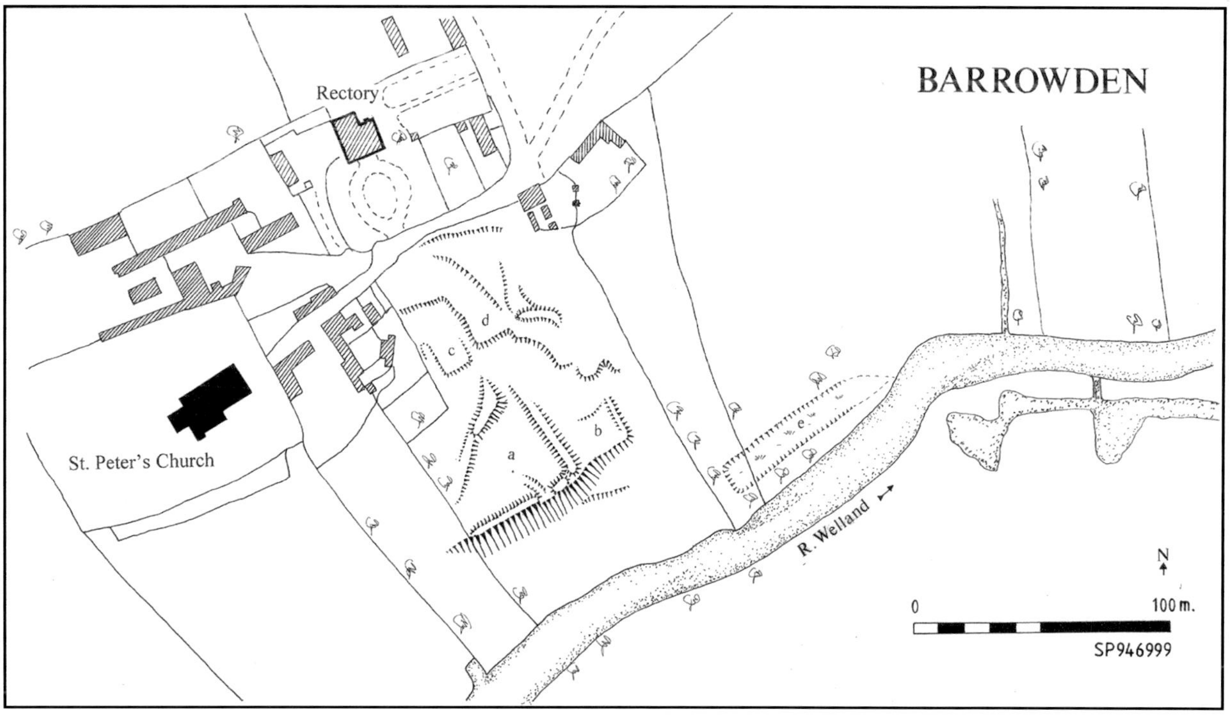

Figure 6: Barrowden

BARROWDEN

Barrowden was one of the last Rutland villages to be enclosed. There were three open fields, Stone, Scrapwell, and East or Nether. The Enclosure Act was passed in 1878 and the subsequent Award and map date from 1882 (Ryder 2006,62).

Fish Pond and Other Earthworks (fig 6) — *SP946999*

Just to the east of St. Peter's Church in Barrowden are clear remains of a "perched" fish pond (a) built into the valley side above the River Welland. Just east of the pond is a level platform (b), and to the north west of the pond are a building platform (c) and a higher terraced area (d). There are remains of another pond, possibly unrelated, further east and close to the river (e).

BEAUMONT CHASE

"Castle Hill" Motte and Bailey (fig 7) — *SK849004*

Beaumont Chase is an historically extra-parochial area to the west of Uppingham, and became a separate civil parish in 1858. It was one of two bailiwicks of the Forest of Rutland (the other being Braunston) (VCHR 1, 235) and occupies part of the Eye Brook valley. Towards it's northern extremity, at the junction of Uppingham and Ayston parishes lies the site of a castle motte, believed to have been constructed during the conflicts of King Stephen's reign by Hasculf, Keeper of the Royal Forest of Rutland. In 1269 one of the bailiwicks of the Forest of Rutland was called Beaumont, and it is likely that the foresters were based at Castle Hill.
Built on a promontory of the westward-facing escarpment, it occupies a site which is naturally defended by a triangular promontory, it's steep slopes falling away to the north, west and south. The motte (a) has steep sides, and is some 10m in height, with a circular platform at the top, originally about 20m in diameter, but somewhat reduced to 12m by subsidence. It is surrounded by a ditch (b), and the counterscarp bank east of the motte is about 4m high. Beyond it is a level field, now ploughed. Some 60-70m from the motte are traces of a defensive bank with an outer ditch (c), which extend in a semicircle across the promontory, forming an outer defended area or bailey. These features have been ploughed almost level now, but appear as soil marks on aerial photographs. Further east still is another concentric ditch (d), which has been recorded as a crop mark in ripening cereals in photographs by J. Pickering now in the Record Office for Leicestershire, Leicester and Rutland.

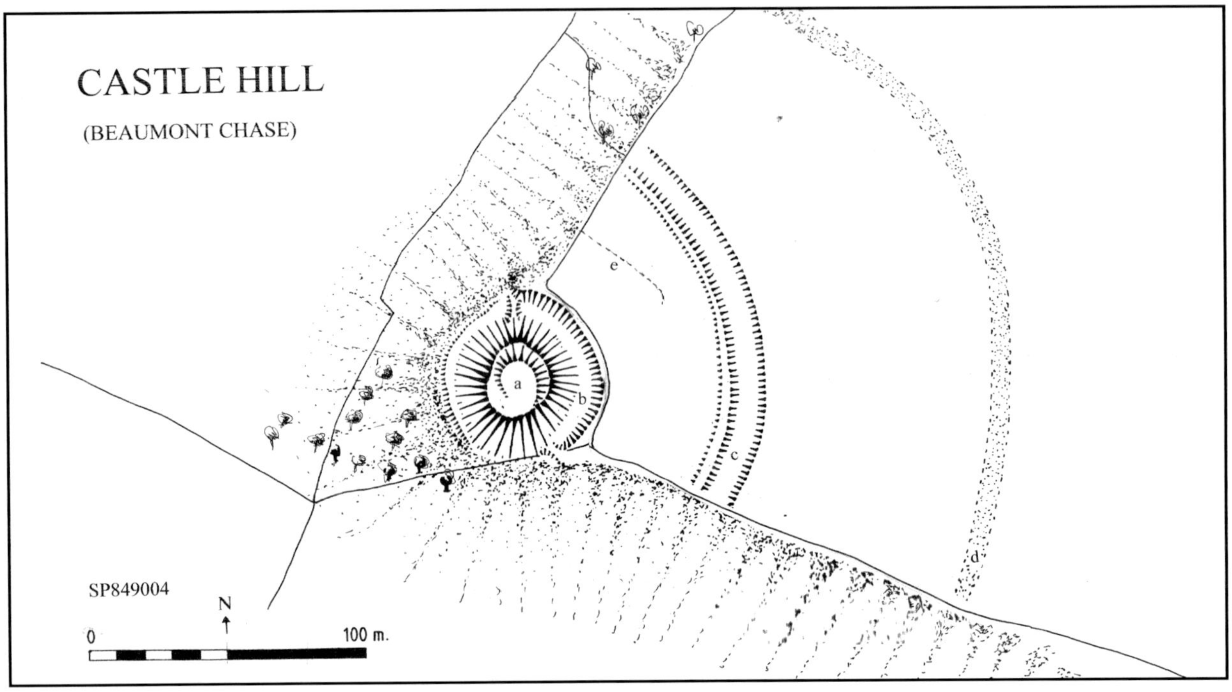

Figure 7: Beaumont Chase: "Castle Hill" Motte and Bailey

The Victoria County History of Rutland, in the chapter on Ancient Earthworks by J. Charles Wall, has a description of the site, including the suggestion that there was a scarp or slope (e), north-east of the motte, forming part of an oblong enclosure. There is now no field evidence to confirm this (VCHR 1, 112).

BELTON-IN-RUTLAND

The parish of Belton-in-Rutland was originally within the bounds of Leighfield Forest and was enclosed in 1794. Ridge and furrow survives in many of the fields.

Pond dam - water mill ***SK811013***

This earthwork site was first noted in 1992, then surveyed and partly excavated in 1997 and identified as the site of a water mill (Ovens & Sleath 1998).

BISBROOKE

Village Earthworks ***SK886997***

Earthwork boundaries of some old village closes are visible on RAF vertical photos CPE/UK/ 1925 2150/1.

BRAUNSTON

Mound ***SK837072***

There is a possible windmill mound at this location, on the north side of the road to Oakham.

Earthworks ***c.SK825020***

A small area of rectilinear earthworks is visible on a vertical air photograph (RAF CPE/UK/1932 3032). The Victoria County History of Rutland (1,118) refers to "entrenchments of no definite form" on the hillside above the north bank of the river Gwash. "They extend to the boundaries of Flitteris Park". The RAF vertical photograph shows this as a particularly impressive area of open field earthworks, with ridge and furrow and headland banks. Parts of this landscape still survive.

Braunston Pond ***SK84050710***

Earthwork banks are visible on a 1945 vertical air photograph (RAF CPE/UK/1932 3032). These appear to be the remains of a pond, also marked on the OS 2nd Series maps of 1904.

BROOKE

At the time of the original survey programme (1981-2) a large area of pasture land used to exist west of Brooke village, containing evidence of various aspects of historical land use. Much of this area has since been levelled. There was evidence of a former area of the village, the formal gardens around the 16th century mansion of Brooke House, a water mill, and also fishponds and "pillow mounds" - likely to be rabbit warrens - associated with Brooke House.

Brooke Priory (fig 9) — *c.SK846062*

There are historical records of a small Augustinian priory, which provided the land on which Brooke House was constructed, but it is not possible to identify any definite features. A house of Augustinian canons was established in Brooke prior to 1153, with land granted by Hugh de Ferrers, then Lord of Oakham (VCHR 1, 159). It was a daughter house or cell of the large Kenilworth Priory in Warwickshire, and there were only three canons. Priors were sent regularly from Kenilworth, but the poverty and remoteness of the establishment did not encourage them to stay long. The last Prior, Roger Harwell, arrived in 1534, and the following year, when the King's commissioners visited he persuaded them that it was an independent house and surrendered it to them in exchange for a pension of £10 a year. Kenilworth Priory later tried without success to have this arrangement revoked.
The original endowment of this small priory or cell included the land on which the religious house was built, and about 228 acres of wood (VCHR 1, 160). The woodland would have provided fuel and grazing land to support the small religious community.

Village Earthworks (fig 9) — *SK847057*

Extending west from the current village are old hollow ways (a, b, c). The modern road cuts through this pattern. Alongside hollow way (a) are what appear to be areas of former village, with building platforms (d, e, f, g).

Earthworks of Brooke House, Gardens (fig 10) and Water Mill (fig 11) — *SK846062*

In 1536 the site and land of Brooke Priory were granted by Henry VIII to Anthony Cope, who sold it on to Andrew Noel in 1549 (VCHR 2, 38). It passed to his son Andrew (d.1607) and then his grandson Edward, who inherited his father-in-law's title of Viscount Campden in 1629. In 1610 Edward Noel had obtained a fresh crown grant of the property, presumably to sort out continuing disputes over its original sale by the last prior in 1535.

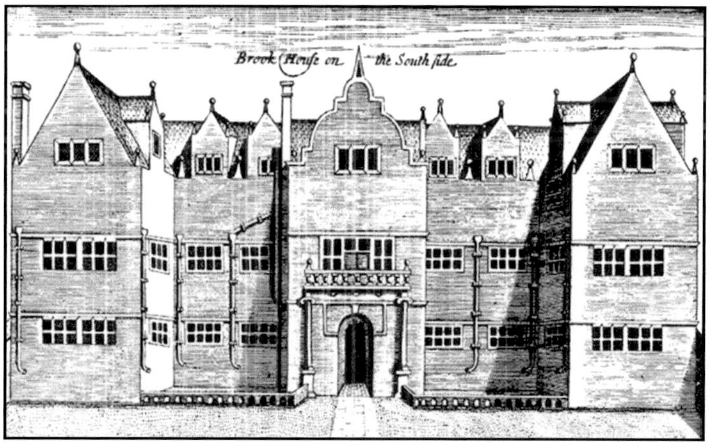

Brooke House (Wright, 1684, 1687 Additions)

A magnificent house and gardens were built on the site by the Noels. The house had the characteristic "E" plan of *c.*1600. Edward Noel's daughter- in-law lived there until her death in 1680, apparently aged 100. The house was depicted in James Wright's History of Rutland: Additions volume, published in 1687, but may already have been disused, and was subsequently demolished (Wright 1687, 6). All that survives to show its grandeur are a gatehouse lodge and the earthworks of the remarkable gardens. They are unusual for the abruptness of the slopes which were created. Ponds and moats at a low level are flanked by levelled parterres, which in turn can be viewed from raised terrace walks and from even further up on the summit of prospect mounds.

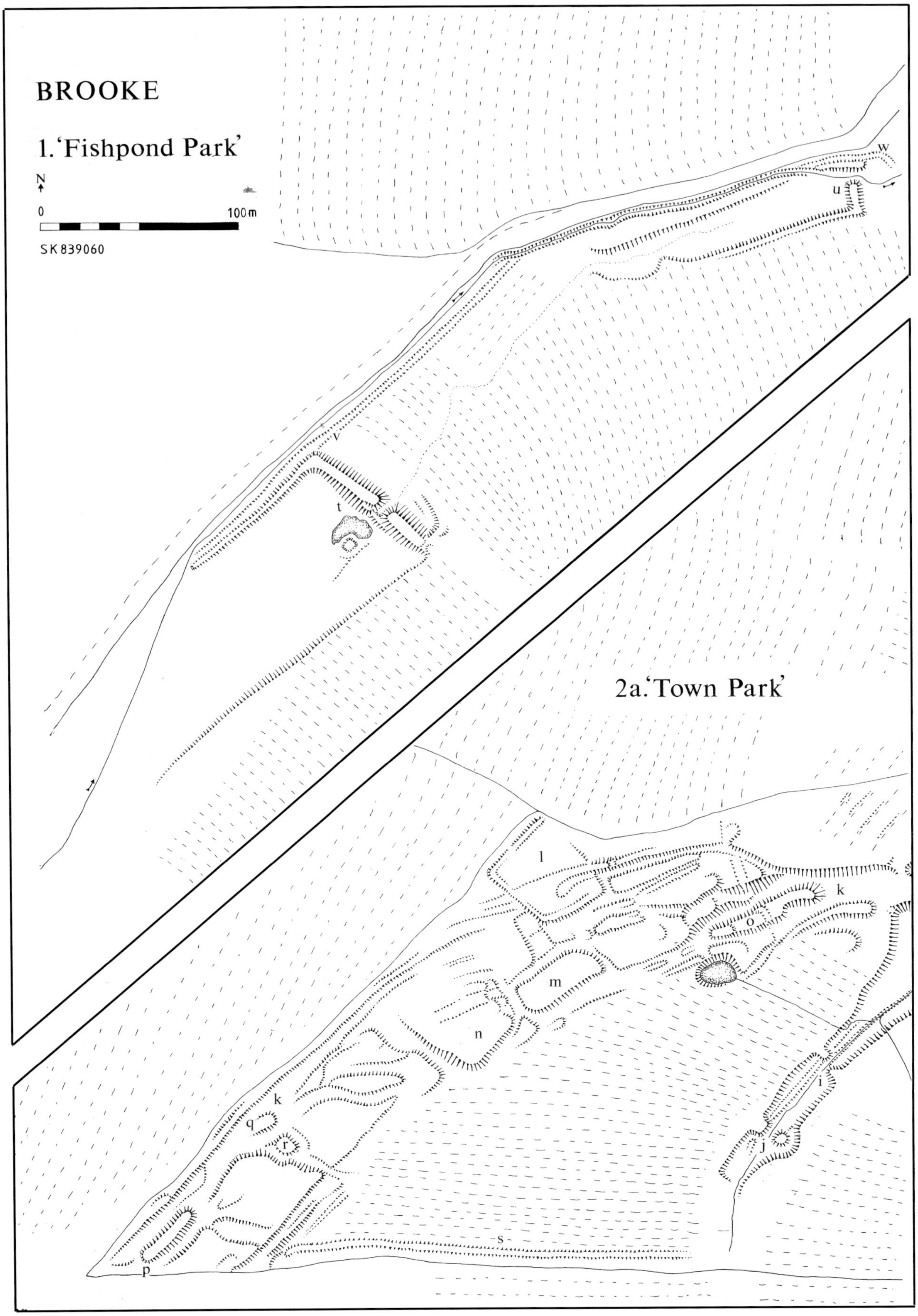

Figure 8: Brooke 'Fishpond Park' and 'Town Park'

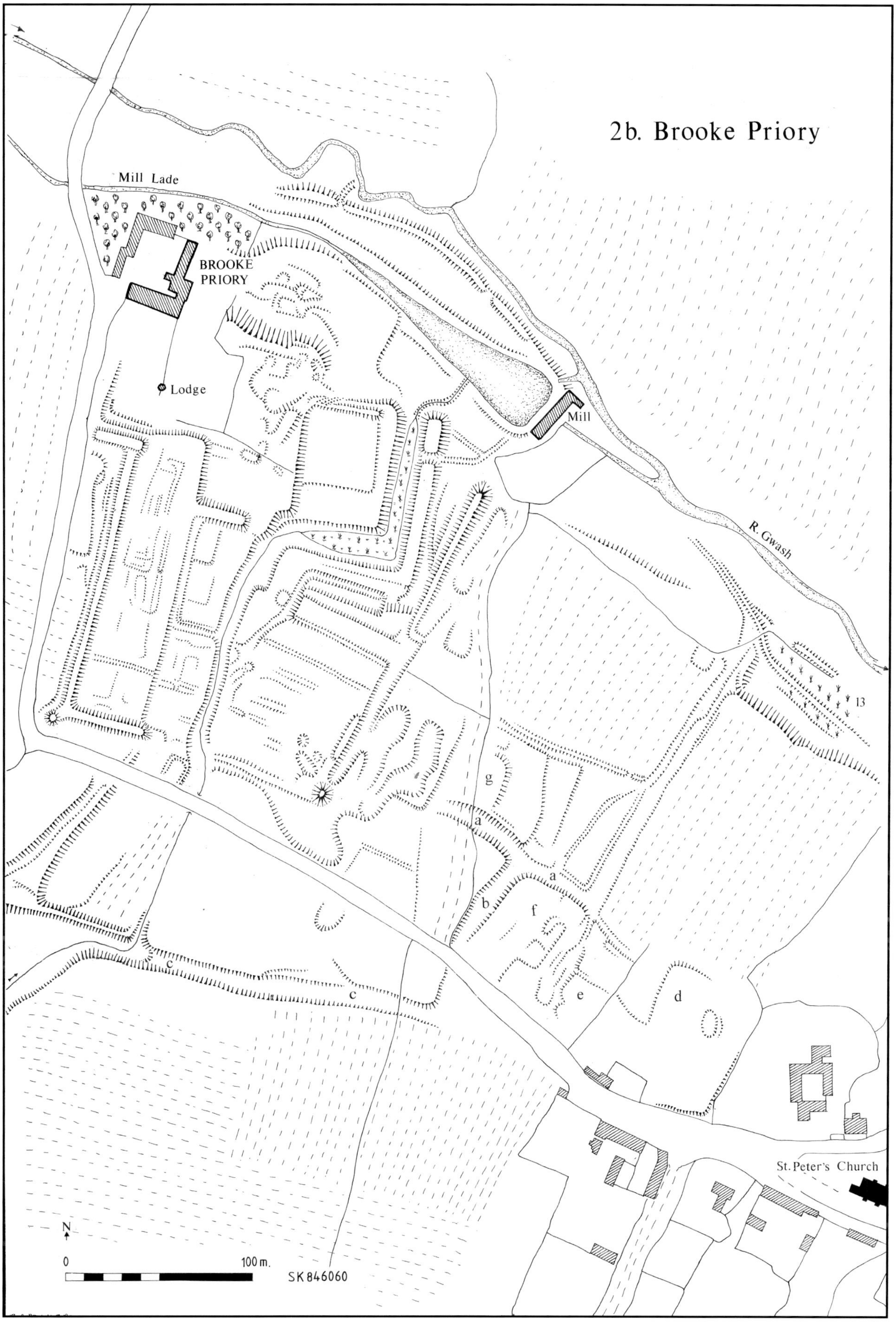

Figure 9: Brooke Priory and Village Earthworks

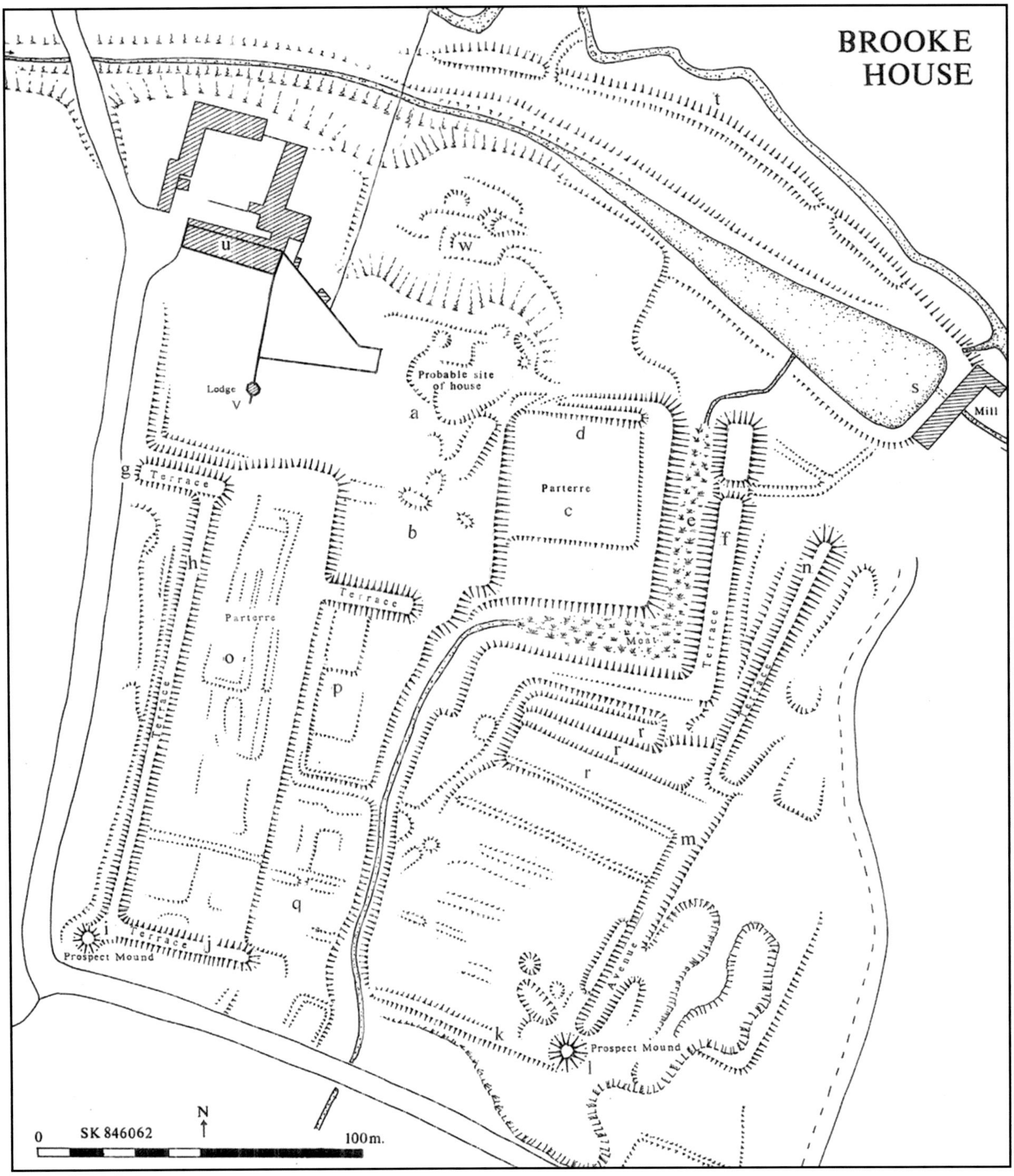

Figure 10: Brooke House

The probable site of the house would have been somewhere near (a), where hollows in the ground suggest that even the foundations of the great house were dug out for re-use as building material elsewhere. To the south the gardens began with a levelled courtyard or garden (b). To the east at a lower level is another parterre (c) which would have had ornamental flower beds. This area could be viewed from a raised terrace walk (d), and was bounded on its south and east sides by an "L" shaped pond or moat (e), beyond which is another raised terrace walk (f).

The formal gardens form a broadly rectangular area, surrounded on three sides by levelled walkways. Beginning on the west side with a short terrace walk (g), a longer one (h) forms the western boundary of the gardens, extending to a raised prospect mound (i). From here the southern edge of the garden is formed by two further sections of terrace walk (j, k.) which lead to another prospect mound (l) in the south-east corner. Extending northwards is a deep cutting (m), forming an alignment with another terrace (n).

The terraces and prospect mounds would have given wonderful views over the gardens, with their ornate geometrical "knot gardens", and also out towards natural contours of the surrounding countryside, giving a pleasing contrast. The southwestern quarter of the gardens had particularly ornate and extensive parterres (o, p, q), while across the stream to the east, on a slope above the moat, is an arrangement of three terraces (r, r, r) which would also have had flower beds.
Below the gardens, by the river, are the water mill and mill pond (s). The mill has some stonework in a style contemporary with Brooke House. It remained in use as a corn mill in the 19th century, being marked as such on the 1885 Ordnance Survey map. The buildings were derelict and largely roofless when photographed by researcher Emilie Gardner in the 1940s (Mills Archive. https://catalogue.millsarchive.org/brook-sic-priory-mill-rutland). The pool seems originally to have been larger, enclosed by a bank (t) which may have suffered from subsidence.
Of the buildings of the present Brooke Priory, there are features suggesting that one (u) could perhaps date from the 16th century or even earlier, but this cannot be confirmed. The lodge (v) with its attached arch would have formed an entrance to the site. It was retained because it was rather crudely converted into a dovecote, with nesting holes cut into the interior stonework.

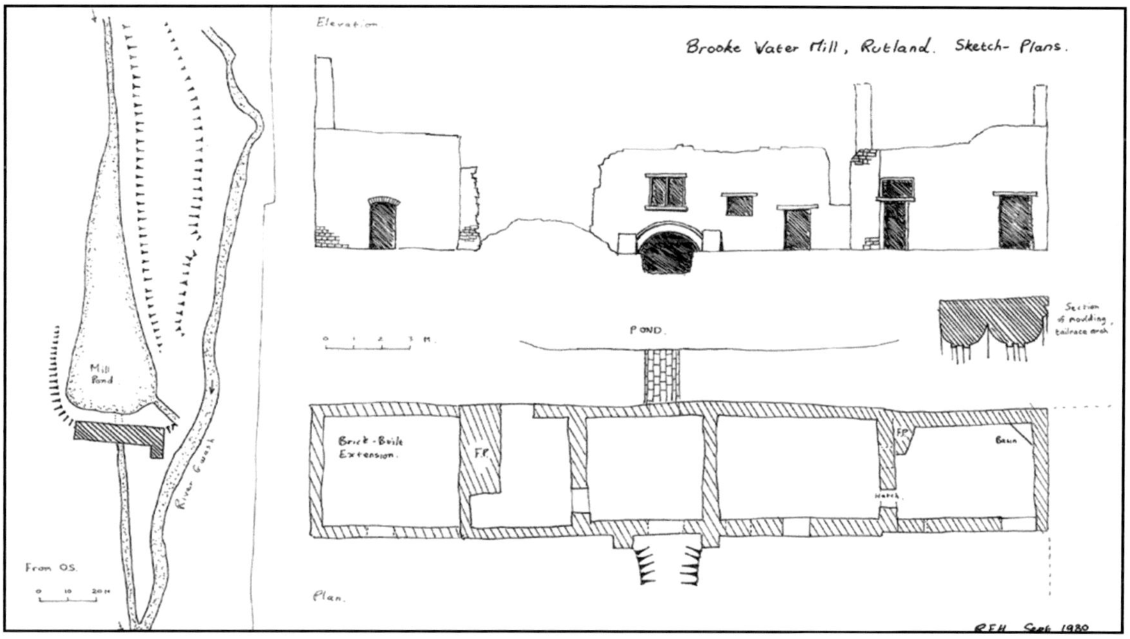

Figure 11: Brooke Water Mill

Earthworks Associated with Brooke Post-Medieval Park

Town Park (figs 8, 9) ***SK845056***

The hollow way (c, fig 9) led to an earthen dam across a shallow valley (fig 8). This dam would have retained a pond, and there were traces of two more dams (i, j) retaining smaller ponds upstream. The hollow way (c) probably predated the dams, and used to extend westwards (k, k), rising up the hillside, through a field named "Town Park", where there used to be a broad band of rectilinear earthworks, including a banked enclosure (l) low flat-topped mounds such as (m) and (n), long narrow mounds (o, p) and very small rectangular mounds (q, r). These earthworks have been removed in recent years, and part of the area has been built on. An inventory taken in 1680 records the existence of the "Greate Park" containing 50 deer (Brown 1975, 4). The dam at (h) has been replaced by a modern dam, retaining a pond.

Fishpond Park (fig 8 top) ***SK842062***

To the west of Town Park is the field called "Fishpond Park" and this indeed used to contain earthwork remains of dams (t, u) which had formerly retained quite large fishponds, with in each case a bypass channel (v, w). These earthworks have been levelled and the field ploughed.

Windmill Mound **SK853072**

On the edge of Brooke parish, where the lane to Oakham crests a low ridge, is the site of Brooke Windmill, marked on maps of 1824 and 1836 but burnt down on the night of 5th November 1874. The site is marked by a small spinney on the east side of the lane, where Brown notes the existence of a low mound (Brown 1975, 4).

BURLEY ON THE HILL

Deer Park

In 1206 there is a reference to a park belonging to Henry de Armenters, who at this time held the manor of Burley on the Hill (VCHR 2, 114). There seems to be no more evidence for the possible existence of a medieval park, but a large area of the parish was later enclosed as an amenity park, developed during the 16th, 17th and 18th centuries.

Burley House and Gardens **SK883101**

Burley has a fine hilltop setting, and in 1573 Sir John Harington of Exton acquired the estate and built a magnificent mansion house with views across Rutland and beyond. This was complete by 1595 when a lavish house party saw the arrival of two hundred guests. A park was created around the house, which was replaced by the Duke of Buckingham's short-lived mansion in the 1640s. A plan of *c.*1680 shows three terraces on the hill slope south of the house, with a bowling green and prospect mound further west.

When the house was reconstructed the terraces seem to have been enlarged, and although the formal gardens were largely erased in the early 19th century, there are still the remains of the terrace slopes, now grassed.

Alstoe "Motte" and Deserted Village (fig 12) **SK895119**

The site of Alstoe lies alongside the main road between Burley on the Hill and Cottesmore, and comprises traces of a village and clear remains of a motte or mound surrounded by enclosures.

There is a hollow way running north to south (a, a, a), which makes a junction with another one extending west to east (b). Alongside the first hollow way are probable sites of houses (c, d, e and f, and perhaps also at g and h). There are also foundations of a rectangular building (i), behind (f). The conical mound (j) called Mount Alstoe is still a prominent feature. The ditch which encircles it is shown as being water-filled on the 1885 Ordnance Survey map, but it is now dry. It is set in an enclosure (k), which could be regarded as a bailey, and has the remains of substantial outer banks. There is another enclosure (l) to the north, and one more on the east side at (m). To the north is another and larger enclosure (n). An archaeological excavation was carried out on the mound in the 1930s by G. C. Dunning (1936).

There is a mound of rubble, perhaps the site of a building (o), and building foundations (perhaps more recent than most of the village features) at (p). West of Alstoe House farm are foundations of a large rectangular building (q), perhaps a barn. Brown notes that there is abundant documentary evidence for the village of Alsthorpe from the Domesday Survey onwards (Brown 1975, 5; VCHR 2,112-119). Alstoe gave its name to a "hundred" - a division of the county of Rutland. Gatherings were presumably held at the strongpoint of Mount Alstoe.

CALDECOTT

Village Earthworks (fig 13) **SP866935**

The Eye Brook has been diverted to provide water to power the mill (a, b), leaving the original channel with less water and rejoining the new channel to the east of the main street.

Snelston Deserted Village (fig 14) **SP865951**

In the northern part of Caldecott parish the main road to Uppingham is crossed by the line of an ancient hollow way. This was once the main street of the village of Snelston, which appears in the Domesday Book and in further references in 1286 and 1316. After 1327 it was included in the tax lists with Caldecott (Brown 1975, 5-6)

Figure 12: Burley on the Hill, Alstoe "Motte" and Deserted Village

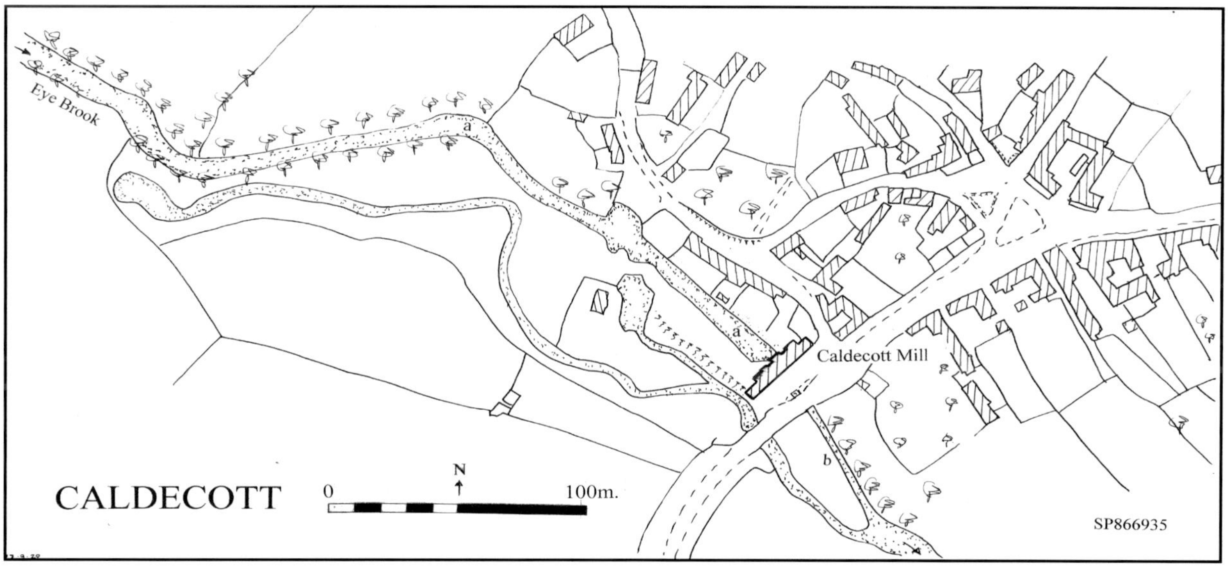

Figure 13: Caldecott

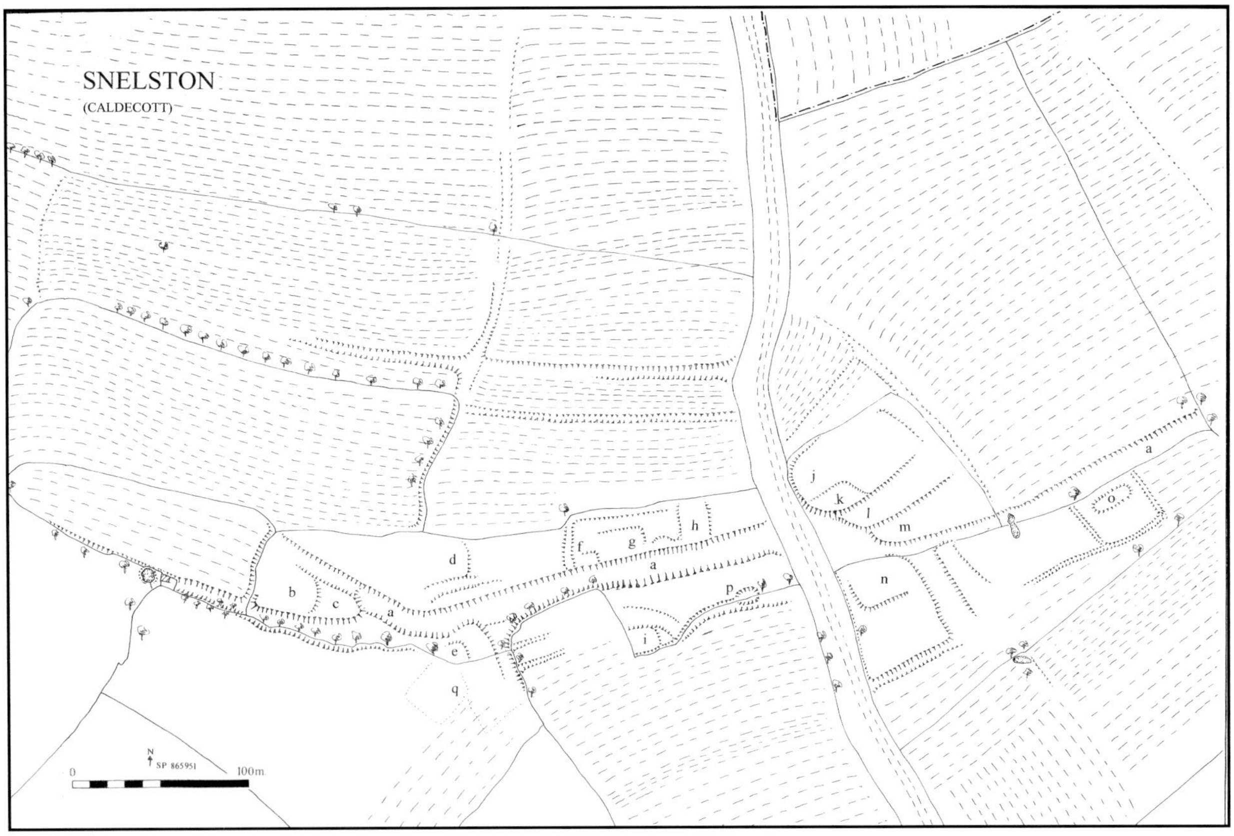

Figure 14: Caldecott: Snelston Deserted Village

The hollow way is flanked by an area of earthwork remains, including platforms where cottages and other buildings would have stood (a, b, c, d, e, f, g, h, i, j, k, l, m) and at the east end foundations of a large and possibly more recent building (o).
Back on the west side of the main road was a small pond (p). The field adjacent to the village site on the south-west side has long been ploughed, but soil marks have been recorded indicating the site of two closes (q) which had been levelled.
The earthworks survive in several small fields with old hedges. One was still named "Long Snelston Field" in the 1940s (Sterndale Bennett 1943). At the time of writing two fields adjacent on the north-east side still have fine examples of ridge and furrow.

Windmill Mound — *SP86589392*

Brown notes the existence of a windmill mound 16m (52ft.) in diameter at the end of a long, narrow close at this location (Brown 1975, 6). This shows on vertical photographs (RAF CPE/UK/1925, 1157-8).

CLIPSHAM

Village Earthworks (fig 15) — *SK971163*

The northern half of the village of Clipsham shows evidence of having been gradually cleared of houses to accommodate the creation of parkland around Clipsham Hall. Two estate maps of 1687-8 (ROLLR DE1175 MA/R/7 & 7a, illustrated overleaf) help understand this process. Although both maps are dated 1687 there are differences, perhaps because one was made for the owner and the other for an estate office. One gives land rent/values, the other does not. The area of the house, village and park from both maps is also shown for comparison with figure 15.
The lane to Clipsham Church used to continue eastwards (a, a, a) to what was in 1687 the Parsonage (b), where the extent of the plot can still be seen as earthworks. To the south, the 17th century map marks a house approximately at (c). Its foundations may lie under the small spinney. Further south again was another lane (d, d).

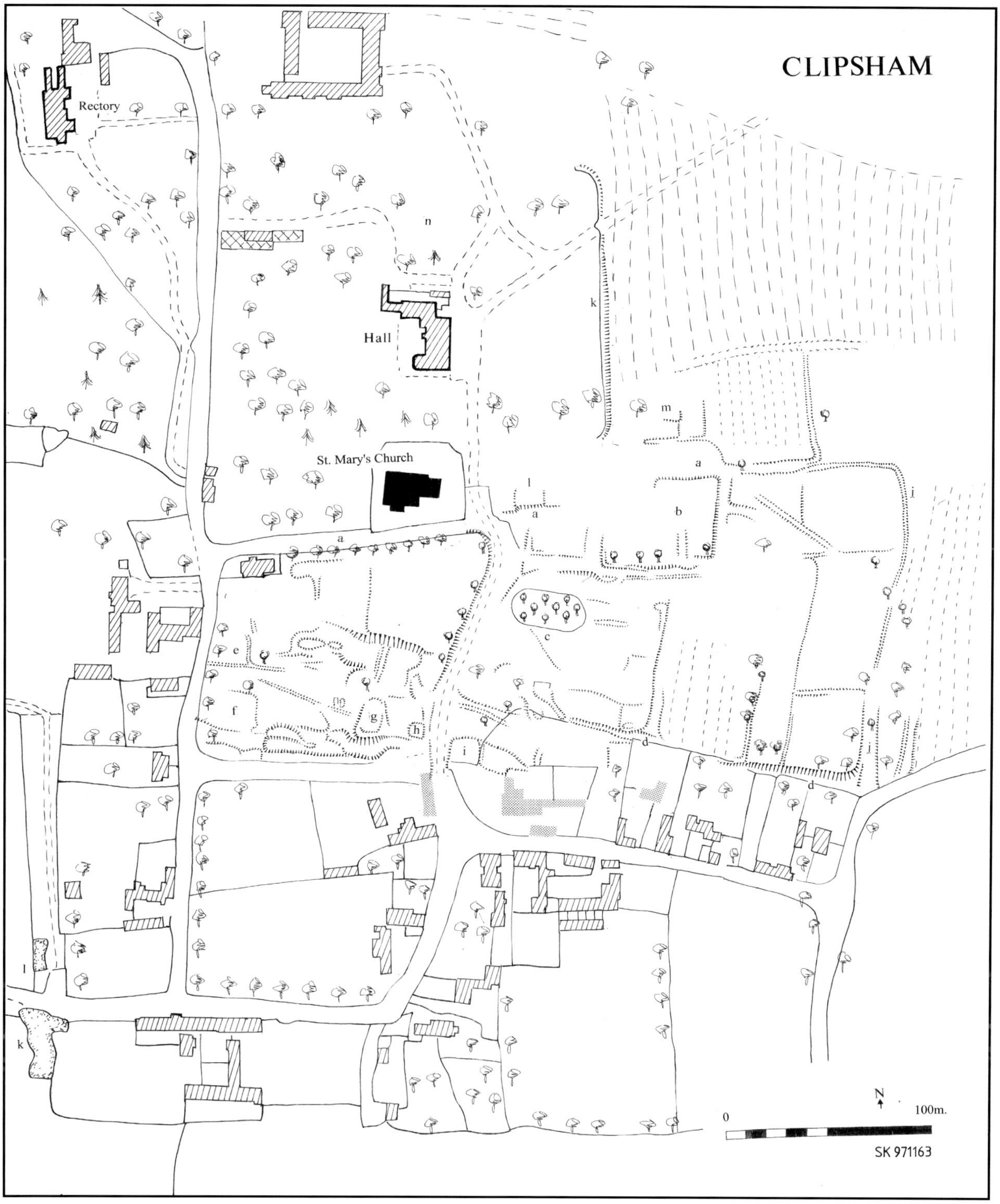

Figure 15: Clipsham: Village Earthworks

The sites of more houses may be identified in the field south of the church, at (e) (marked on the 1687 map) and (f, g, h and i). The eastern edge of the village can be traced by a hollow way and then a low bank (j, j).
East of Clipsham Hall is a ha-ha (k), probably created in the 18th century to give an uninterrupted view out over the parkland. There are other rectilinear earthwork features nearby which could be garden features, or village earthworks (l, m).
The map gives us another clue to the past, because the orchard north of the Hall (or Manor House as it was then) is called "Mott Close", probably indicating the earlier existence of a garden with ponds or a moat.

Above: Full plan of Clipsham cum Membris Lordship 1687 by John Wing, nephew of (and successor to) Vincent Wing. (© Record Office for Leicestershire, Leicester and Rutland, DE1175 MA/R.7-7a)

Both of the Clipsham plans seem to have been done when the manor was sold by Ezekial Johnson in 1686/7 (shortly before his death) to Richard Snow of Staple Inn (the last surviving Inn of Chancery in Holborn, London). A cartouche on one plan reads::

To his worthy and much honour'd friend Mr Richard Snow Lord of the Mannor of Clipsham in the county of Rutland and one of the members of ye six Clerks Office in Chantry Court. Health, Happiness and length of days here, and Eternal Happiness hereafter be ever yours by John Wing.

In 1699 Richard Snow purchased more property in the parish. The manor was rebuilt in local stone early in the 18th century and clearance for the park may have continued at this time. The manor continued in the Snow family until sold in 1865 (VCHR 2, 42). The plans are oriented slightly north-west.

Right: Detail of the Manor House and village of Clipsham from both surveys, showing the differences in illustration, lettering and legibility. (© Record Office for Leicestershire, Leicester and Rutland, DE1175 MA/R.7-7a)

East Stone Meadow
A R P
5 03 13
9 01 15
Mannor House
The Park
Cow Close
A R P
25 1 18
Hither Lownd
A R P
21 02 13
East Gleab
A R P
17 02 17
West Gleab
A R P
35 01 20

Moll Close
A R P
3 3 21
The Gleab Homsted
A R P
4 1 20
Long Close
A R P
4 2 35
Mannor House
Parsonage

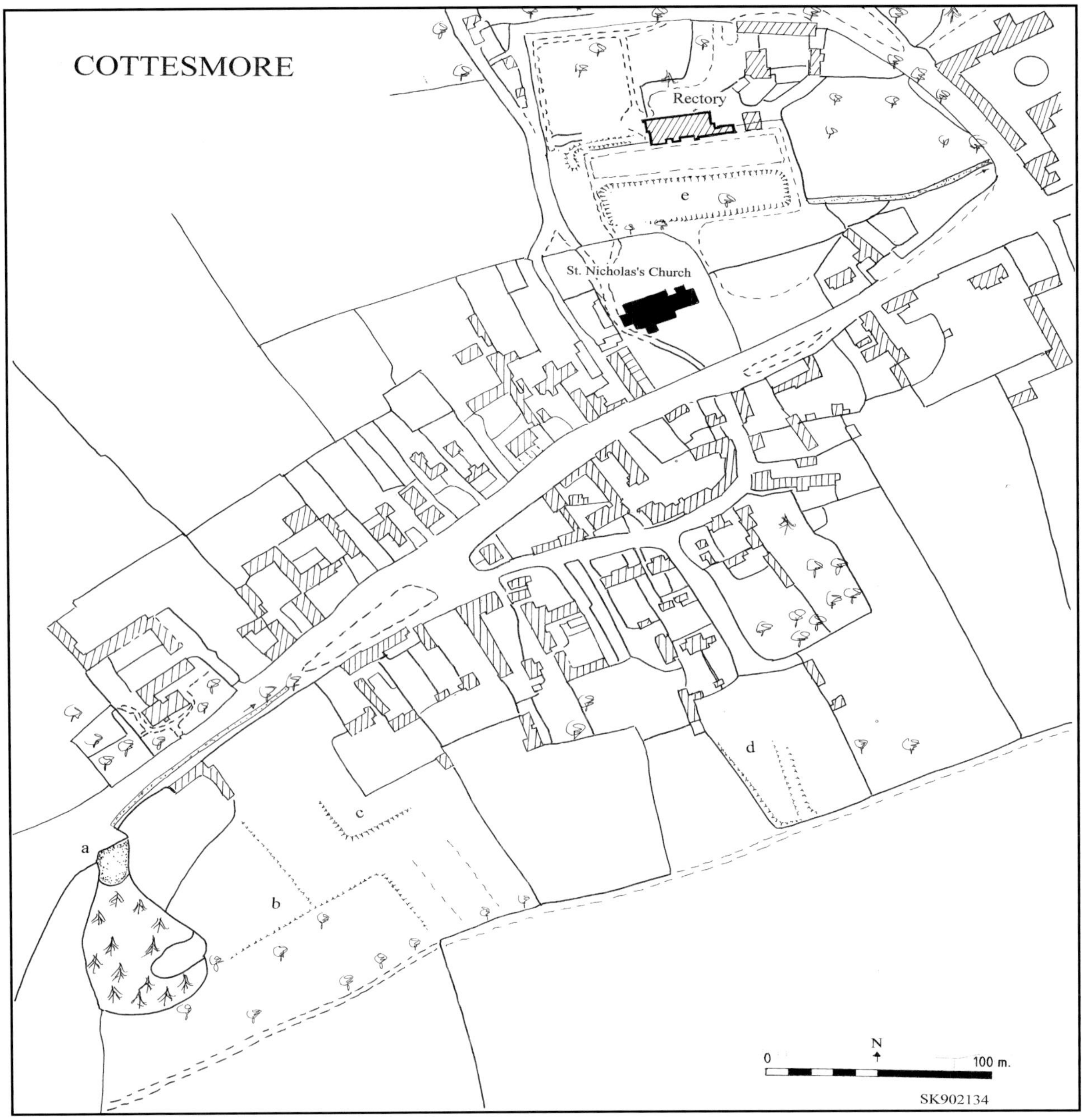

Fig 16: Cottesmore Village Earthworks

COTTESMORE

Village Earthworks (fig 16) — ***SK902134***

Some faint earthwork features have been noted on aerial photographs of Cottesmore village. A pond (a) (at SK 900133) is named as a "Public Watering Place" on the Enclosure map. South and east of it are earthworks of old closes (b) and a building platform (c).

Garden Earthworks (fig 16) — ***SK903136***

There are more faint earthwork remains further east in Cottesmore village (d). A rectangular fishpond (e) formed part of the Rectory gardens, and was in existence in 1730. The area is recorded on RAF vertical photo CPE/UK/1932 3139.

Wenton Deserted Village (figs 17, 18) — ***c.SK888141***

A map dated 1730 from the Exton collection (ROLLR DE3214/4571) gives a number of field names which indicate the area of the former village, which was on the spring line on the west-facing escarpment, between Barrow and Cottesmore. The heart of the village would seem to

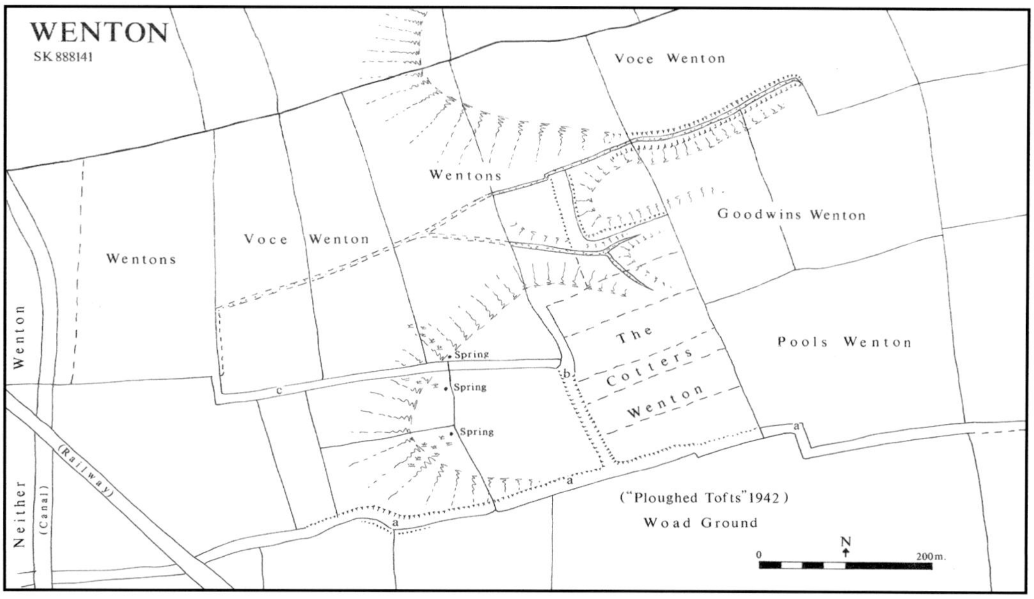

Figure 17: Cottesmore, Wenton deserted village and field names

have been "The Cotters' Wenton", and there is a junction of three old lanes (a, b, c.). Just to the south was the Woad Ground, which on the field name map of 1943 is called "Ploughed Tofts", making it even clearer that a village used to exist here (Sterndale Bennett 1943). Surrounding The Cotters' Wenton are Goodwin's Wenton, Pool's Wenton, and three fields called Voce Wenton, all presumably named after the families holding the tenancies in 1730. Wenton is mentioned in records of 1402 and 1407, when it was held jointly by the Sherard family and St Michael's Priory, Stamford. In 1537-8 the grange was leased to Roger Radclyff (VCHR 2, 123-124).

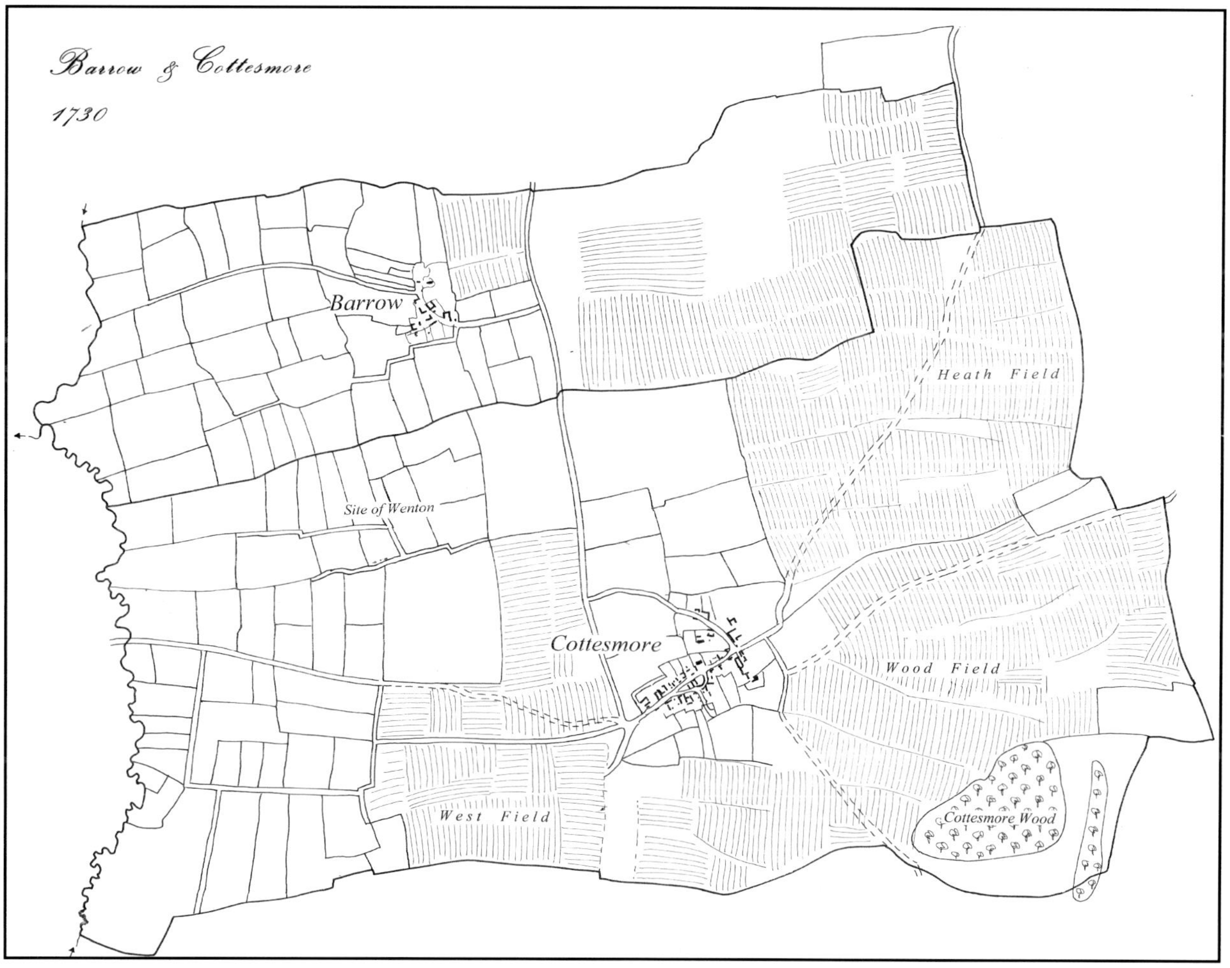

Figure 18: Barrow & Cottesmore, Ridge and Furrow, 1730

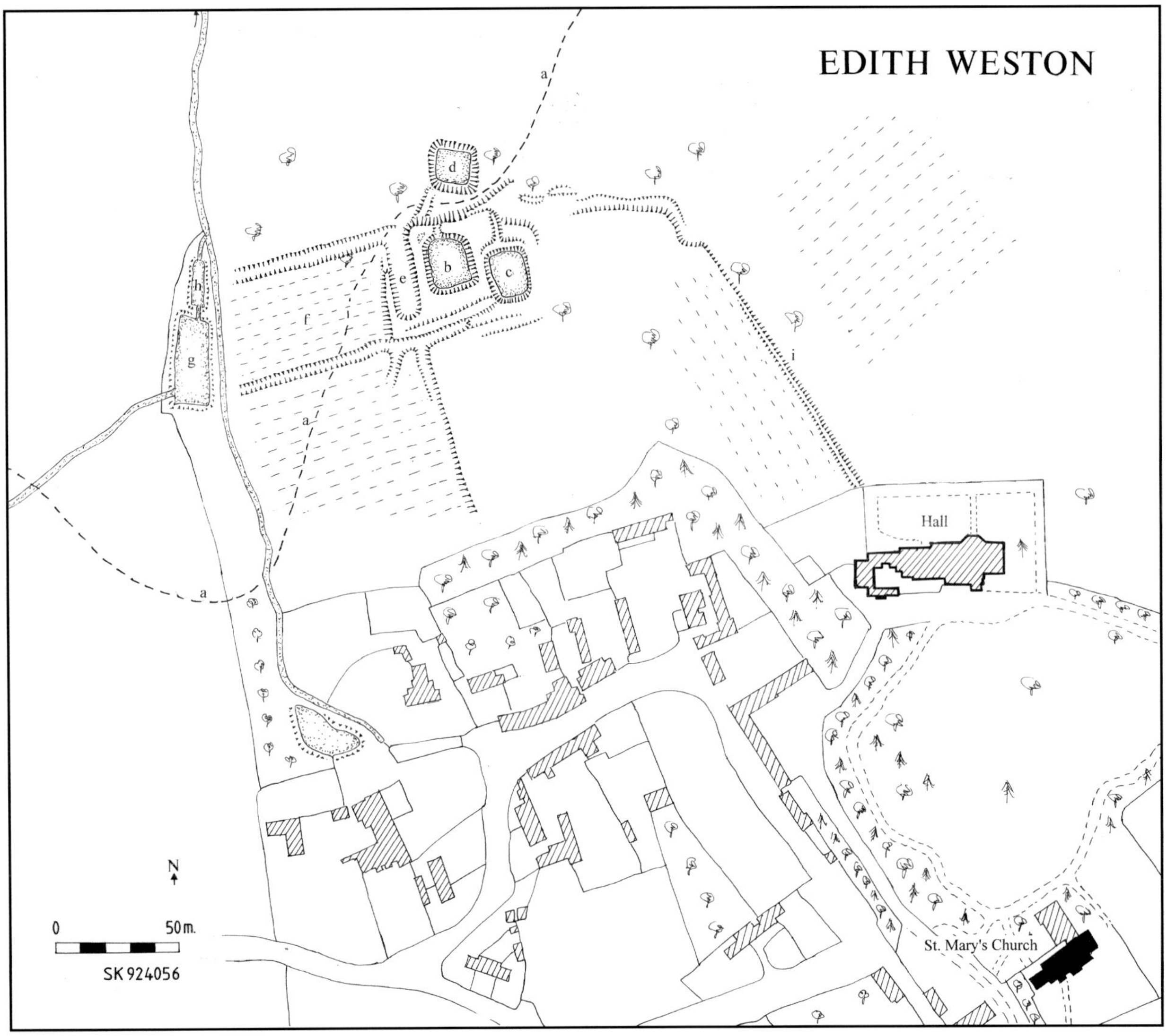

Figure 19: Edith Weston

EDITH WESTON

Fishponds (fig 19) **_SK924056_**

The edge of Rutland Water (a, a, a) comes close to the village, and has cut through an area of historic earthworks comprising three rectangular ponds (b, c, d). There was possibly a fourth, narrower, pond at (e). An old close (f) on the west side of this site, used to lead down to the site of two more ponds (g, h) marked onOrdnance Survey maps. The eastern boundary of this complex of features is a bank (i) beyond which is evidence of the ridge and furrow of the open fields. These several fishponds would seem to have been part of the gardens of a manor house at this end of the village. The site appears on RAF vertical photos CPE/UK/1932 2045, CPE/UK/1925 2064-6, and was recorded by the Ordnance Survey in 1969 (Brown 1975, 7). There is an alternative, perhaps less likely, explanation that the ponds might have been created as part of the structure of a small Benedictine priory. The great Abbey of St Georges de Boscherville, in the Seine Valley near Rouen, was given the manor and church of Edith Weston as early as 1114, and a prior is mentioned here in 1276. The community was small - no more than two or three monks - and in the 14th century was frequently in the King's hands on account of the wars with France. At some date before 1394, the Abbey of St. Georges sold their possessions here to the Carthusians of St. Anne's Priory, Coventry, and there are no further references to a priory in Edith Weston (VCHR 1, 163-4).

Figure 20: Egleton Village Earthworks

EGLETON

Village Earthworks (fig 20) **SK875072**

The old lane leading south out of the village (a, a) is flanked by areas of village earthworks. On the west side are building platforms (b, c, d), and a possible crew-yard (e). Further south are traces of a substantial walled enclosure, containing evidence of former buildings (f). There are remains of a stone-walled extension (g) to this enclosed area, and more foundations of buildings to the south at (h). Across the lane on the east side is another house platform (i) surrounded by other earthworks.

Further north in the village a hollow at (j) seems to be the old course of the stream. Above it on the hillside at (k) are slight earthworks. There is evidence of small quarries, (l) and (m) probably for gravel, with some traces of old closes at (n), and on the east side of the village (o) and (p).

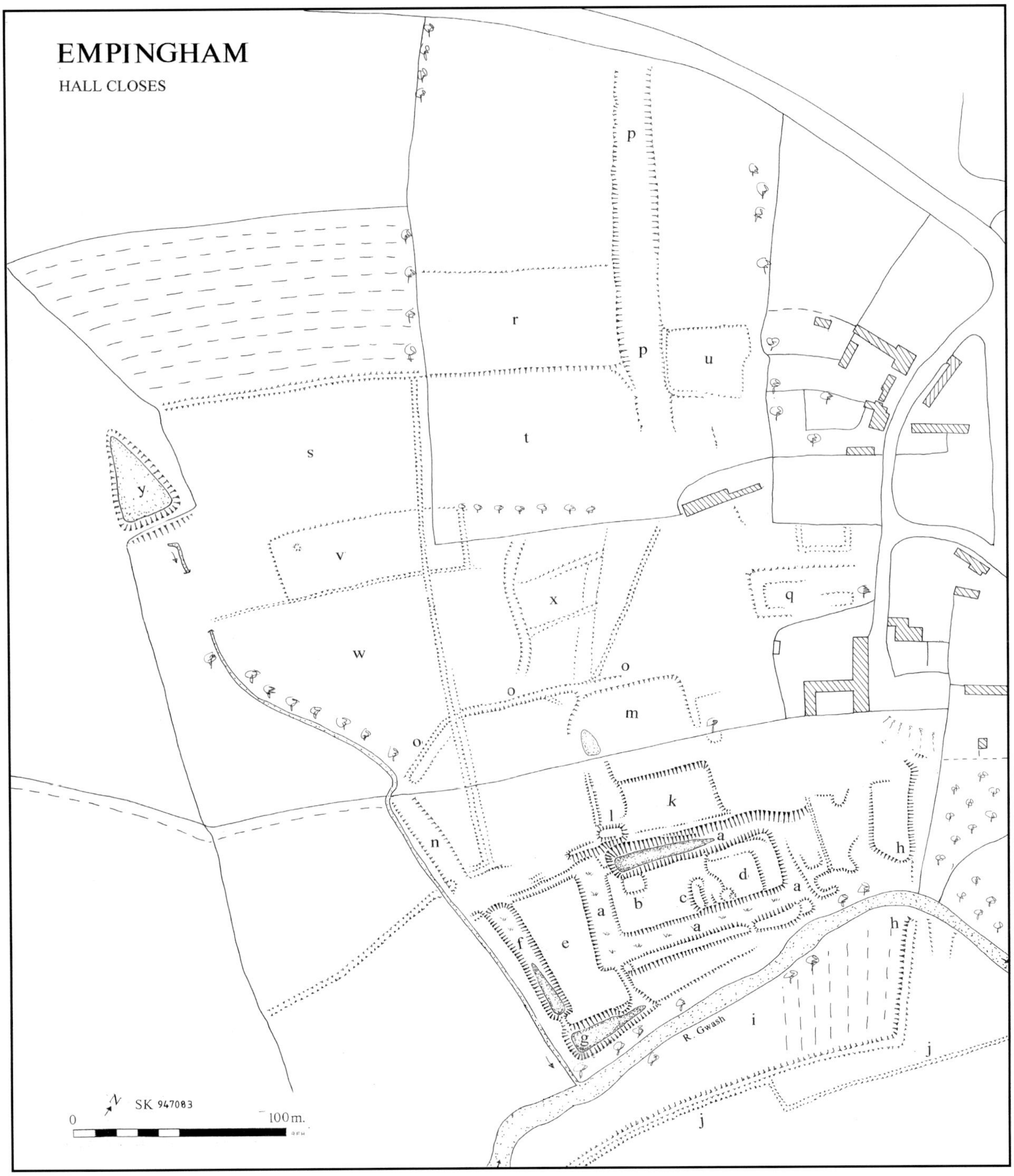

Figure 21: Empingham, Moated Site and Village Earthworks, "Hall Closes"

EMPINGHAM

Moated Site and Village Earthworks, "Hall Closes" (fig 21) ***SK947083***

Near the south-west corner of Empingham village is an area of pasture land with evidence of an abandoned manorial site. The most prominent feature is a moat (a, a, a) surrounding a rectangular platform with traces of building foundations (b, c, d). To the west is a levelled area (e), perhaps once the site of an orchard, surrounded by two fish ponds (f) and (g). South of the moat the River Gwash appears once to have been retained by a dam (h, h).

Forming a large pond around (i), with a bypass channel (j), north of the moat is a terrace (k), probably once the site of a garden, with a mound (l) perhaps marking the foundations of the gatehouse to the moated site. Further north are more features, with another garden terrace (m), another possible fishpond (n) and a bank and ditch enclosing these (o, o).
The original road access to the site may have been via the hollow way (p, p, p). Aerial photographs show the foundations of a large building nearby (q), perhaps the later site of the manor house, transferred from the low-lying moat.
Further north are more old closes (r, s, t, u, v, w, x) defined by banks and ditches, with another fishpond (y) which is still water-filled.

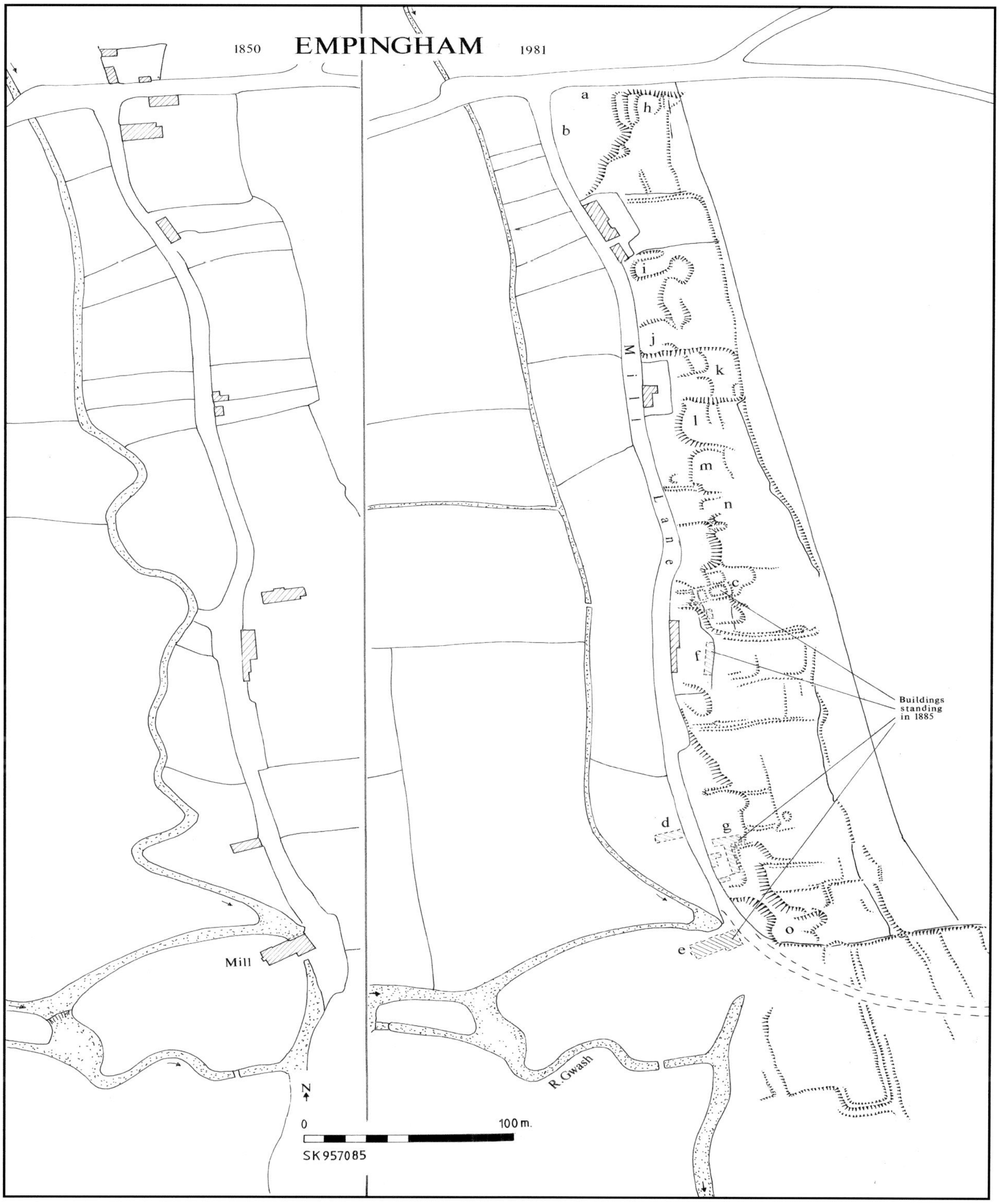

Figure 22: Empingham, Village Earthworks and Water Mill "Mill Lane", 1850 & 1981

Village Earthworks and Water Mill, "Mill Lane" in 1850 & 1981 (fig 22) **SK957085**

The eastern end of Empingham village shows signs of gradual depopulation of the area alongside Mill Lane. The Enclosure Map of 1852 (ROLLR EN/MA/R16/1) shows that buildings used to exist at several locations (a, b, c, d, e) which are now empty. In most cases there is no sign of these buildings, but at (c) there are very clear wall foundations. Site (e) is the water mill.

At least two other buildings, constructed between 1850 and 1885, have also since been demolished (f, g). There are platforms perhaps indicating the sites of earlier village houses (h, i, j, k, l, m, n), and around them all are remains of old enclosure boundaries.

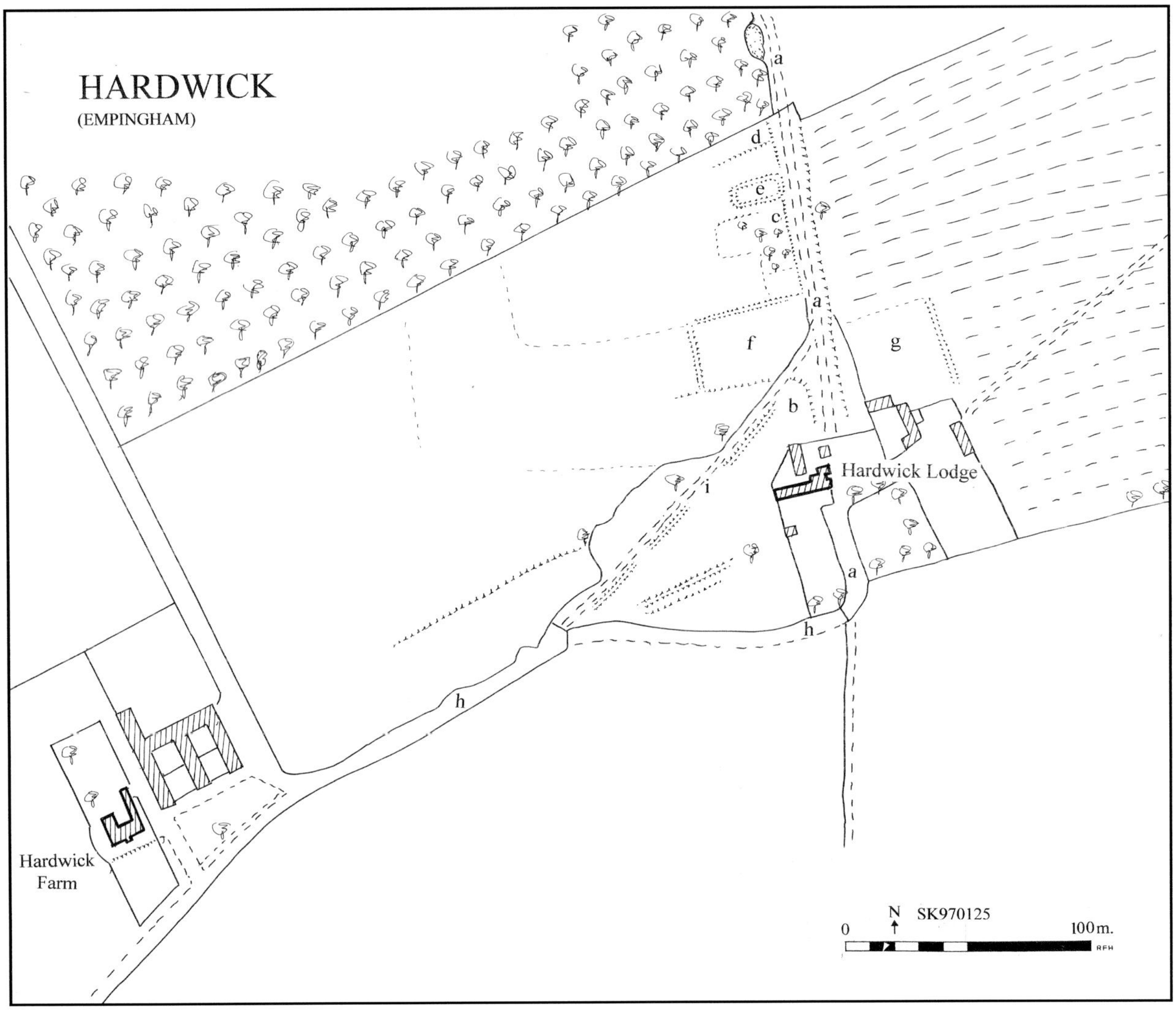

Figure 23: Empingham: Hardwick Deserted Village

Hardwick Deserted Village (fig 23) **SK970125**

The site of Hardwick village has been the subject of some speculation. James Wright, the County's first historian, noted that it was "formerly a Village, though now the Name only of some certain Grounds adjoining to Empingham" (Wright 1684, 69). In 1295 there was a capital messuage with pond and dovecote "worth only half a mark because of great deductions for the houses". In 1383-4 the village was described as waste and destroyed, and in 1495 as uninhabitable (VCH 2, 242, 246). The Ordnance Survey marked the site as southwest of Hardwick Farm, but this seems to have been an area of quarrying.

Earthwork evidence can be seen on an RAF vertical photo taken 17th January 1947 (reproduced in Bonser 2001, 347). An old lane (a, a) runs south to north past Hardwick Lodge, forming a slight hollow way. It is flanked by faint traces of village earthworks. There are slight platforms (b, c, d) and actual foundations of a building (e). There are also old closes (f) and (g).

The lane (h, h) linking Hardwick Lodge to the Great North Road seems at some time to have

been replaced by a cut-off (i), and although it had become disused the hedge banks alongside it survived as earthworks.
Remarkably the earthwork features noted above can still to some extent be seen on current Google Earth online aerial views. The area is a pasture field adjacent to a golf course to the east, where the pattern of ridge and furrow is still visible along the fairways.

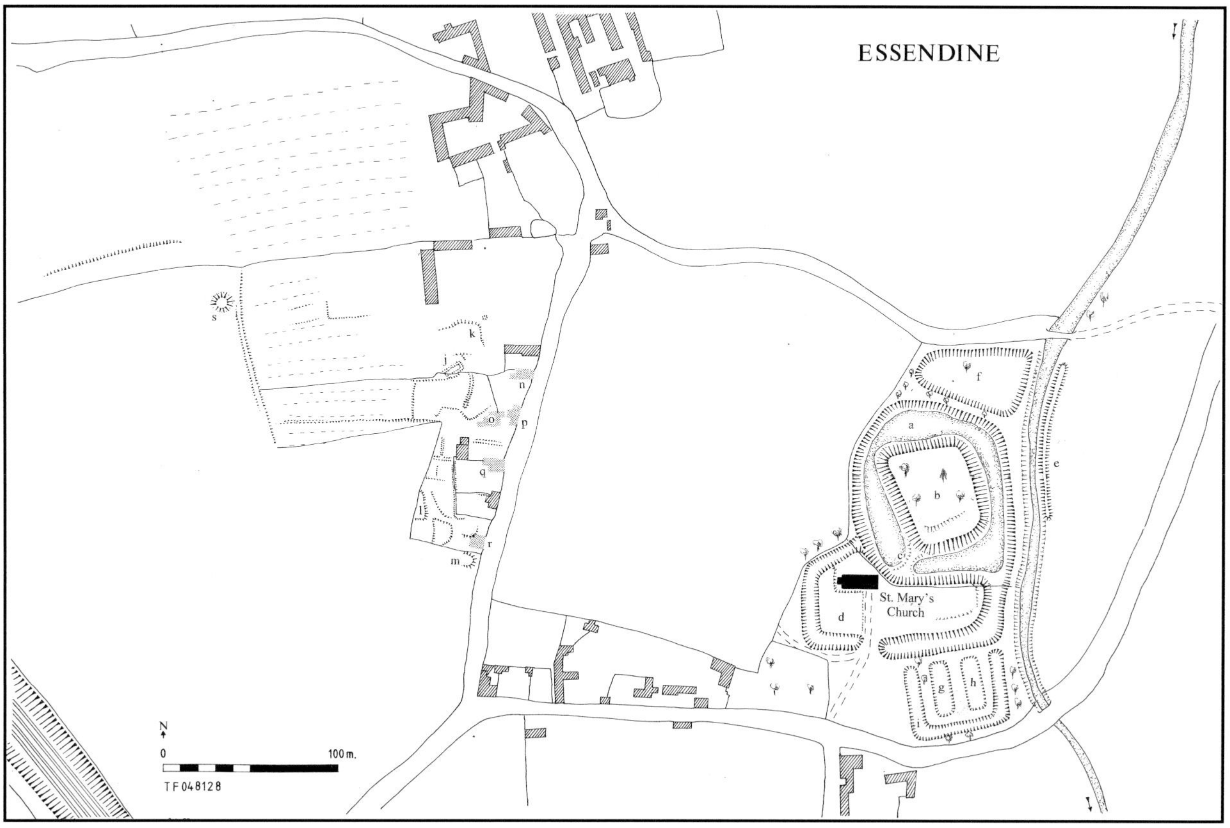

Figure 24: Essendine "Castle" and Village Earthworks

ESSENDINE

"Essendine Castle", and Village Earthworks (fig 24) ***TF048128***
The plan is based on the Ordnance Survey map as trees have grown up around the site. There is a large and deep moat (a), surrounding a platform (b), with possible evidenceof a former bridge or causeway at (c). Adjoining this to the south is a ditched enclosure containing a chapel, now the parish church (d). There is an embankment (e) to the east of the river. with a fishpond to the north (f), which may represent attempts to keep the river close by in order to fill the top pond. A complex of small fishponds is now ploughed away (g, h, i).
The village earthworks consist of truncated remains of what was until recently an extensive area of earthwork features (l, m, n, o, p, q, r). There is at least one building site (j, k), and a possible windmill mound (s) to the west.

Essendine Castle Deer Park
Associated with the fortified manorial site of Essendine Castle is a deer park. It was in existence in 1296 when Roger de Clifford stocked it with deer. It is mentioned further in 1318, when John de Cromwell complained that his park had been broken into and deer stolen, and again in 1333 (Cantor 1976-7, 75). In 1447 it was granted to Cecily, duchess of Warwick, and comprised 200 acres of wood, 20 acres of land, and an additional 20 acres of meadow and hay across the county boundary in Lincolnshire (*ibid*). In 1548 it was granted to Sir Edward Fynes, Lord Clinton, and was described as "a wood called Essendine Park", suggesting that it had by this time been disparked (VCHR 2, 250).

EXTON

Exton Park Cuckoo Farm Dam (fig 25) **_SK942105_**

The western arm of the North Brook flowing from the village and park was dammed by 1685. The water may have been used as catchment in dry times for Horn Water Mill.

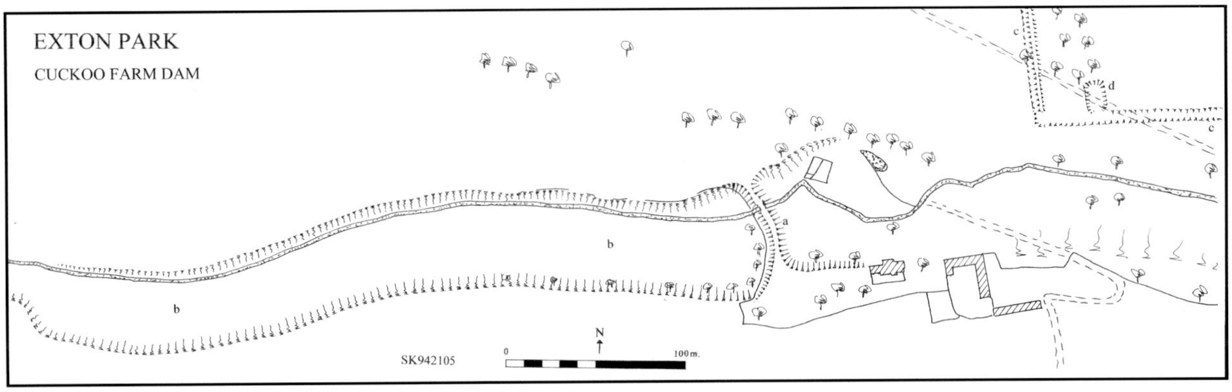

Figure 25: Exton Park Cuckoo Farm Dam

Village Earthworks and Old Hall Gardens (figs 26, 27) **_SK922111_**

Most of the earthworks are to the west of the village around the Old Hall and church (fig 27). Figure 26 shows the area before the construction of the present Hall and figure 28 the east side of the village where there are no remains of note to be seen. Earthwork features survive alongside the lane (a) leading to the parish church. The tithe map of *c.*1807 (ROLLR DE2459/66/1-4) shows houses alongside this lane (a, b, c, d, e, f, g, h, i and j). Only at (b) is there a clear platform surviving. Another building marked on the tithe map (k) may have been associated with the Old Hall. The earthwork survey suggests probable additional sites of cottages (l, m, n) and shows the wall footings of a small building (o). There are earthworks suggesting the former existence of a back lane along the western edge of the village (p, p) and a possible small pond (q). South of the 16th century Old Hall are two level garden parterres (f, s) shown in use with ornate flower beds on a late 17th century bird's eye view. They are linked by a terrace (t). North-east of the Old Hall in the late 18th century was a geometrical water garden with a moat. This area (u) was landscaped in a more informal style in the late 18th or early 19th century. The Old Hall was severely damaged by fire in 1810, and replaced by the present Hall, some distance to the north. This was begun in 1811 but mostly dates from 1850-51. The creation of this building and its surrounding gardens required the clearance of another area of the old village, which used to exist around (v) and (w). The large pond further to the west (x) was in existence as least as early as the 1690s.

Deer Park (figs 29 a/b/c) **_SK932121_**

There is reference to a park in 1185, when it was owned by David, Earl of Huntingdon (VCHR 2, 130). The location seems likely to have been "Todyngley" or Tunneley Wood. A map of 1633 (fig 29a) seems to show a rather larger amenity park of which Tunneley Wood forms the centre. In 1639 a new Exton Park was created by Royal Licence (Cantor 1976-7, 75). A birds-eye view in the Exton papers, dated about 1685 (fig 29b), shows this much larger park extending from the village nearly to the Great North Road. Much of the eastern half of the former open field of Exton village was enclosed in the process. The amenities included a large lake made by damming the east arm of the North Brook (fig 26 opposite). It was described in the late 19th century as "a noble...park of 800 acres with a herd of fallow deer" (Cantor 1976-7, 75).

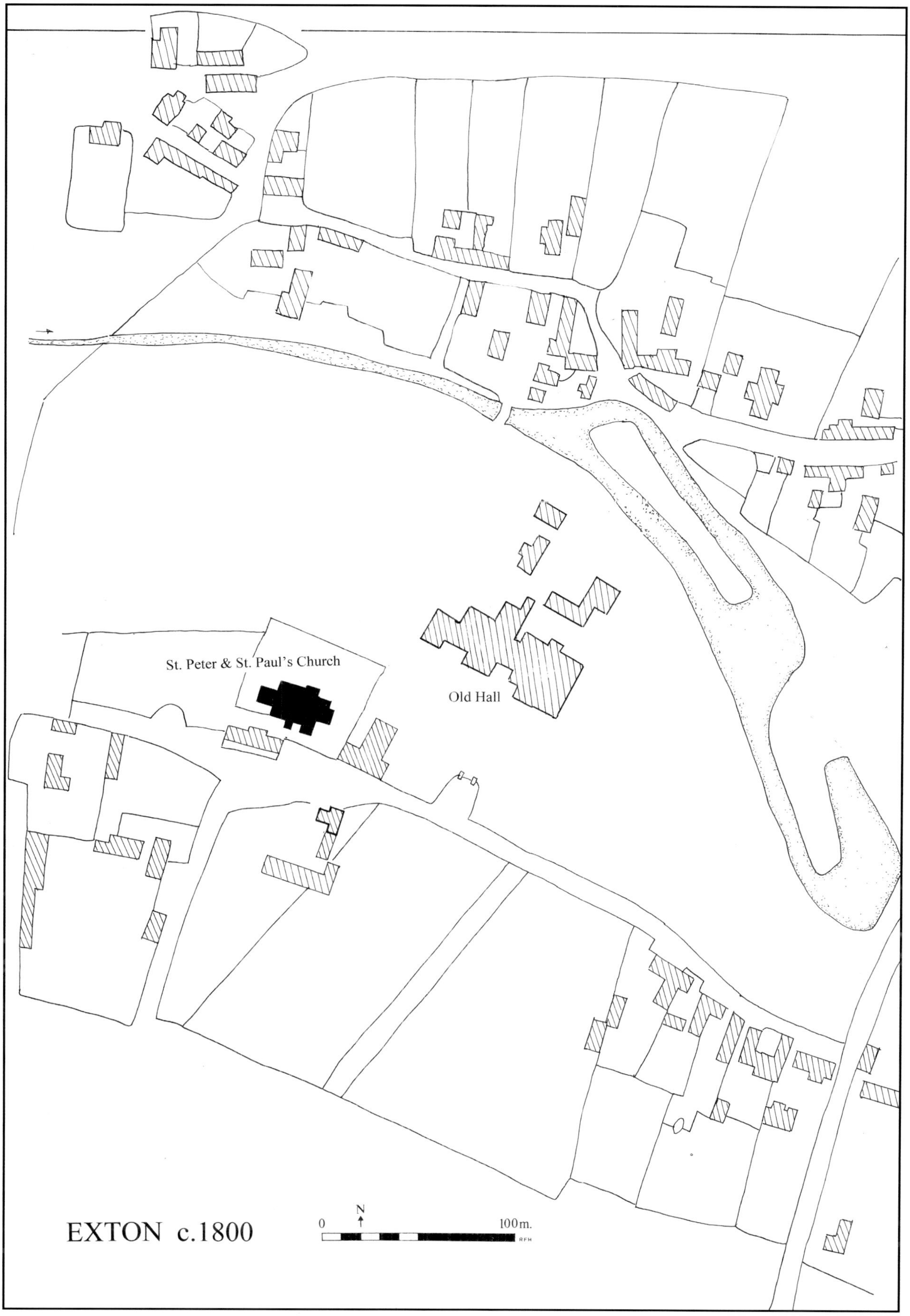

Figure 26: Exton village in 1800

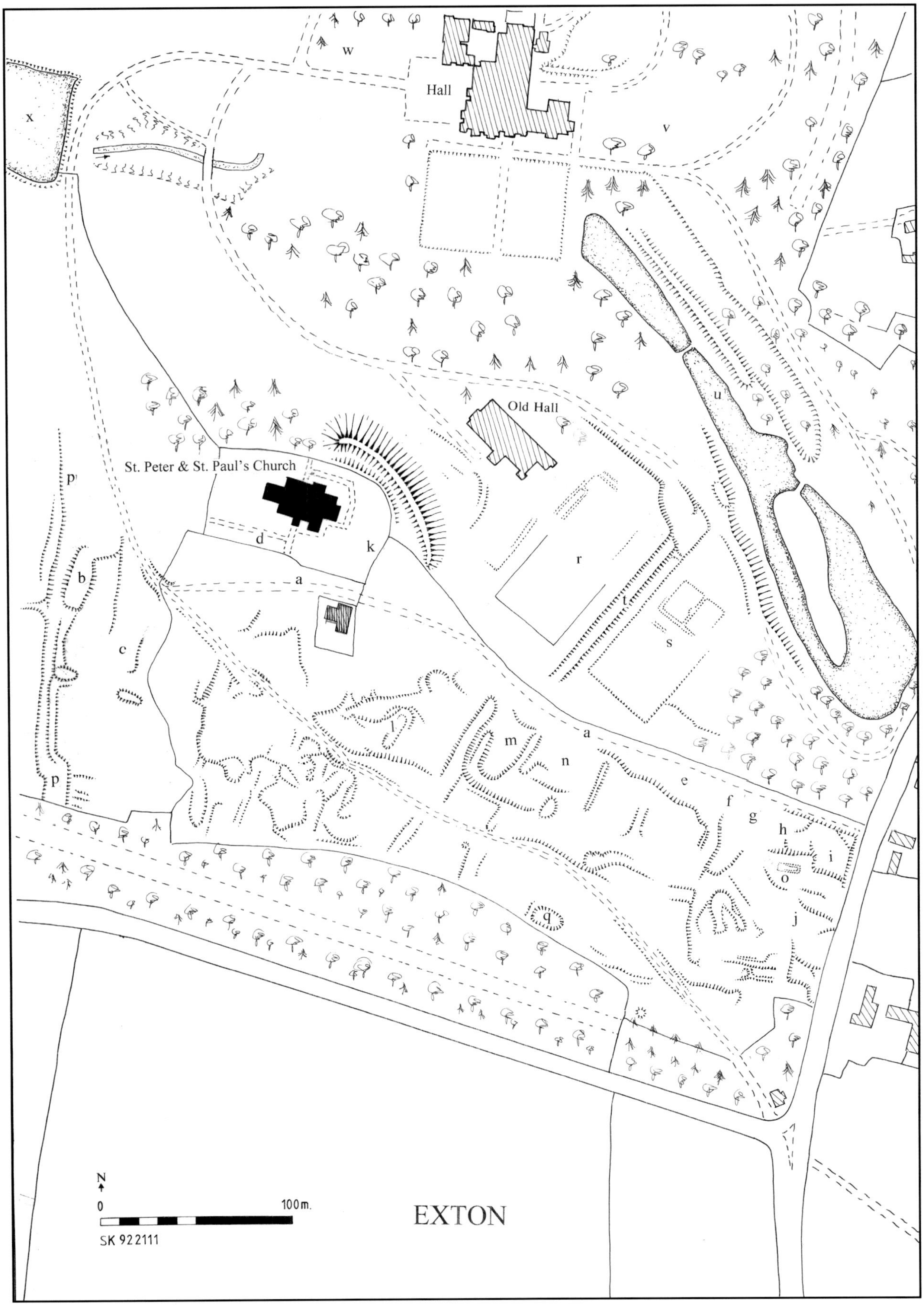

Figure 27: Exton Village Earthworks West

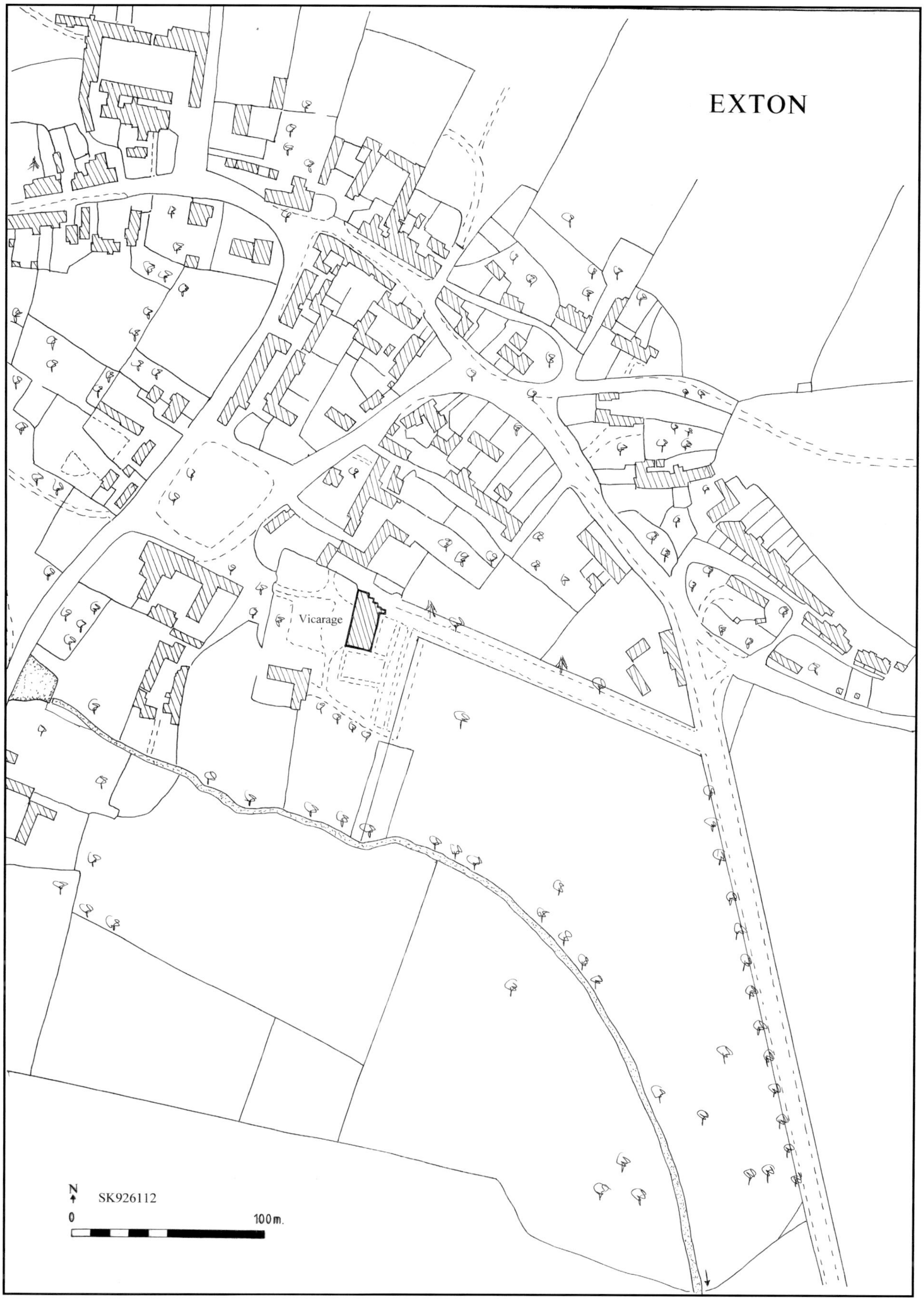

Figure 28: Exton Village Earthworks East

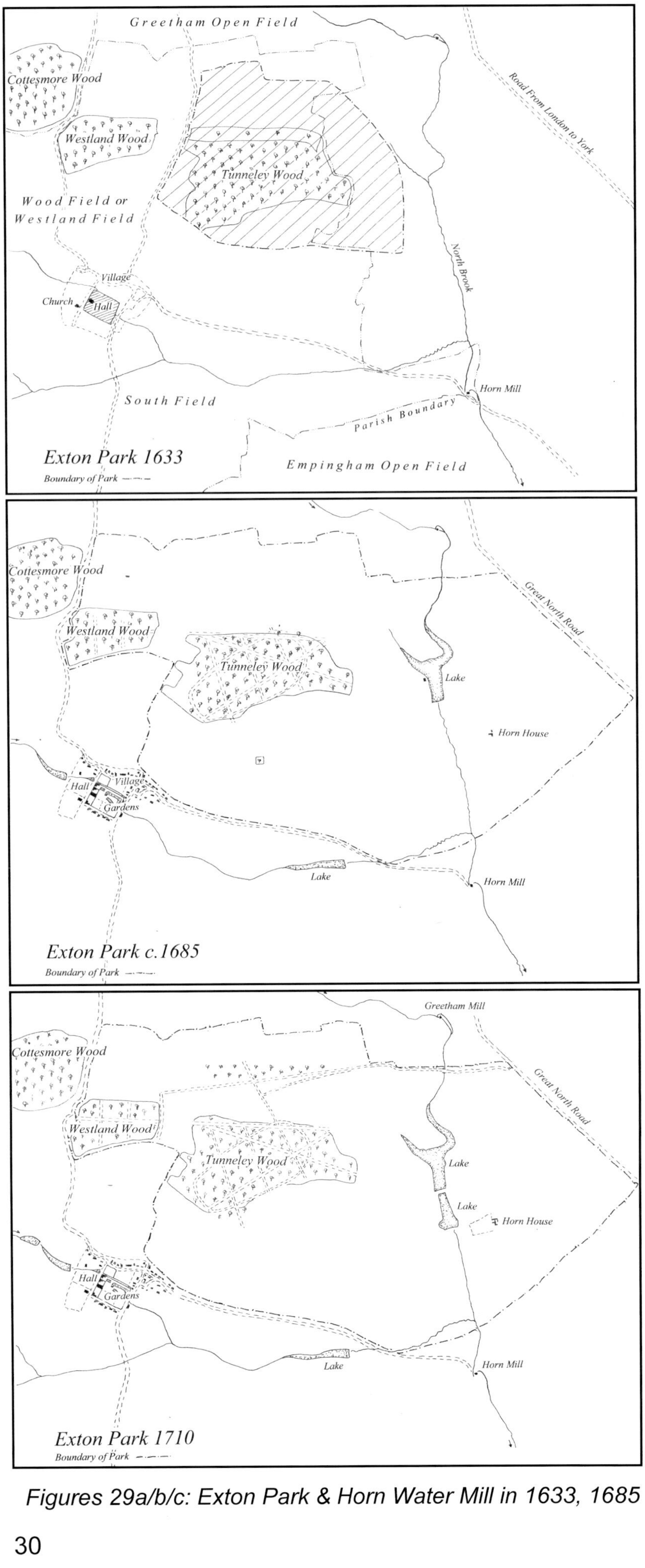

Figures 29a/b/c: Exton Park & Horn Water Mill in 1633, 1685 and 1710.

Horn Water Mill, Exton Park (figs 29a/b/c) SK95231049

In the extreme south-east corner of Exton parish is the site of Horn water mill, mainly in Exton parish, partly in Empingham.

The parish of Exton seems to have been deliberately extended at some point so as to include the mill, and it is depicted on the late 17th century bird's eye view of Exton.

Five photographs taken by Emilie M Gardner in the 1940s are on the online Mills Archive https://catalogue.millsarchive.org/horn-mill-rutland

Deer Park, Barnsdale SK910083

A notable oval extension of Exton parish used to protrude southwards between the open fields of Whitwell and Hambleton. This area contained Barnsdale Wood. The park is mentioned as "the park of Bernardeshull" in 1282, and "Barnardeshilpark" in 1421. A park is shown in this area on Saxton's map of 1576 and an anonymous map of 1602 (Cantor 1976-7, 75). The map of 1633 however, merely shows an area of wood-pasture.

The shape of the boundaries, and the topography, in a valley bottom, are strongly indicative of a park, and sections of pale have been recorded (Brown 1975, 11). Most of the area was destroyed by the construction of Rutland Water. A discussion of Barnsdale by Sue Howlett, especially pages 45-8, is in Ovens & Sleath, The Heritage of Rutland Water (Howlett 2007a).

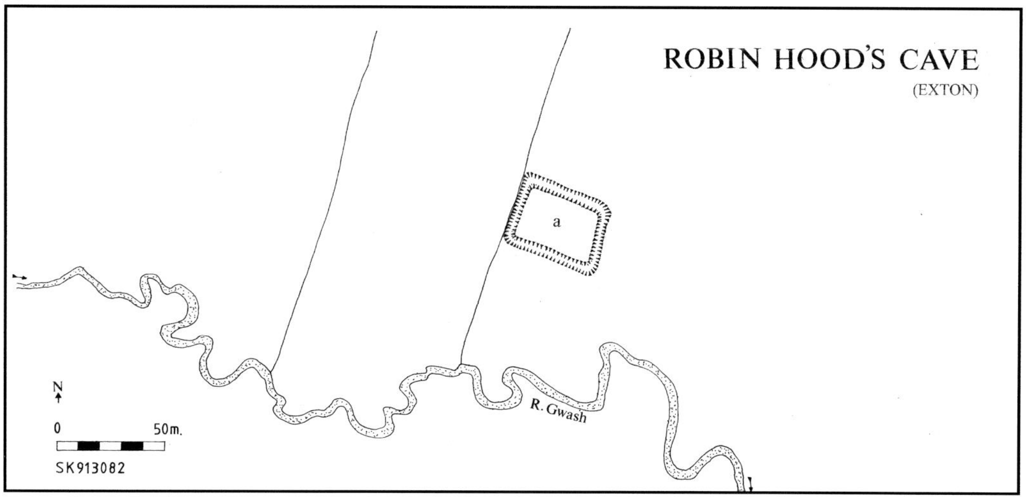

Figure 30: Exton, Robin Hood's Cave

Moated Site, "Robin Hood's Cave" (fig 30) **SK913082**

In the middle of the area of Barnsdale Park there used to be a rectangular earthwork site. This was also destroyed in the 1970s by the construction of Rutland Water but was almost certainly the site of a moated park lodge. It appears clearly on 1945 aerial photographs, with a small platform (a), about 35 x 25 metres, surrounded by a moat about 5 metres wide. (RAF CPE/UK/1932 3043: Brown 1975, 11).

GLASTON

No specific sites are recorded in Glaston. The parish was enclosed in the 17th century, prior to which there were three open fields, North, Mill and South (Ryder 2006, 64).

GREAT CASTERTON

"Woodhead Castle" (fig 31) **SK996116**

This was a strongly defended manorial site, on the eastern end of a low ridge. It would have

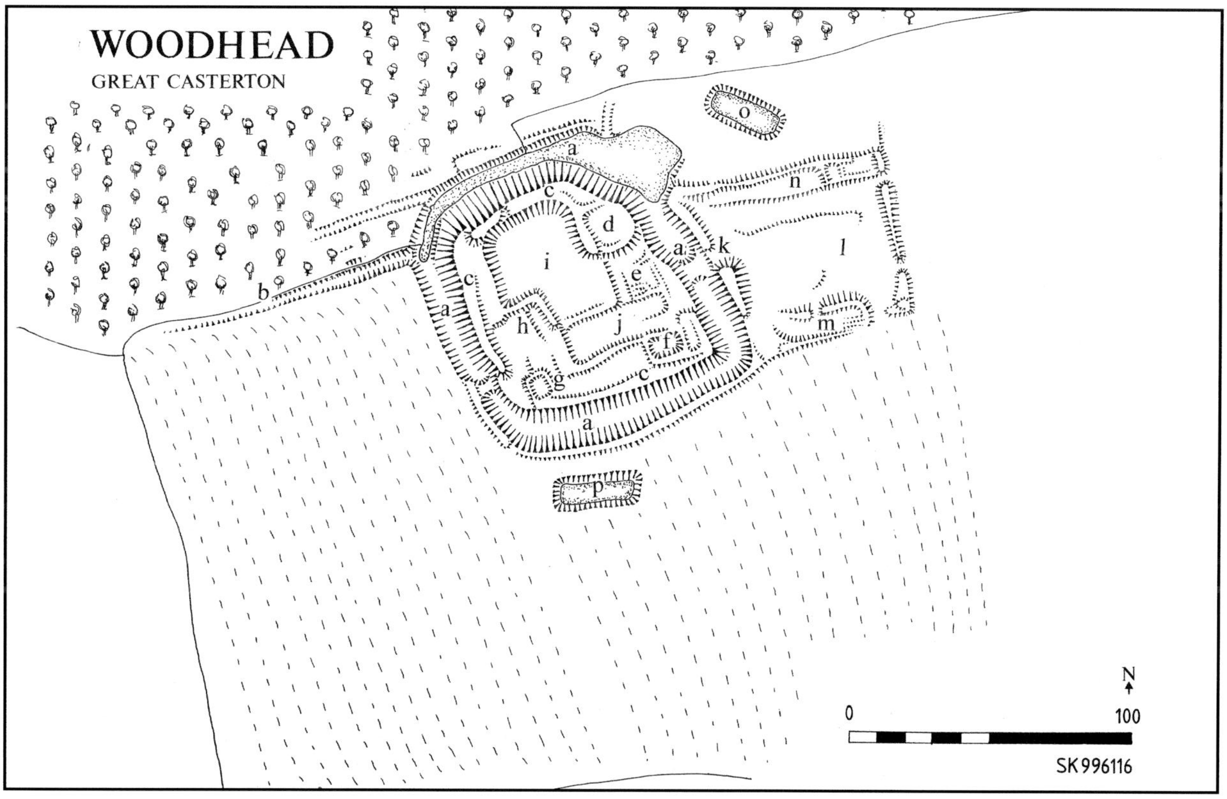

Figure 31: Great Casterton, "Woodhead Castle"

commanded views over the Roman road from London to York, and the lower part of the Gwash Valley, including the site of the Roman town of Great Casterton. Comparison with the sites of known Iron Age enclosures in Rutland suggests that Woodhead Castle may well stand on the site of such an Iron Age farmstead. It is unlikely that there would have been complete continuity of use, but the builders of the castle might have begun by making use of existing earthworks.
The site has a broad moat (a, a, a), fed by a small supply channel bringing any surface water from further west along the ridge. There is a very substantial rectangular platform, with remains of a defensive wall just inside the moat (c, c, c). Within the platform area are foundations of a possible tower (d) and wall foundations indicating rooms (e, f, g, h). Between them are two internal courtyards (i, j) separated by a wall.
The entrance to the site would have been at (k), where there are foundations, perhaps indicating the site of the gatehouse. This lies within a walled outer enclosure (n) with a large building (o), perhaps a barn, to the south, and a range of smaller chambers on the north side of the yard at (p). Outside the two enclosures are two fish ponds, (q) and (r).

GREETHAM

Village Earthworks and possible Manorial Site (fig 32) **SK925145**

There are two areas of earthwork evidence in the village of Greetham. West of St. Mary's Church is an area thought to be the site of a manor house. There are clear wall footings of several linked buildings (a, b, c, d) and a walled yard (e).
Towards the east end of the village, and east of the existing Manor House, is a compact area of remains with wall footings of two buildings (f, g), a building platform (h) and a hollow (i), perhaps a crew-yard. To the north is an enclosure (j) with a bank dividing it from the old back lane (k).

Deer Park

A park belonging to Greetham Manor House is recorded in 1446, when because of the minority of the heir of the Duke of Warwick to whom the manor belonged, the Crown appointed a park keeper (VCHR 2, 136). This may have been in the area of Greetham Wood, but the pale has not been traced (Brown 1975,13).

Water Mill

This water mill on the North Brook is shown on the 1680s birds-eye view of Exton Park.

Windmill **SK95141314**

The Mills Archive has a drawing by Karl Wood in 1932 showing the base of this tower mill. https://catalogue.millsarchive.org/greetham-tower-mill (shown left).

Greetham Tower Mill

GUNTHORPE

Village (fig 33 overleaf) **SK870056**

The Hall and its outbuildings comprise most of the buildings in this small parish. Alongside the access road are some earthworks probably indicating part of the former village. There is a rather irregular hollow way (a-a-a) flanked by building platforms (b, c, d, e, f, g). There are more substantial building foundations to the north (h) within a ditched enclosure (i), and another enclosure to the east (j).
To the south of the access road is an area (k), bounded by a ditch, which could indicate the southern edge of the village, or the boundary of a now-cleared ornamental plantation. There is a pond at (l), and another (m) set in a garden terrace (n) near the Hall.

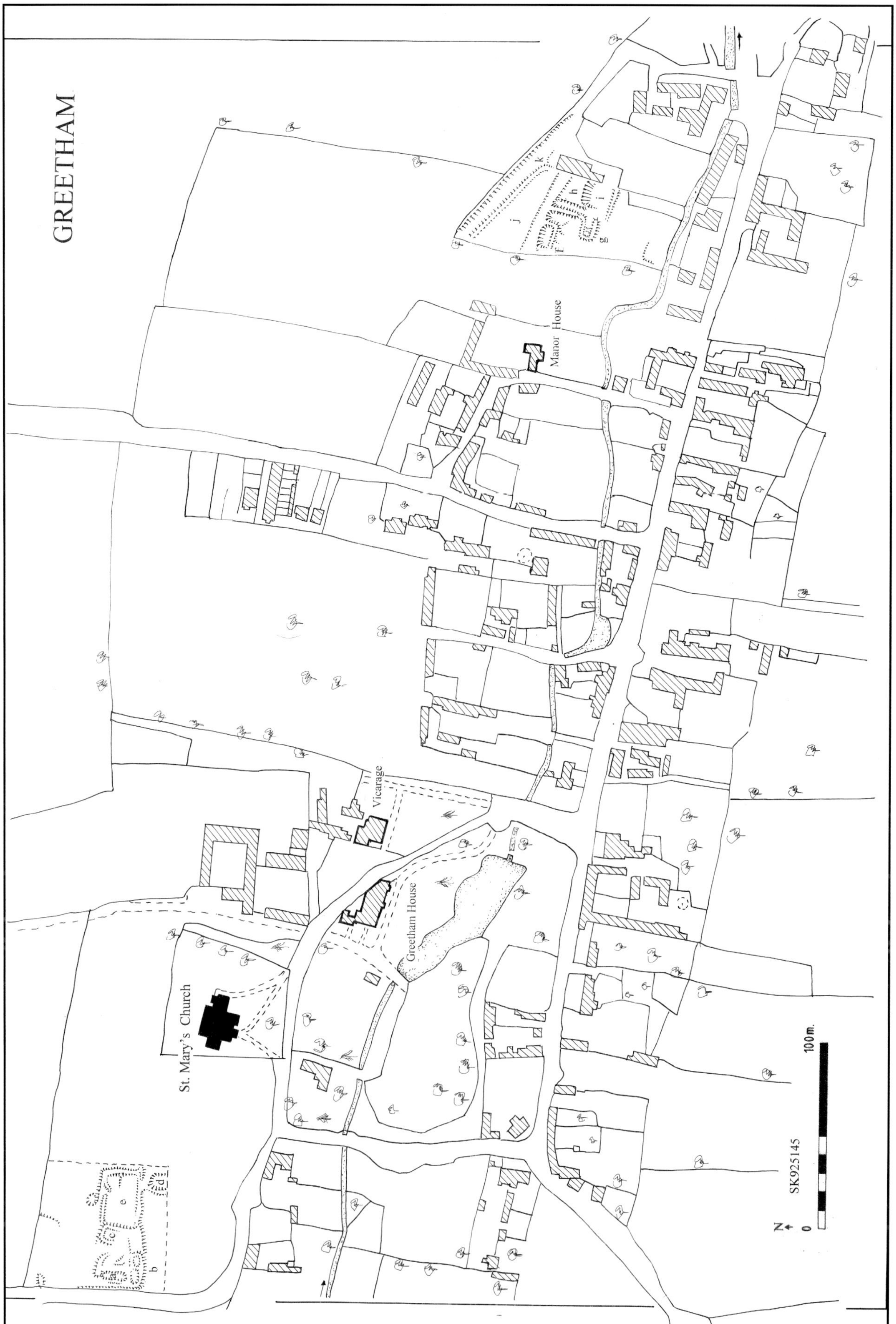

Figure 32: Greetham, village earthworks

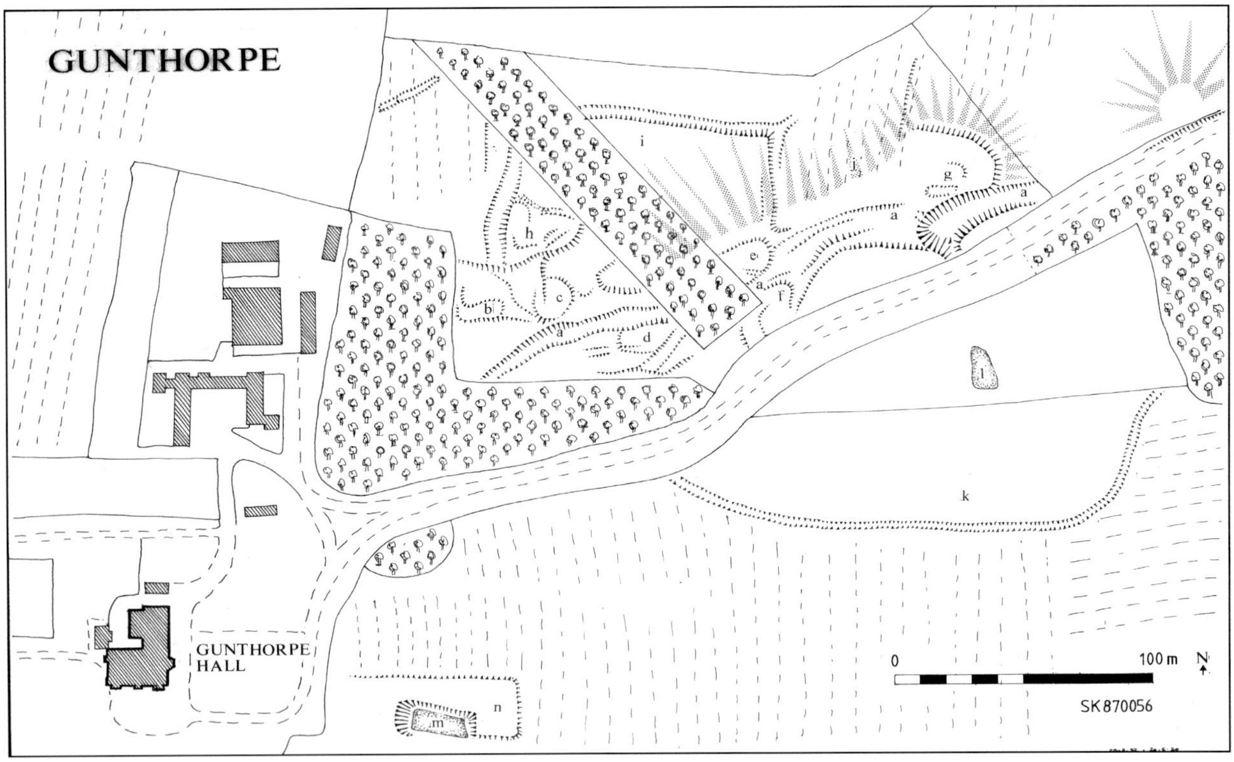

Figure 33: Gunthorpe Village

HAMBLETON

Hambleton Wood is marked on Speed's map of 1611 as a small park. A stretch of bank is visible on vertical photographs (RAF CPE/UK/1925 2063-4) running NE from SK 9105 0635 (Brown 1975, 14). This is now under Rutland Water. The village at the centre of this parish formerly had three distinct foci - Upper, Middle and Nether Hambleton. The parish church is in the largest settlement, Upper Hambleton. Much of the parish, including the site of Nether Hambletonm was flooded to create Rutland Water in the 1970s.

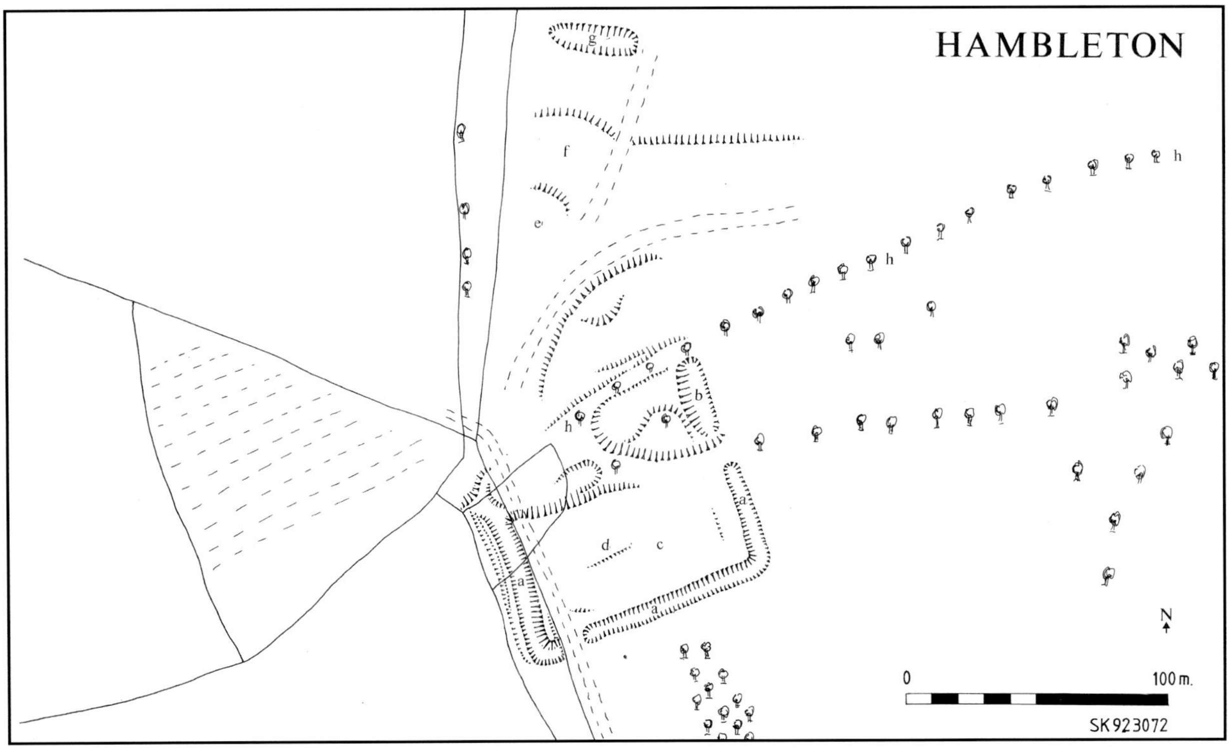

Figure 34: Hambleton "Moat" Site, Barn Hill

Moated Site, Barn Hill (fig 34) **SK923072**

Near the end of what is now the Hambleton Peninsula are the earthworks of a moated site. The moat (a, a, a) is approximately 8m wide, enclosing the west, south and east sides of the site. The north-east corner (b) is marked by a separate hollow, presumably once a pond. The rectangular platform (c) has slight traces of possible building foundations (d). Down the slope to the north are terraces (e, f), and another pond (g). To the west of the moat the field has traces of ridge and furrow which appear to have been truncated by construction of the moat.

Sited as it is on a ridge, in terms of topography, this "moat" could be the remains of the manor of Hambleton Parva/Little Hambleton. The First Edition Ordnance Survey maps show that it was then in the north-west corner of the splendid sweep of parkland surrounding Normanton Hall. This portion of the parkland is named as New Park and was probably created in the 1760s for Sir Gilbert Heathcoat, 3rd Baronet. A line of large trees shown on the First Edition maps (h, h) seems to have defined part of the boundary of Normanton Park so it is also possible that the "moat" may have been created as the site of some picturesque parkland feature as a building visible on the skyline when viewed from Normanton Hall.

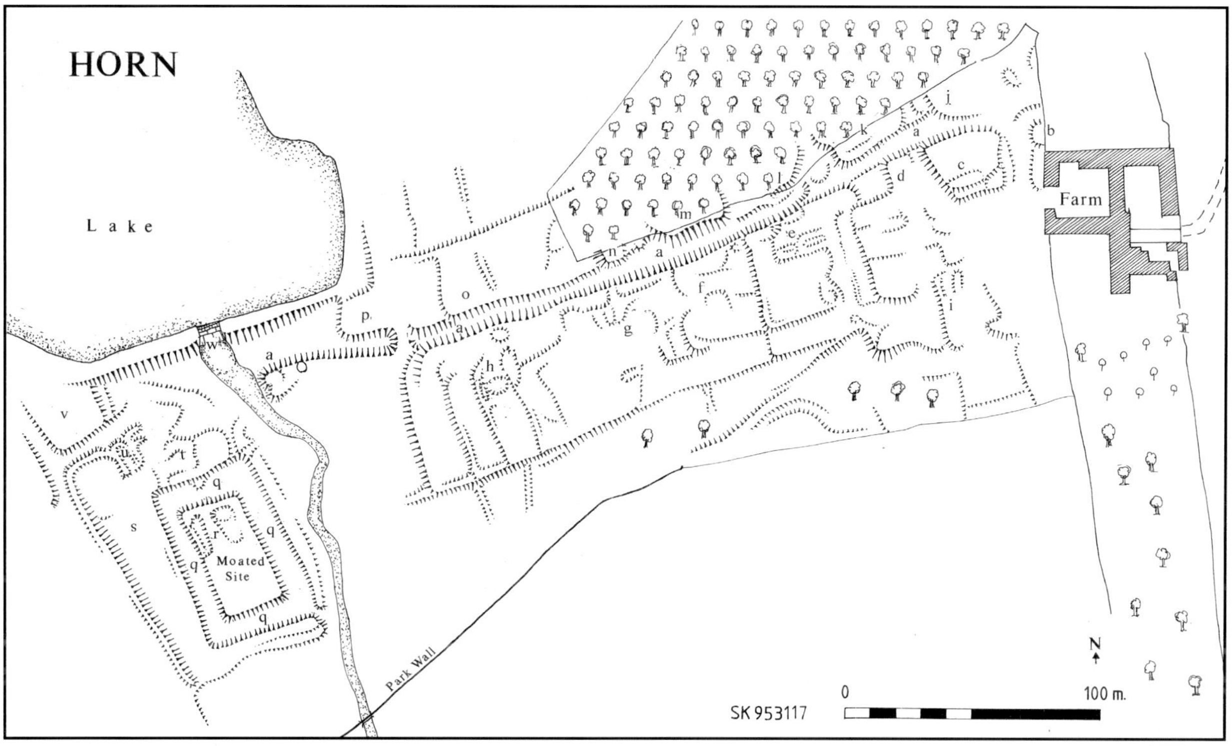

Figure 35: Horn Deserted Village

HORN

Deserted Village of Horn (fig 35) **SK953117**

A fine area of earthworks survives to mark the site of the village and manor house of Horn. A hollow way (a, a, a) marks the course of the village street. Most of the earthwork evidence lies to the south of this, with house platforms (b, c, d, e, f, g, h and i). Wall foundations may be discerned at (e), (h) and (i).

There is a plantation of trees on the north side of the hollow way, but along its fringes evidence of more building platforms can be seen (j, k ,l, m, n, o, p). To the west, across the North Brook, is a moat (q) some 10m wide, surrounding a platform approximately 40m x 20m. This probably marks the location of a manor house, and there are signs of building foundations (r).

To the west, outside the moat, is an enclosure (s), probably once containing a garden or orchard, while north of the moat is an area of building foundations (t), probably the site of the manorial farm buildings. Wall footings at (u) may indicate the site of a gatehouse.

There is another building platform (v) to the north, probably another of the village crofts which used to extend all along the north side of the hollow way, but in this area they are partially obliterated by the construction of a large earth dam. This was constructed in about 1700 to form a second large lake in the Exton Hall parkland. An engraved view dated 1749 shows that the overflow (w) at that time had ornamental cascades, of which there is now no obvious sign. The village of Horn appears in the Domesday Survey in 1086, but by 1376 the principal manor was declared to be valueless, and a reference in 1384 notes that "the whole village was then wasted and destroyed". It was given taxation relief in 1445 and 1489 (VCH 2, 139-40, Brown 1975, 15).
In the later 17th century Exton Park was enlarged to include the site of Horn and the adjacent farm of Horn Lodge. A fine stretch of park wall bounds the southern side of the site. It used to cut across the village site near its mid-point, but this section has been removed.

Horn Water Mill **SK95231049**
The site of the water mill is mainly in Exton parish, and is referenced there.

KETTON

Garden Earthworks, "Hall Close" (fig 36) **SK982043**
200m north of St. Mary's Church is a field named Hall Close on a map of 1768 (ROLLR EN/MA/R23/1 overleaf). Just intruding into this field is a levelled platform (a), possibly the site of a large building. Hall Close contains various earthworks. There is a fishpond (b), with an overflow channel (c-c) which has been laid out to enclose a rectangular area, probably once a garden. There is the site of another pond (d) and levelled terraces (e, f, g, h).
Near the river are the embankments of a raised pond (i), and on the far side of the river are possible remains of another one, in a field named "Ponds Bank" (j). Just to the north, beyond the footbridge, are foundations of a small rectangular building (k), perhaps a dovecote.

Water Mill Channel (fig 36) **SK978036 - SK981041**
Further south, beyond Ketton Hall, is the long mill-leet (l) which formerly supplied the Ketton water mill. The mill building is marked on the map of 1768 (overleaf) sited just south of St. Mary's Church at SK98150415 , marked 'site of mill' on the plan.

Garden Earthworks, "Towns End Close" (fig 37 overleaf) **SK983047**
North-east of Hall Close there is a substantial rectangular dovecote at Manor Farm. Adjacent to it is a field named Towns End Close on the map of 1768, containing some earthwork evidence. The upper part of the field has ridge and furrow, and below it are several levelled terraces (a, b, c), possibly once a garden. Nearby are the footings of a small circular building (d), probably a dovecote or summer house. The River Chater has been diverted from its original course (e) to allow the construction of a large ornamental lake (f) in the 18th or 19th century.

Fregthorpe Deserted Village Earthworks (figs 38, 39, 40, pages 39-40) **SK990048**
The map of 1768 marks a series of small closes at this location, and names them as "Fregthorpe". On vertical photographs taken in 1947 the main elements of this deserted village can be seen and plotted. The lane through the village still appeared as a hollow way (a-a-a), flanked by small closes. There was a rectangular building platform (b) with traces of a circular building nearby (c), and another possible building at (d). To the north was a fine sweep of ridge and furrow. The 1768 map shows no surviving buildings in Fregthorpe, but does indicate another small lane (e-e) leading southwards.
The site of Fregthorpe was ploughed prior to the 1980s, but subsequently permission was granted for fieldwalking, which produced a good scatter of early medieval pottery from the site.

Geeston Village Earthworks (fig 41, page 41) **SK988041**
An old lane (a-a-a) between Kilthorpe and Fregthorpe formed the main street of another small village at Geeston. Three quite old houses survive at (b), and to the north of them are

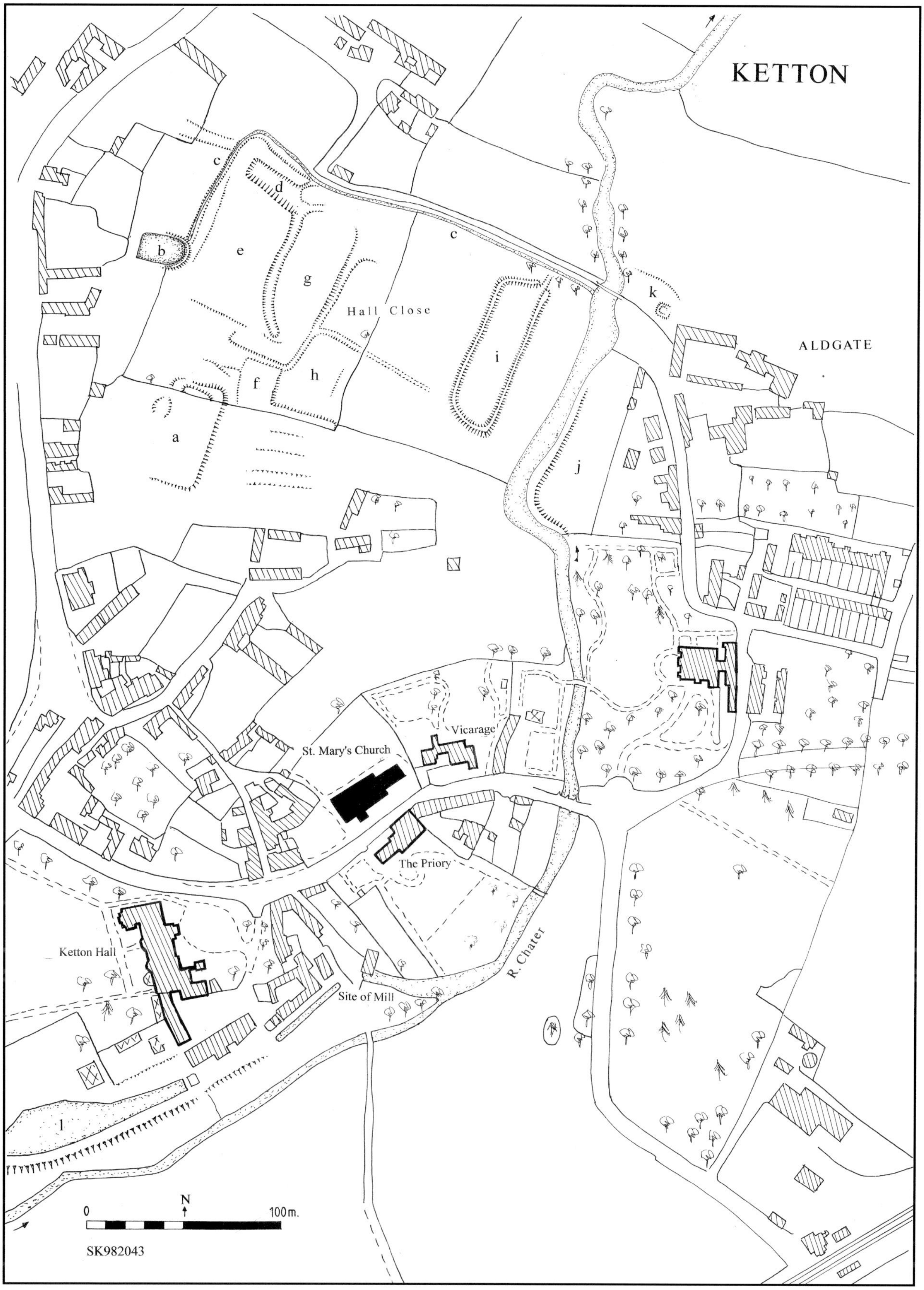

Figure 36: Ketton Garden Earthworks "Hall Close"

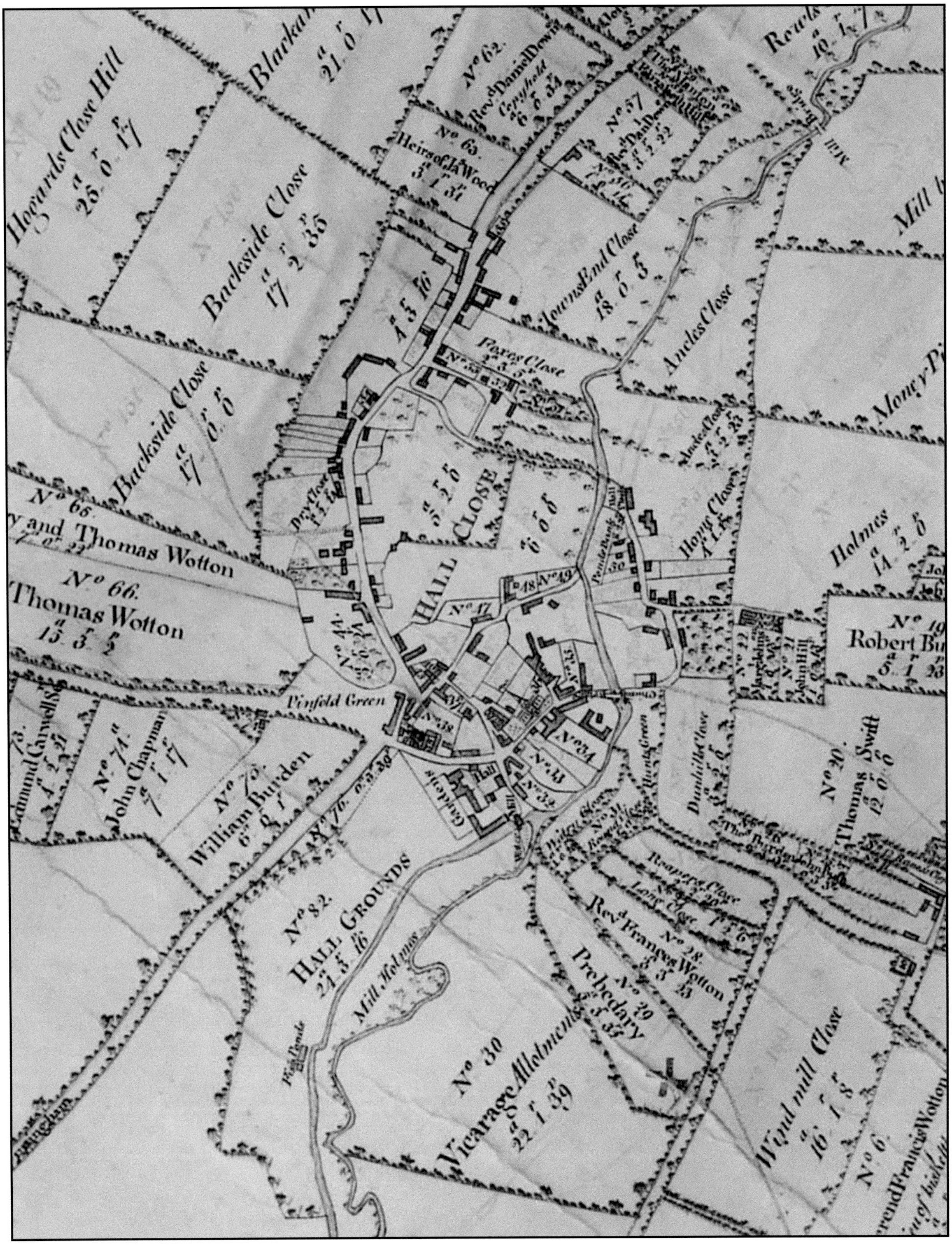

Central part of the estate map of Ketton and its fields 1768 showing the village, hall and church (centre). © By permission of the Record Office for Leicestershire, Leicester and Rutland, EN/MA/R23/1. The map above has been rotated to make comparison with the other plans easier. On the original plan west is at the top of the map and the river Chater runs west to east rather than the current flow south-west to north-east as figure 36.

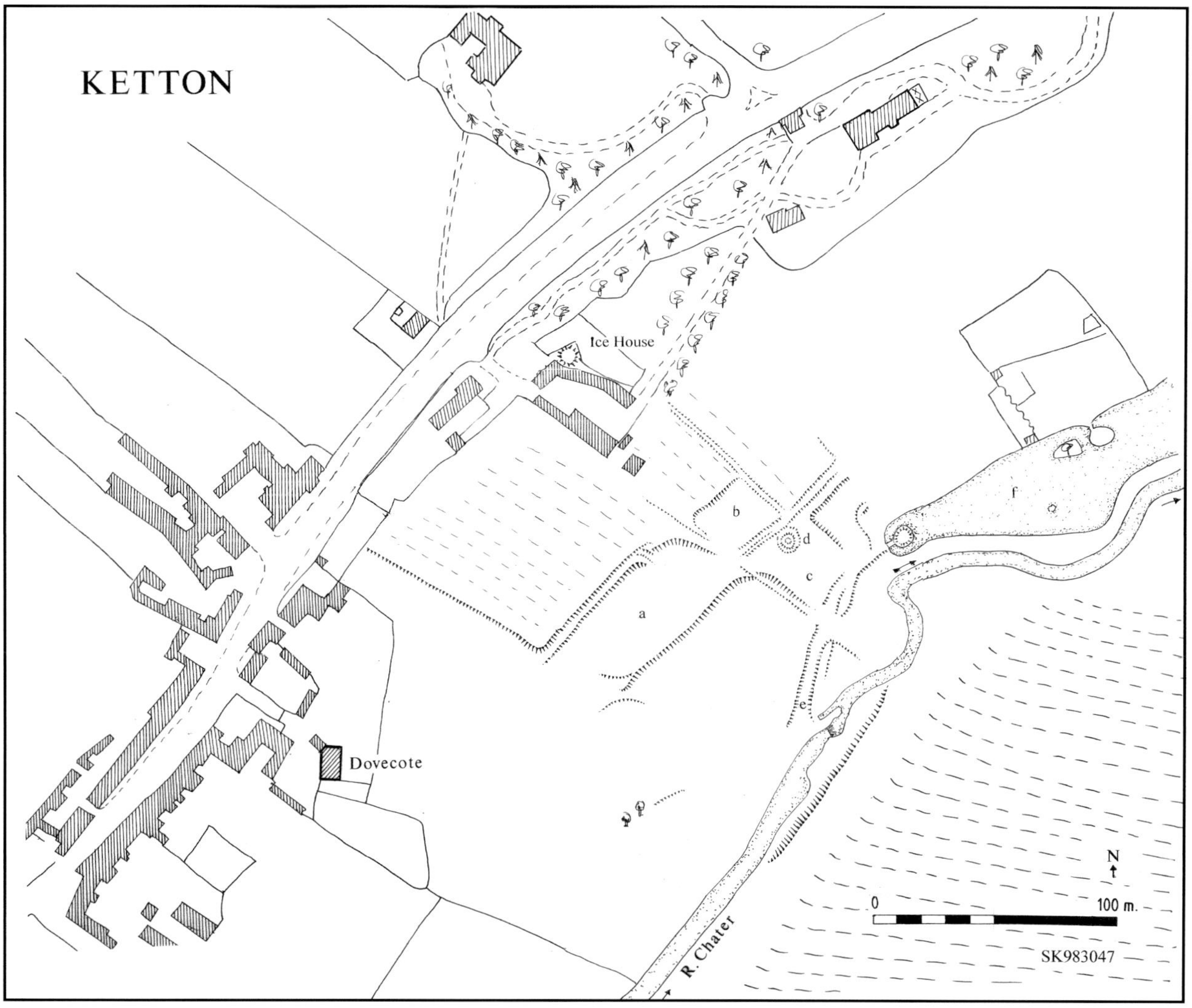

Figure 37: Ketton: Garden Earthworks "Towns End Close"

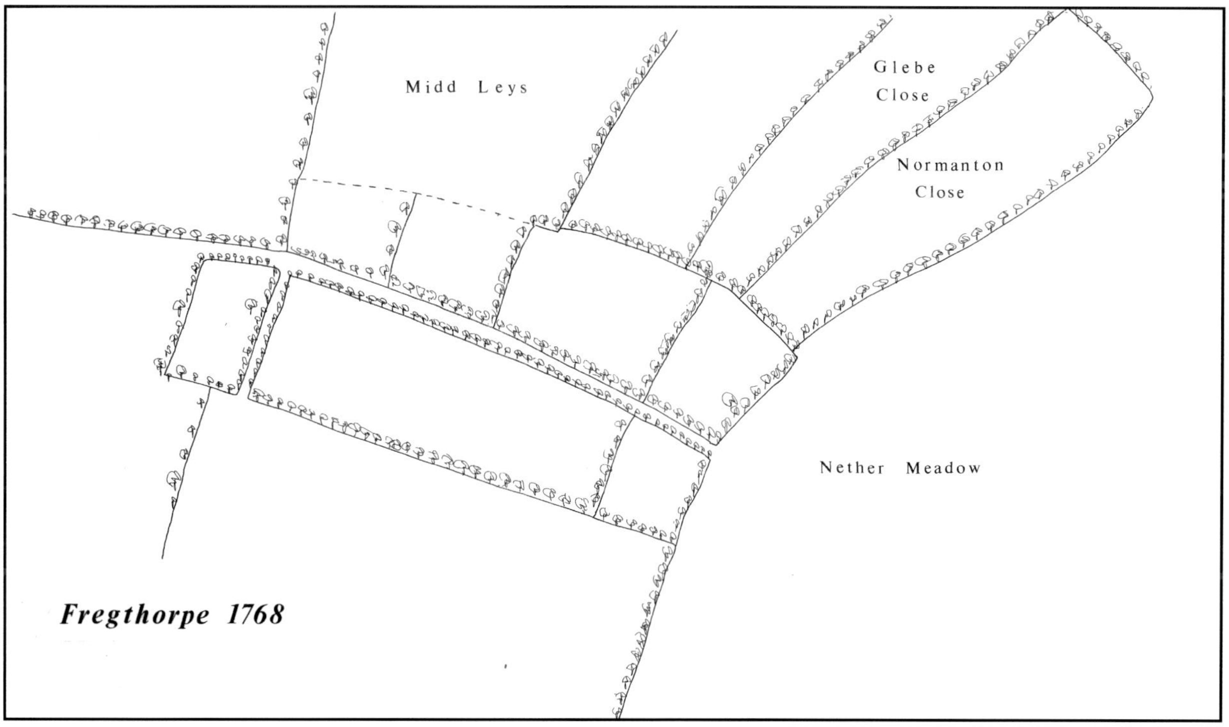

Figure 38: Ketton, Fregthorpe Deserted Village Closes

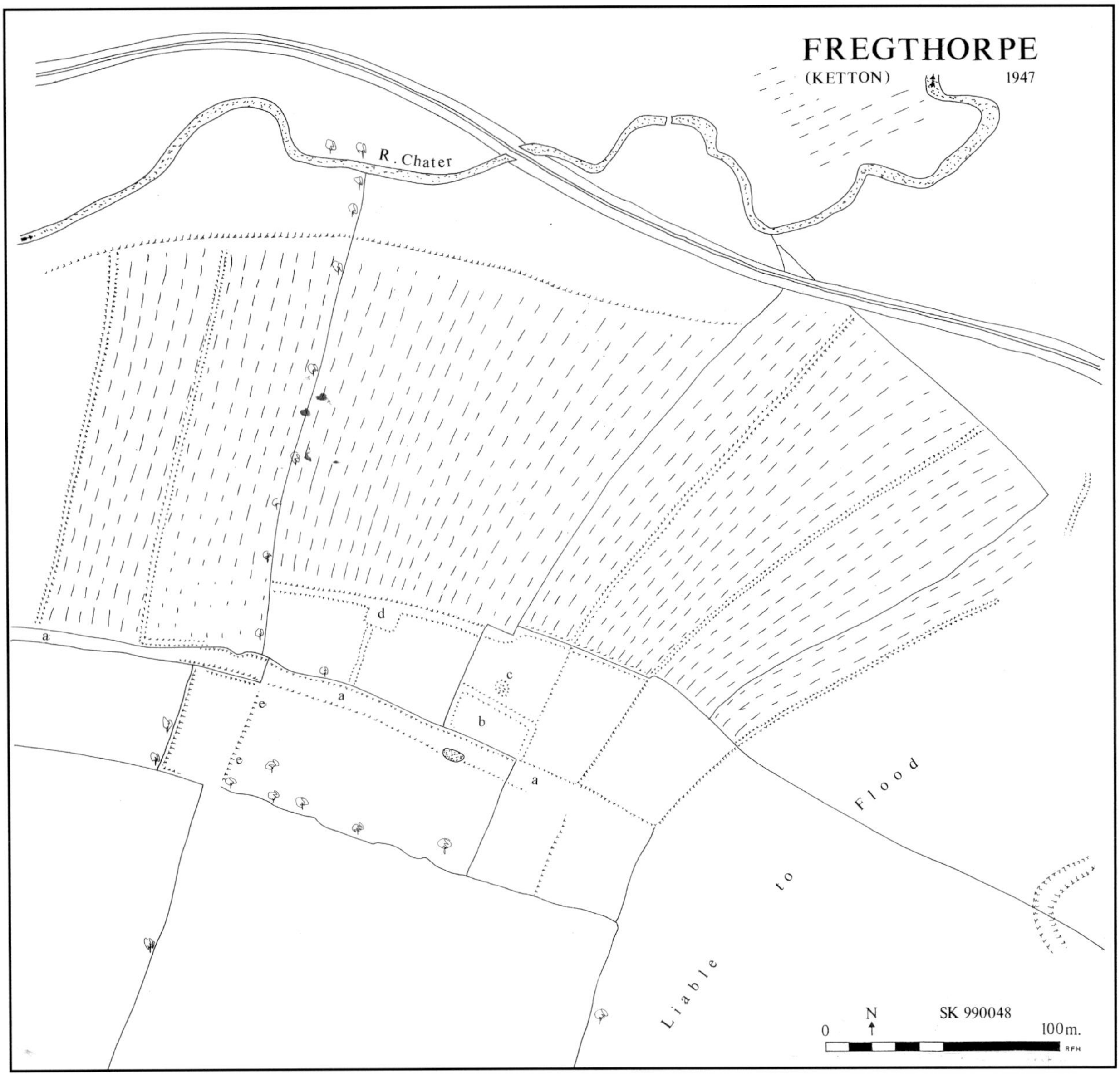

Figure 39: Ketton, Fregthorpe Deserted Village 1947

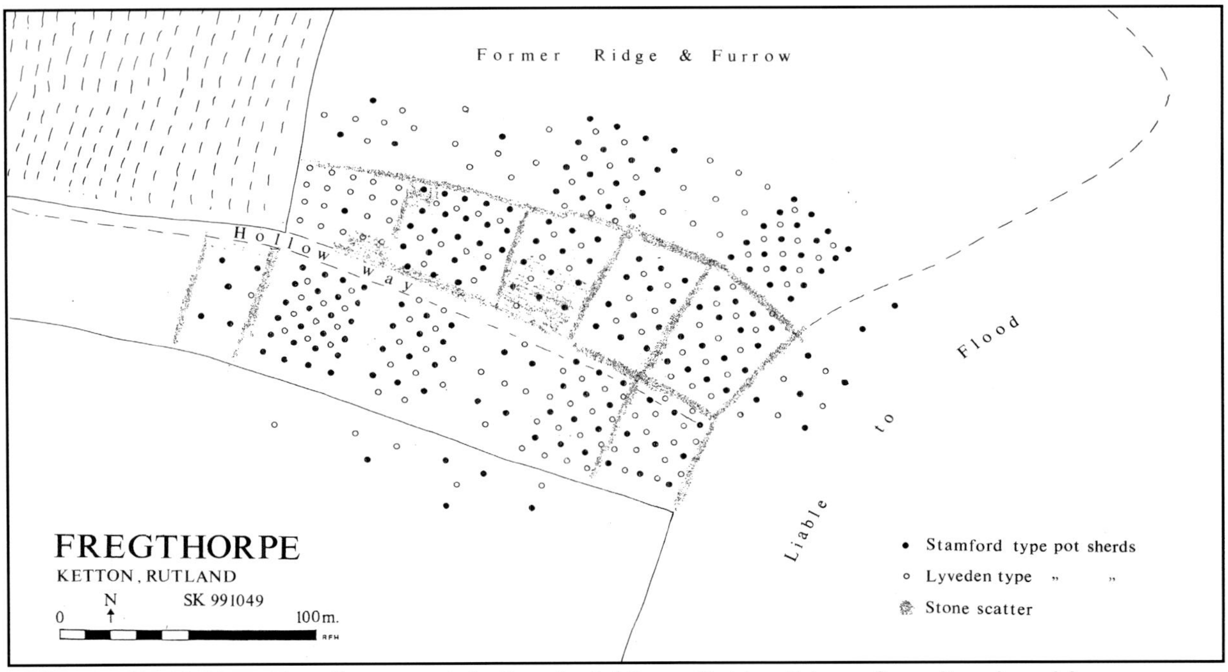

Figure 40: Ketton, Fregthorpe, plot of material from fieldwalking after site ploughing

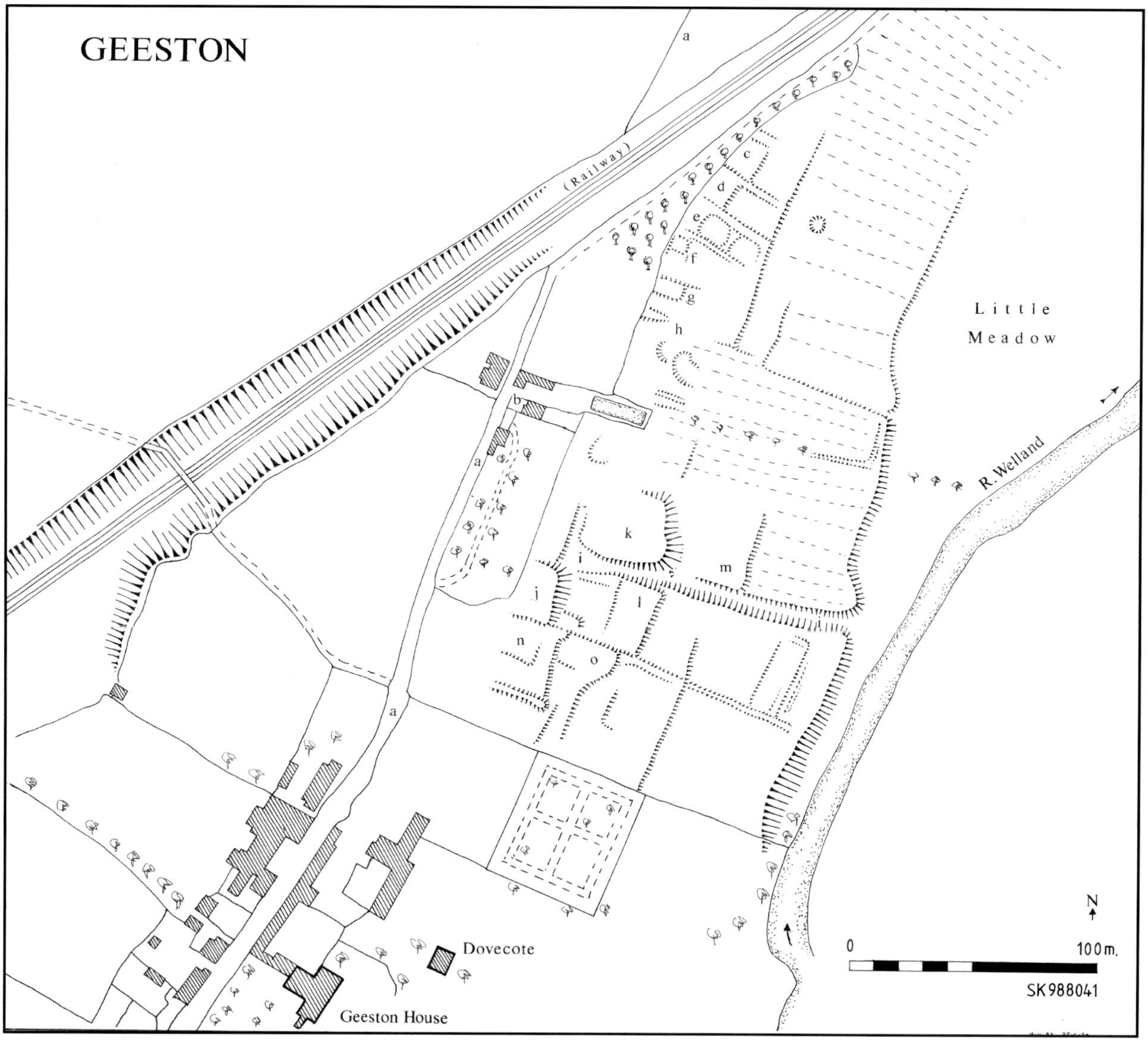

Figure 41: Ketton, Geeston Village Earthworks

foundations of possible buildings (c, d, e, f, g, h). To the south a hollow way (i-i) indicated the site of a lane leading to Little Meadow. Alongside this lane are more building platforms (j, k, l, m). The earthworks at (j) and (k) seem to show particularly substantial buildings. There are two more possible building platforms to the south at (n) and (o). Further south still are the gardens and parkland of Geeston House, including an historic dovecote. The site was probably truncated by the construction of the railway line in the mid-1840s.

Ketton: Kilthorpe Grange (fig 42 overleaf) ***SK985033***

When surveyed in 1981, Kilthorpe Grange Farm was surrounded by evidence of an impressive post-Medieval garden. The view east from the house, across the Welland, looks over three areas of levelled terrace (a, b, c) separated by fish ponds. Below the east side of terrace (b) were clear remains of another pond, and partial remains of a fourth one (d). To the east of terrace (c) was another pond, mainly retained by raised banks. These banks extend eastwards as a raised terrace, containing two more small ponds (e, f). These gardens were clearly intended to make a visual display, in a way that is characteristic of the late 16th or early 17th century.

The manor of Kilthorpe is mentioned in records from the 12th century (VCHR, 2, 259). It was owned by the College of Tattershall. Brown notes that in 1709 there is reference to two messuages and three cottages (Brown 1975, 16). The garden earthworks described above however suggest that between these two periods Kilthorpe Grange was a reasonably large and important manor house. A likely candidate as the man behind its rise in status is John

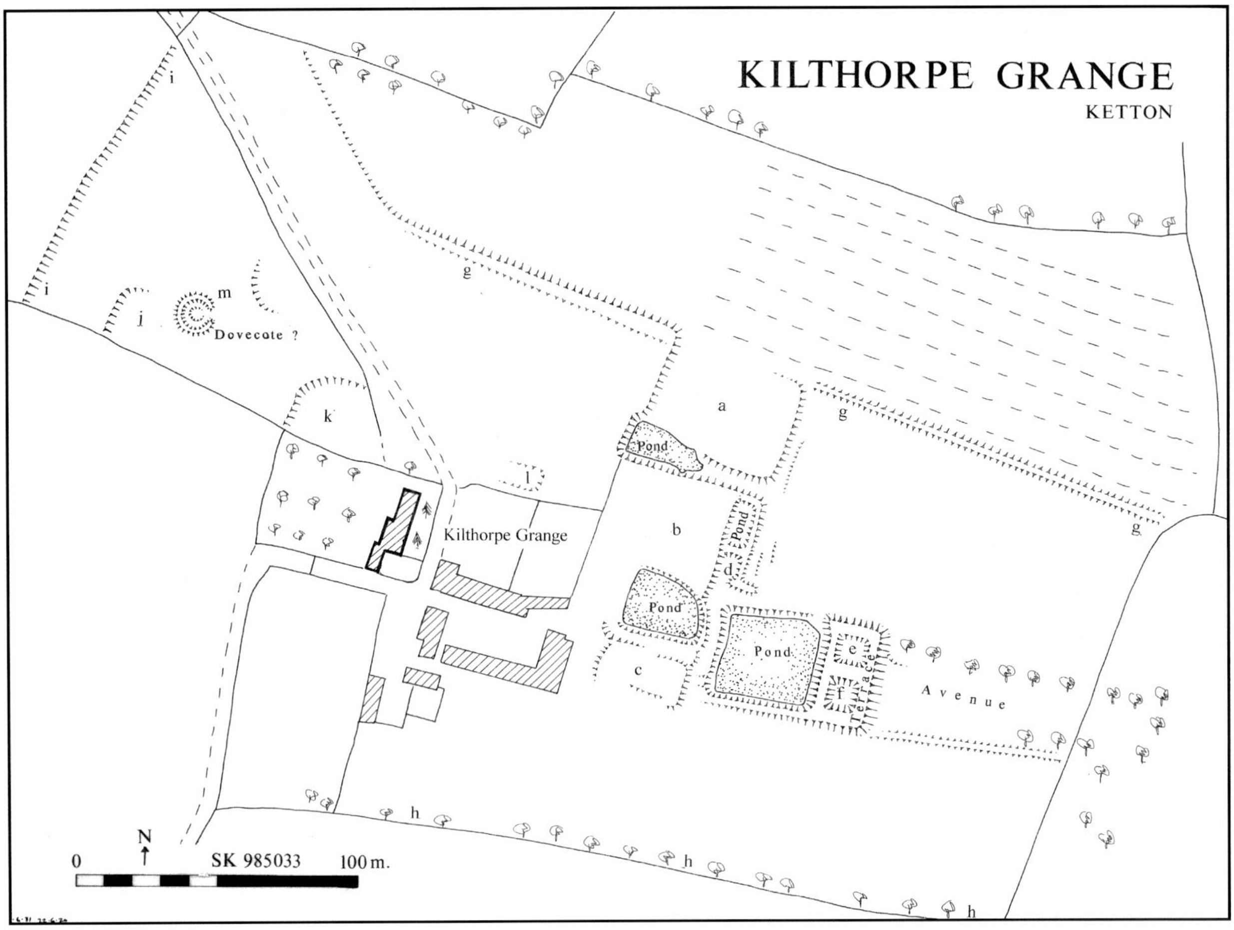

Figure 42: Ketton, Kilthorpe Grange

Houghton, who bought the manor in 1563 and lived until 1583. He "built the Guildhall in Stamford, and represented the Borough in Parliament" (VCHR 2, 260). Kilthorpe is just 3 miles from Stamford and would have made an ideal residence.

LANGHAM

Water Mill Site — *SK838510870*

"A mound and curved leet" at this location "might be connected with a water mill". The field at SK838108 is called Mill Close on the Tithe Map of 1841 (Northants Record Office T282: Brown 1975, 16).

LEIGHFIELD

Deserted Village and Leigh Lodge (fig 43) — *SK829040*

In his History of Rutland, published in 1684, James Wright says Leighfield was "Formerly a Towne and Mannor, now only a lodge, in the 'Forest', which no doubt was named the 'Forest' of Lyfeild from this town" (Wright 1684, 75). This may have been an area where land was still being newly cultivated after the Norman conquest. In the 12th century Leighfield manor was described as a messuage and three carucates of land with pasture, but there was a grant of view of frankpledge in 1312, and in 1357 the homage of tenants is referred to (Brown 1975,16, VCHR 2, 15-16). There clearly was a substantial community here in the early 14th century, for aerial photographs taken in the 1940s show plentiful evidence of ridge and furrow in the parish, as well as traces of the village (RAF CPE/UK/1932 4034: CPE/UK/1925 2050).

Most of earthworks around Leigh Lodge survived to be surveyed by the author in May 1982. North-east of the house was part of the deserted village, with a hollow way (a-a-a) which would have been the main street. On the north side of the hollow way are probable sites of buildings

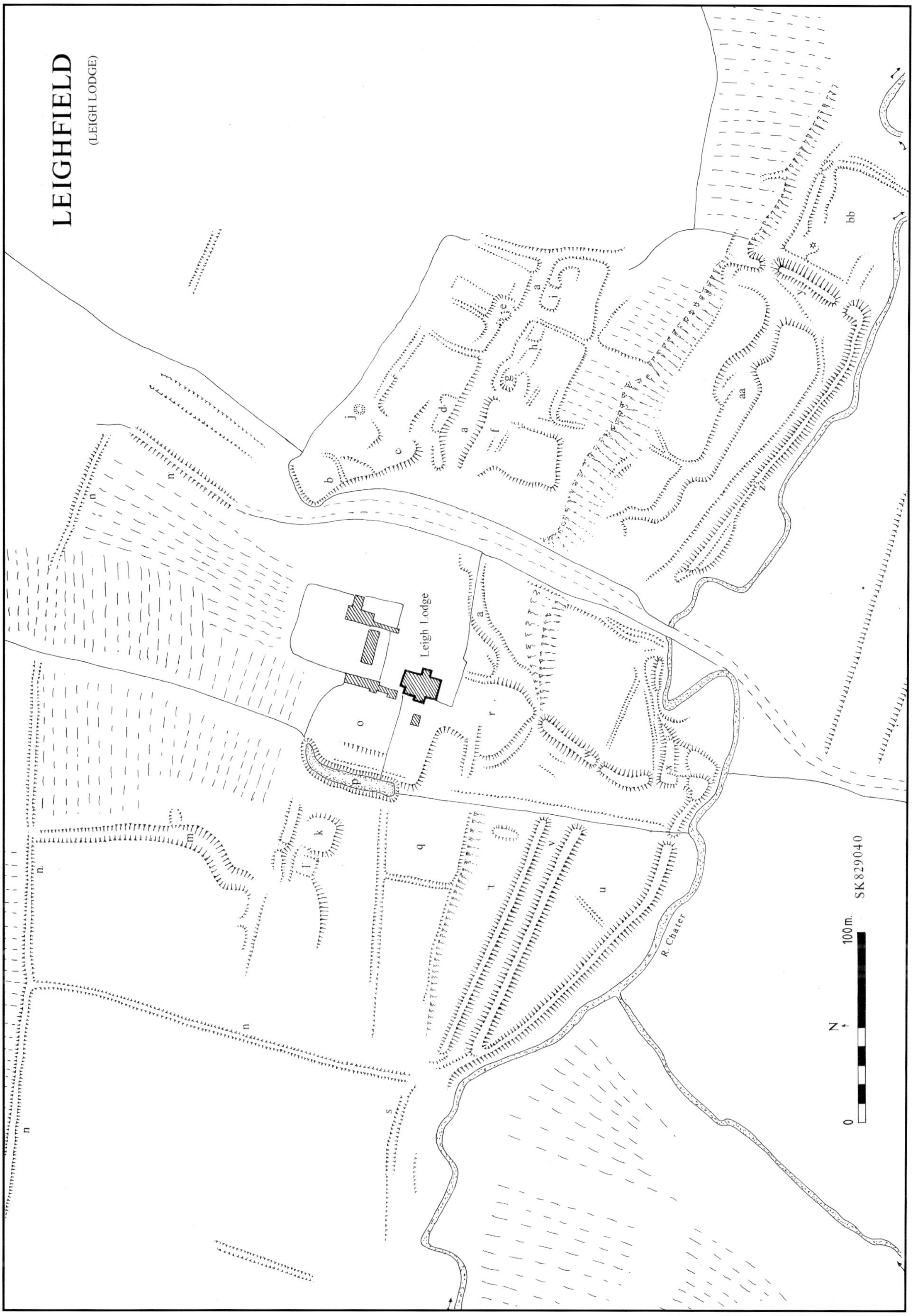

Figure 43: Leighfield, Deserted Village and Leigh Lodge

(b, c, d, e), while on the south side are more, at (f, g, h and i). There are footings of one small circular building (j) – perhaps a dovecote, and from the clarity of its survival it was presumably in existence long after the other buildings had been abandoned.
The aerial photographs show another area of possible village earthworks west of Leigh Lodge, with at least two possible building platforms (k, l) and another hollow way (m) leading north. Medieval pottery has been found in the ploughed soil in this area.
The mansion house of Leigh Lodge seems to date from the early 17th century, built perhaps for the first Lord Harington, who died in 1613, or for Edward Noel, bart., who bought the estate in 1614. It is surrounded by the earthwork banks of a large enclosure (n), with another to the west. Immediately west of the house was a garden terrace (o), and an ornamental pond (p). A map of 1772 shows this as originally two ponds, a round basin and a longer rectangular pond (Lincs Archives, 5 Anc. S/B/3/3/7). South-west of the house is evidence of more enclosures (q), and south of the house is a large building platform (r). These features may well be elements of the medieval village.
In the bottom of the valley, south of the lodge, are the remarkable fish ponds. A supply channel (s) would have supplied water from the small River Chater to two large ponds (t, u), separated by a "canal" (v). The water in all three was originally retained by a large dam (w). At the south end of this dam are building foundations (x), presumably the site of a water mill.
Downstream, to the east, was another large pond, retained by a dam (y), and with a long bank (z) on its south side, forming a by-pass channel for the stream. It is possible to see the original river course in the middle of the pond (aa). Below the dam was another enclosure (bb).
This complex of ponds represents an enormous investment. The evidence for a water mill suggests that there was still sufficient arable farming in the area to make good use of it. The ponds must also have produced a valuable supply of fish.

Prior's Coppice Wood **c.SK832052**

This piece of woodland once belonged to Brooke Priory. Squires notes that there are ancient banks and ditches along two sides (Squires 2014, 166).

LITTLE CASTERTON

Village Earthworks (fig 44) ***TF016097***

All Saints' Church stands close to the River Gwash, and the churchyard forms a raised mound of some size. South of the church is the site of a vanished building (a) indicated by a rectangular platform. To the west, beyond the gardens of the old Rectory, was a mill pool (b), enclosed by a dam which provided a head of water to operate a mill, which must have been located approximately at (c), and accessed by a lane from the village.
At the west end of the village is a field with substantial earthwork features, including a levelled terrace (d), flanking by three large building platforms (e, f, g). This may be the site noted by Blore as having "strong traces of the site of an ancient mansion house" (Blore 1811).

Tolethorpe Hall Earthworks (fig 45) ***TF022103***

The manor of Tolethorpe is mentioned in the Domesday Survey. There was a chapel here in the 14th century, but in 1375-6 "the houses and edifices of the manor were worth nothing yearly" (Brown 1975, 17, quoting Blore 1811, 92), and the chapel is last mentioned in 1496. Tolethorpe Hall dates back to around 1600, with major alterations in the 18th century and in the 1860s.
There are earthworks to the north of the house, where a steep slope (a-a-a) defines the edge of a large rectangular terrace, probably part of a formal garden of 16th/17th century date, which would have had pleasing views over the river. Within the area of the levelled terrace is a rectangular platform (b) and two small enclosures (c, d). There are possible building foundations (e) and the area levelled for gardens extended east around (f).
Nearer to the Hall are a wide garden terrace (g), and a south-facing parterre (h), probably dating from the remodelling of the site in the 1860s. There is a walled garden (i) to the east.

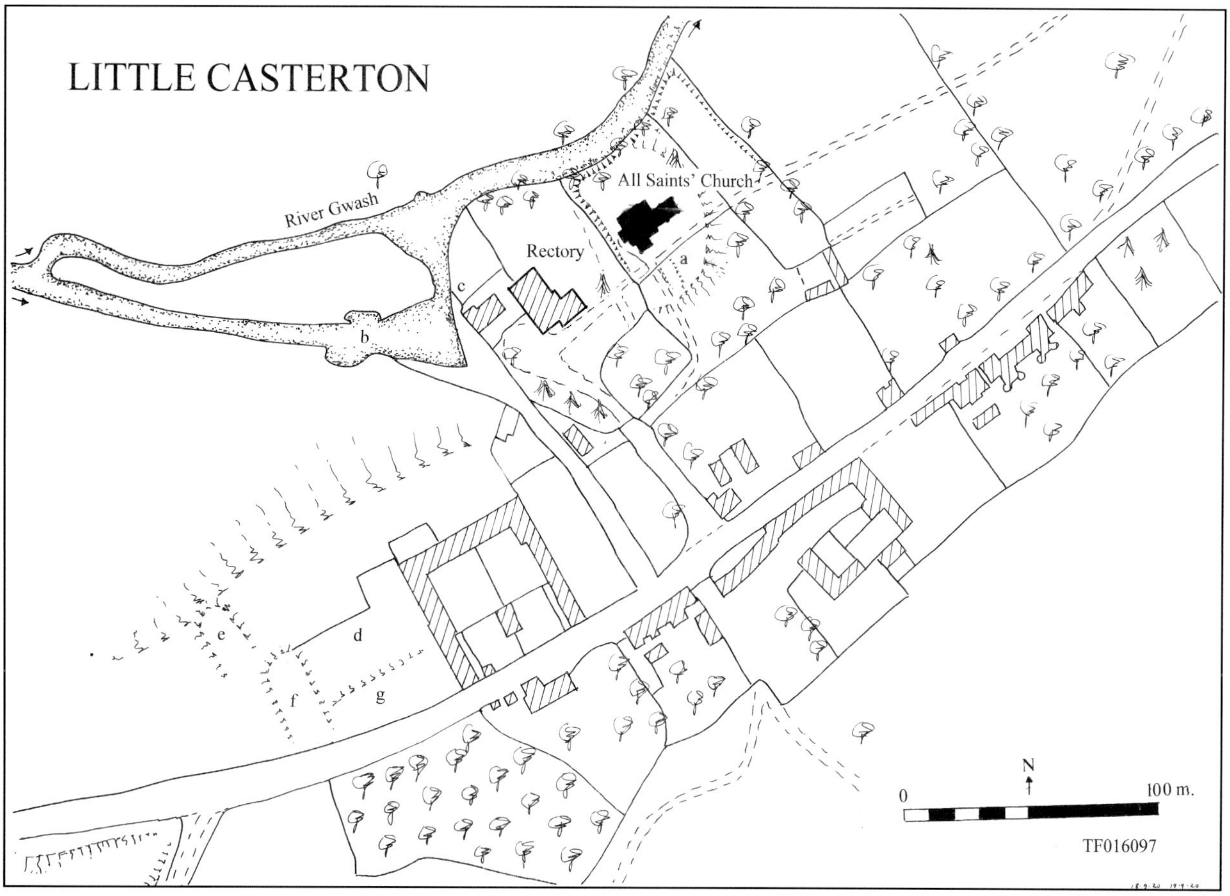

Figure 44: Little Casterton, Village Earthworks

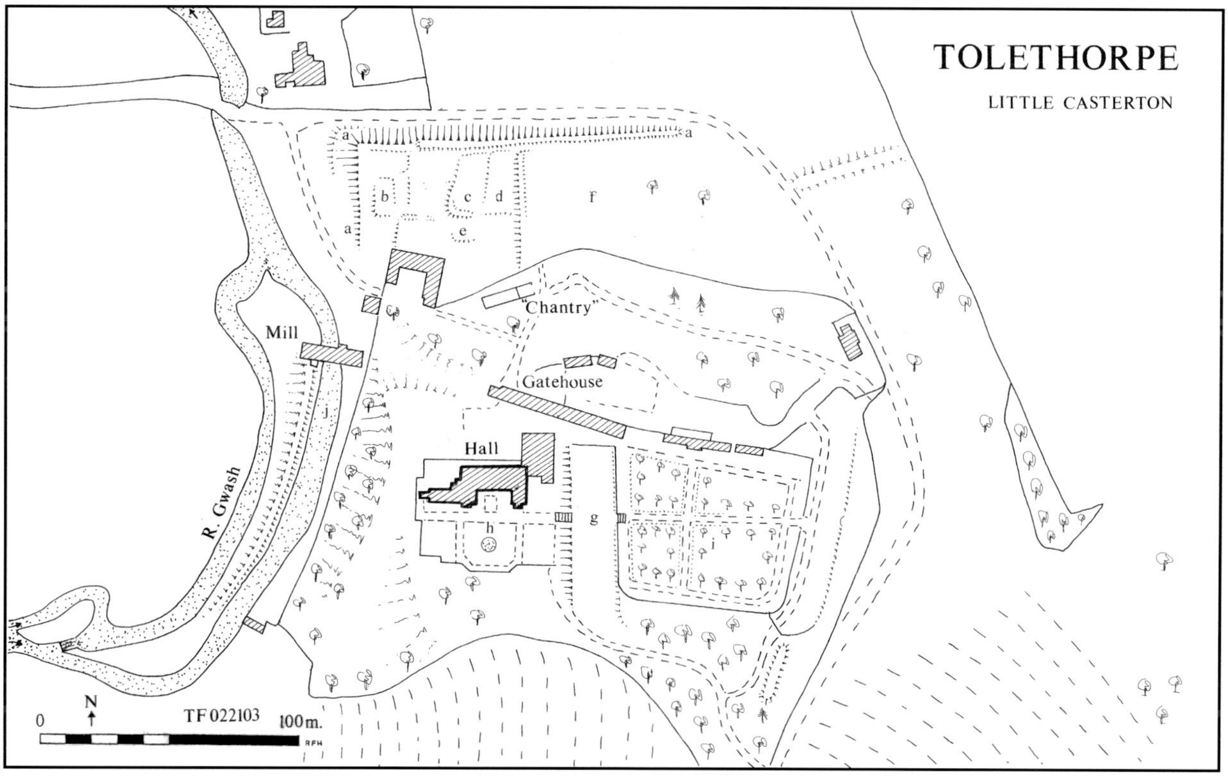

Figure 45: Little Casterton, Tolethorpe Hall Earthworks

Water Mill (fig 45) **_TF021104_**

West of the Hall the river has been channelled into a mill pond (j) to supply the water mill. The site probably has a long and complex history. Four mills are mentioned in the Domesday Survey of 1086.

LUFFENHAM, NORTH and SOUTH

NORTH LUFFENHAM

Village Earthworks and "The Motts" **_SK928032_**

Extending out from the present west end of the village are two old closes (a, b), leading down to a stream, alongside which is a hollow way or perhaps an old pond (c.) To the south of this feature is a substantial building platform (d).

Further south a bank and ditch (e-e) cross the stream, defining an area to the south which contains a rectangular moat (g-g-g-g), now largely drained, which was retained by outer banks, and encloses a platform (h). Within the platform are indications of an old fish pond (i), and four smaller depressions around (j) - perhaps the robbed-out foundations of buildings.

To the south of the moat the stream has been diverted from its original course (k) into an artificial channel (l-l-l). The area between the original and the replacement stream courses has at one time been divided up by a bank and ditch (m). The ditch was probably once water-filled, and enclosed an area (n) which may have been an orchard or garden.

Extending east from the moat, on the east side of the stream, is a ditch (o) indicating another old enclosure boundary. An avenue of trees (p-p) indicates that this area was once parkland, probably associated with Luffenham House.

Luffenham House and Park (fig 48) **_SK935033_**

Luffenham House had gardens extending to north and south, shown on an 18th century map, illustrated bottom right. There seems to have been a post-Medieval amenity park to the south of the village, with a field name "Bottom Parks".

Morcott Spinney Earthwork (fig 46) **_SK928023_**

On the crest of the ridge, on the southern boundary of North Luffenham parish, is a flat-topped conical mound, up to 3m high. The platform on the top of the mound is approximately 20m in diameter, and it is encircled on the west, north and east sides by a ditch about 10m wide.

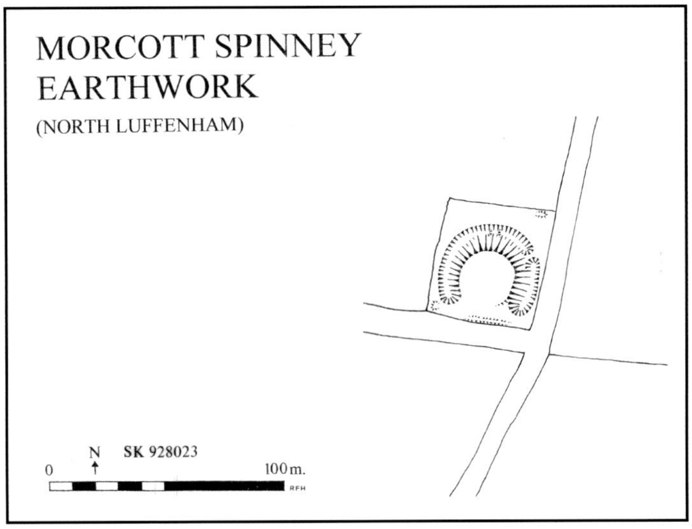

Figure 46: North Luffenham, Morcott Spinney Earthwork

Sculthorpe Village Earthworks (fig 49) **_SK925028_**

A village named Sculthorpe is mentioned in connection with North Luffenham in the Domesday Survey of 1086, but later became deserted. The site was still identified by several 'Sculthorpe' field names, including "Sculthorpe Close", on the North Luffenham Tithe Map.

There are clear remains of Sculthorpe surviving on either side of the nineteenth century brickworks which took out the centre of the village site. Towards the west side of the village are two possible hollow ways, (a) and (b-b), with another towards the east side (c-c). Banks and ditches define part of the western boundary of the village (d-d) and part of the eastern boundary (e-e), with ridge and furrow beyond them.

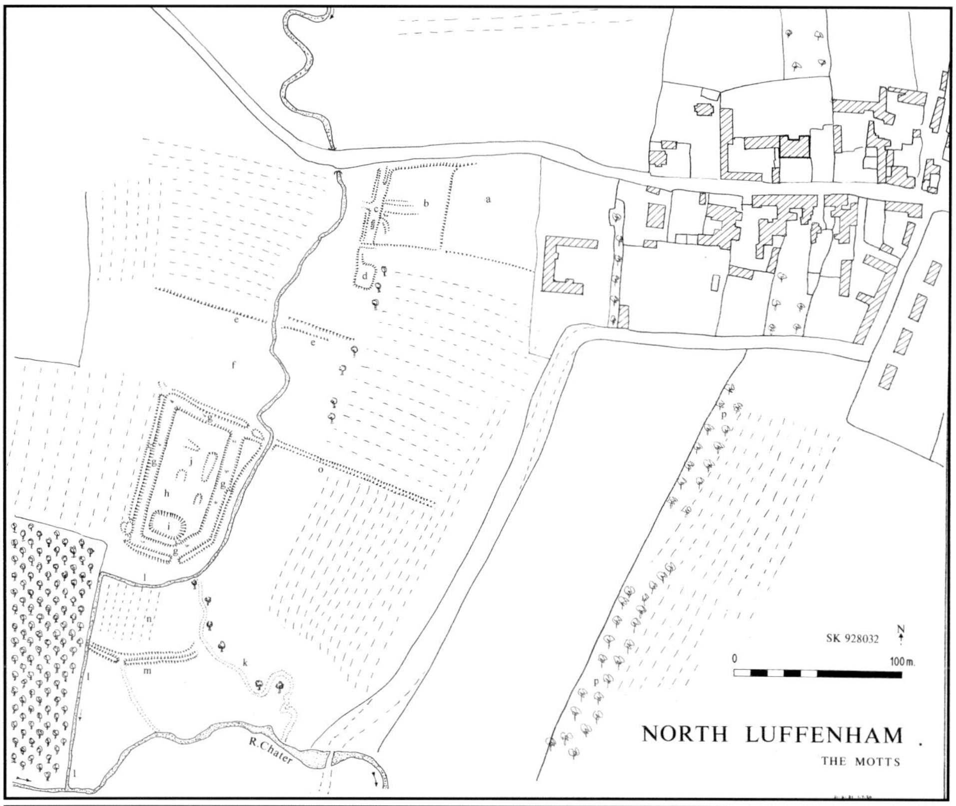

Figure 47: North Luffenham: Village Earthworks & "The Motts"

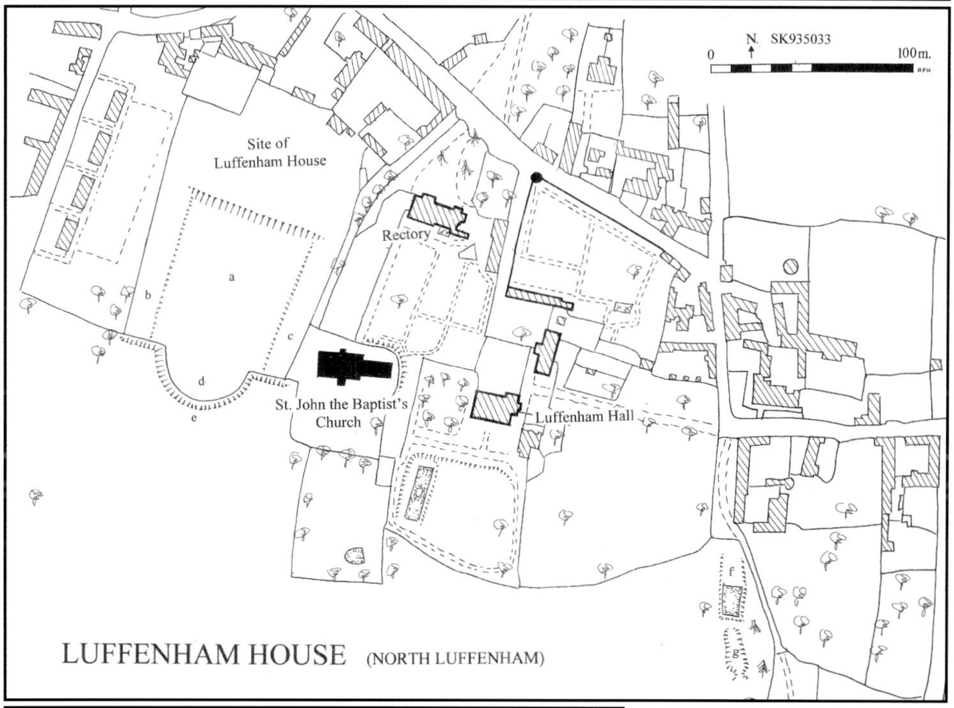

Figure 48: North Luffenham, Luffenham House

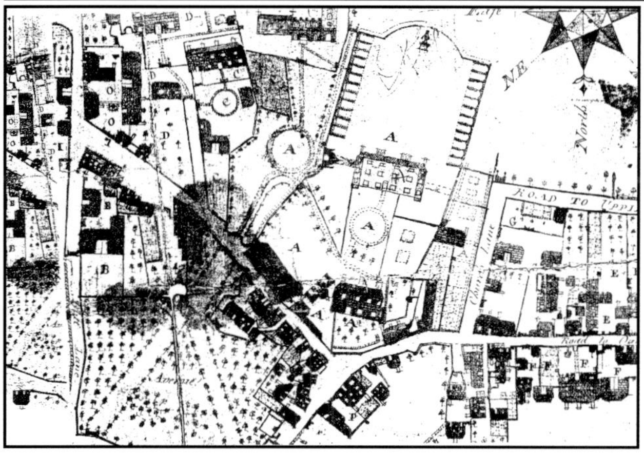

North Luffenham 18th century map

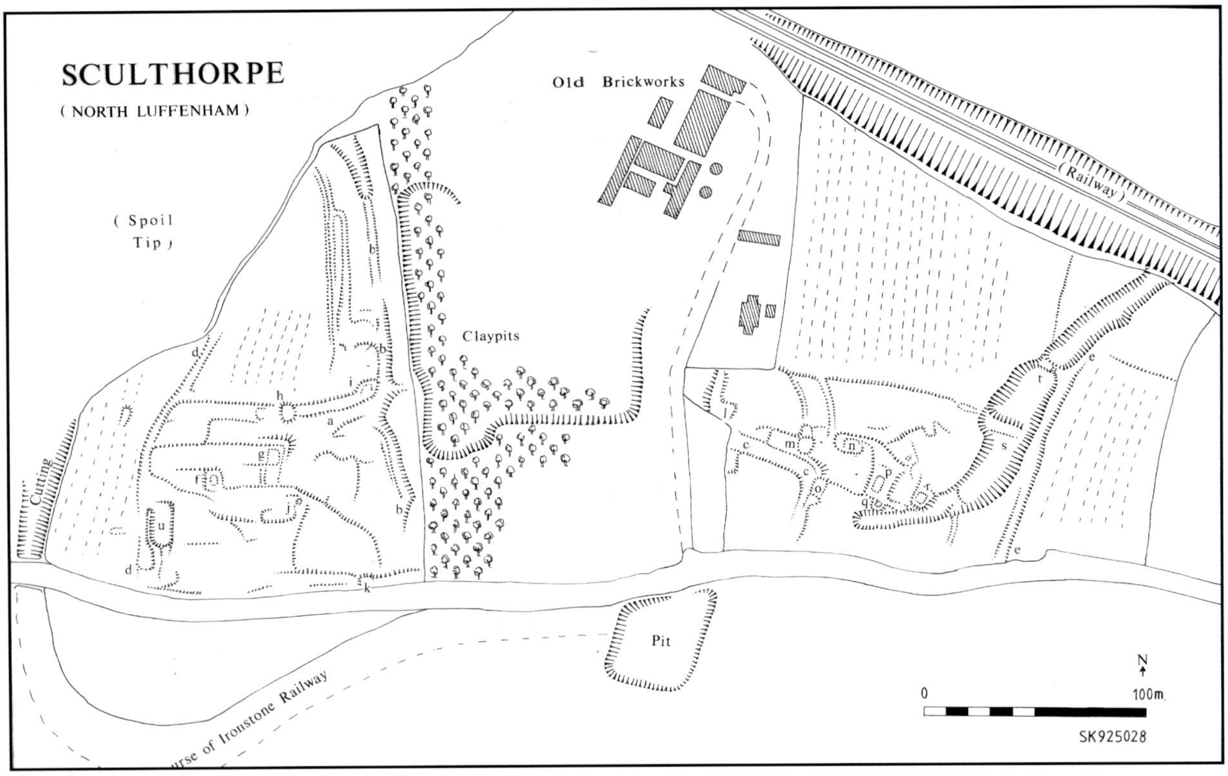

Figure 49: North Luffenham: Sculthorpe Village Earthworks

There are foundations of several buildings, mostly with clear footings of stone walls, (f, g, h, i, j, k, l, m, n, o, p, q, r). At (m) there are probably four buildings joined together, while the building at (q) is remarkably small. At the east end of the village is a small valley, with indications of dams for two ponds (s, t). There is another probable pond near the west end of the village site at (u).

SOUTH LUFFENHAM

Village Earthworks (fig 50) — *SK941019*

There is plentiful evidence for changes in land use in the centre of the village. To the east of West Farm is an old field boundary (a), and a terrace (b), perhaps the site of a vanished building. Further down the slope is a levelled terrace (c) containing an old fish pond (d). Following the contour along the field northwards is a substantial ditch (e), possibly once the supply leet to a vanished water mill further downstream. Across the valley is another fish pond (f), and slight hollows in the ground represent the sites of two more ponds (g, h).
North of the church is a paddock with sites of former buildings at (i) and (j). The small green to the west of the church is slightly raised and may have contained the site of another building (k). Further south, the lane leading west out of the village runs in a deep hollow way (l).

LYDDINGTON

Fish Ponds (fig 51 overleaf) — *SP877972*

The historic building now known as the Lyddington Bede House was largely built in the 15th century as a residence of the Bishops of Lincoln. The amenities of the manor included a deer park, and, east of the Bede House, a complex of fish ponds. There is slight evidence of village earthworks (a), and beyond them, just below the confluence of two streams (b, c) is a substantial bank (d-d-d-d) which would have retained a flooded moat (e-e-e-e). Within the moat platform is a series of linked ponds of different depths (f, g, h, i, j, k), presumably designed to provide specific conditions for rearing fish of different ages and species. Immediately to the west of these features is a much deeper and more conventional fish pond (m).

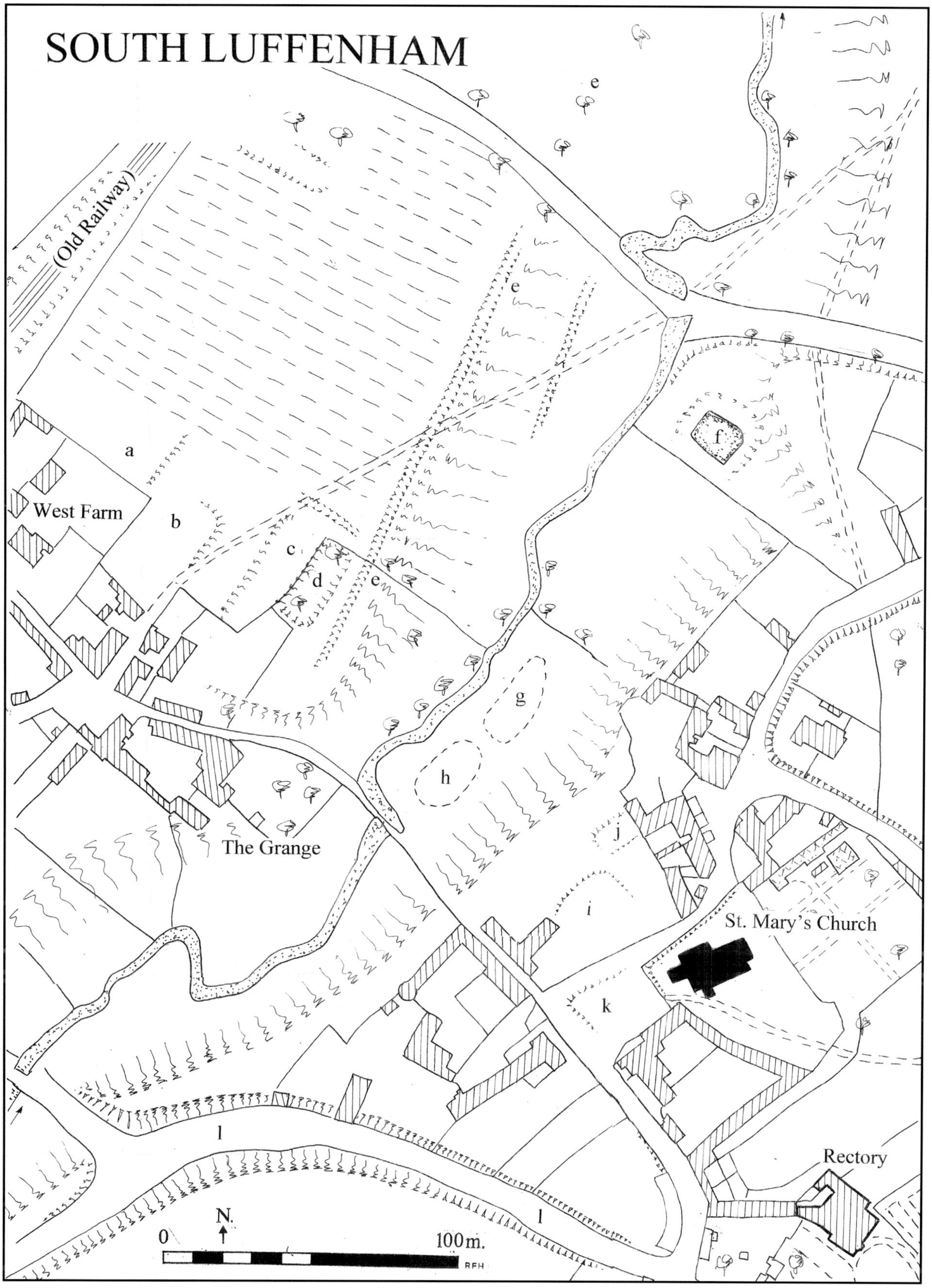

Figure 50: South Luffenham, Village Earthworks

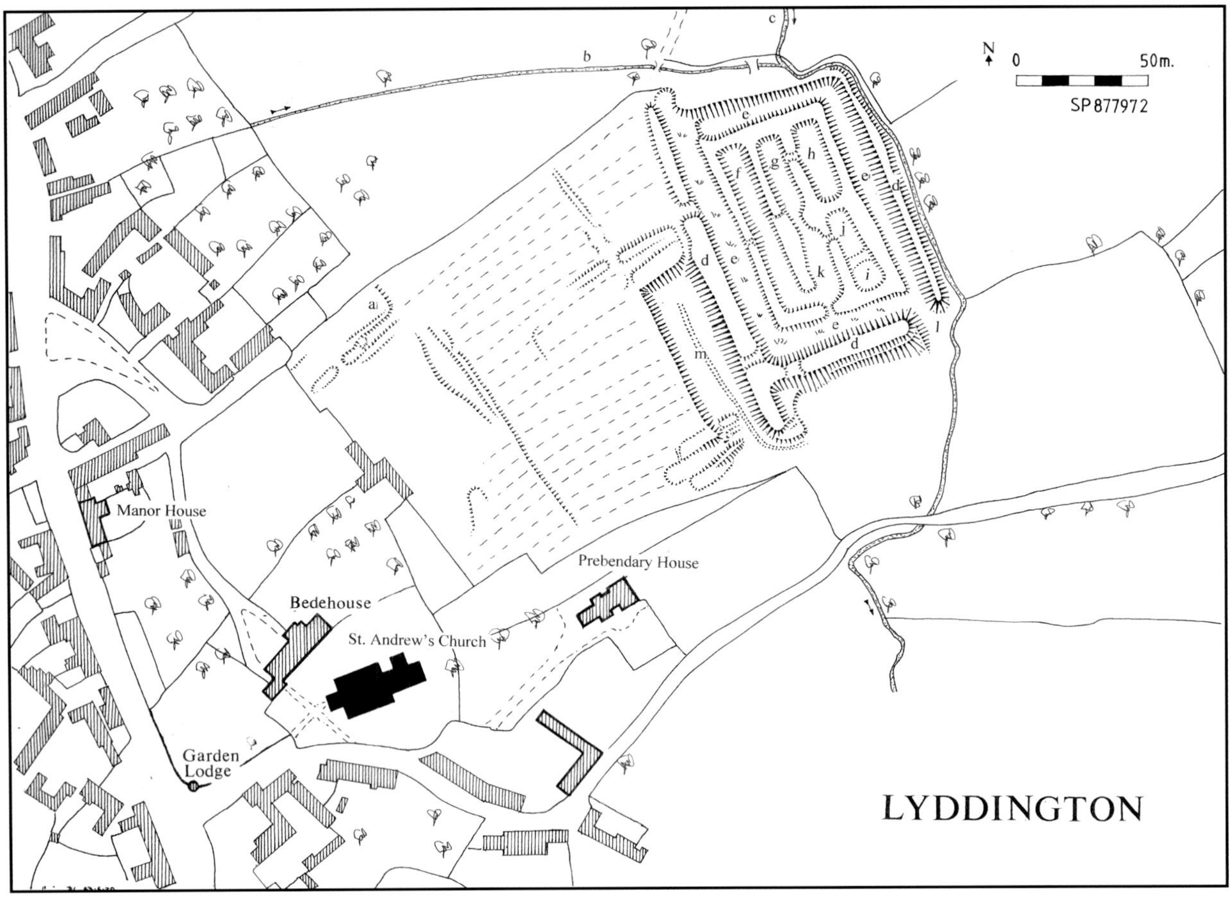

Figure 51: Lyddington Fish Ponds

Deer Park **_SK8698_**

There are references to the Bishop of Lincoln's park at Lyddington from the early 13th century. The bishop obtained permission from the Crown in 1227 to have a deer-leap, and the park is mentioned in 1229. In 1331 it was increased in size by 60 acres and enclosed by a stone wall in place of the old bank and paling fence. No further references to it have been found, although a park is shown here on a map of 1602 (Cantor 1976-7, 85).

There is a series of "park" names around SP856981 and "Long Park" at SK859875 (Sterndale Bennett 1943). A straight stretch of bank extends from SP862976 to SP863980. There is a mound on aerial photographs at SP85809825, perhaps a rabbit warren (RAF CPE/UK/1925 2155-7).

LYNDON

Village Earthworks (fig 52, illustration opposite and page vii) **_SK908043_**

A plan of the village (opposite - rotated so North is at the top for comparison purposes, and in full unrotated view on page vii with associated information) was drawn by Vincent Wing, mathematician, surveyor, astronomer and astrologer who lived in North Luffenham and published a plan of Lyndon in his work *Geodaetes Practicus: or, the Art of Surveying,* in 1664. The Wing plan clearly shows the close or field names around the village and can be compared with houses and roads today. Thomas and Abel Barker bought the manor in 1662 and Sir Abel began building Lyndon Hall in 1665 to his own design (finished 1677), having pulled down the earlier manor to the east of the site. The Wing plan shows a manor house. The current manor house is in the Jacobean/classical style and so the house on the plan must be a fanciful representation. As the plan was published in Wing's book in 1664 he was probably commissioned to prepare the plan of the manor for the Barkers when they purchased it and before building commenced. There are signs of village earthworks (a, b, c) on vertical RAF

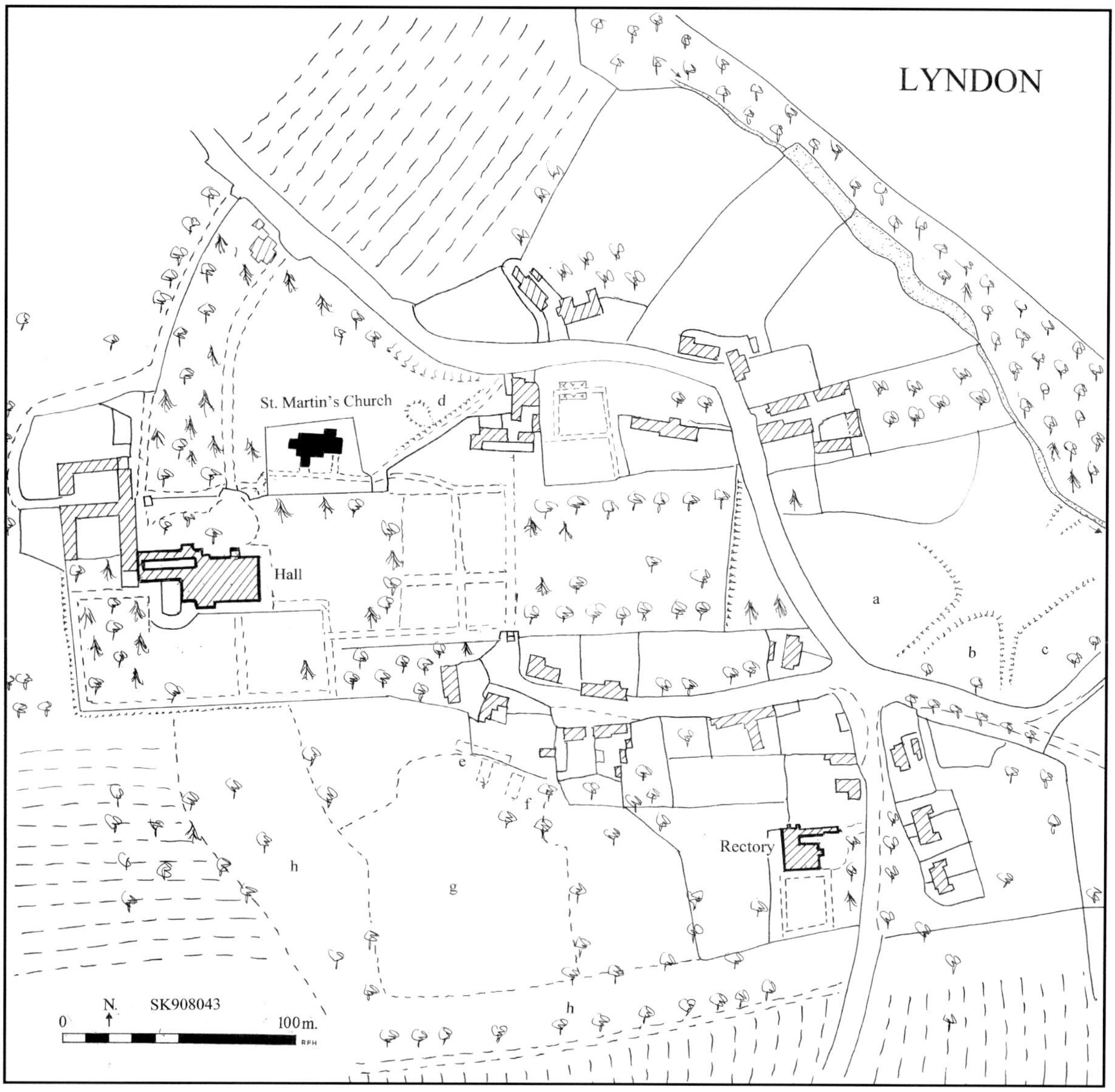

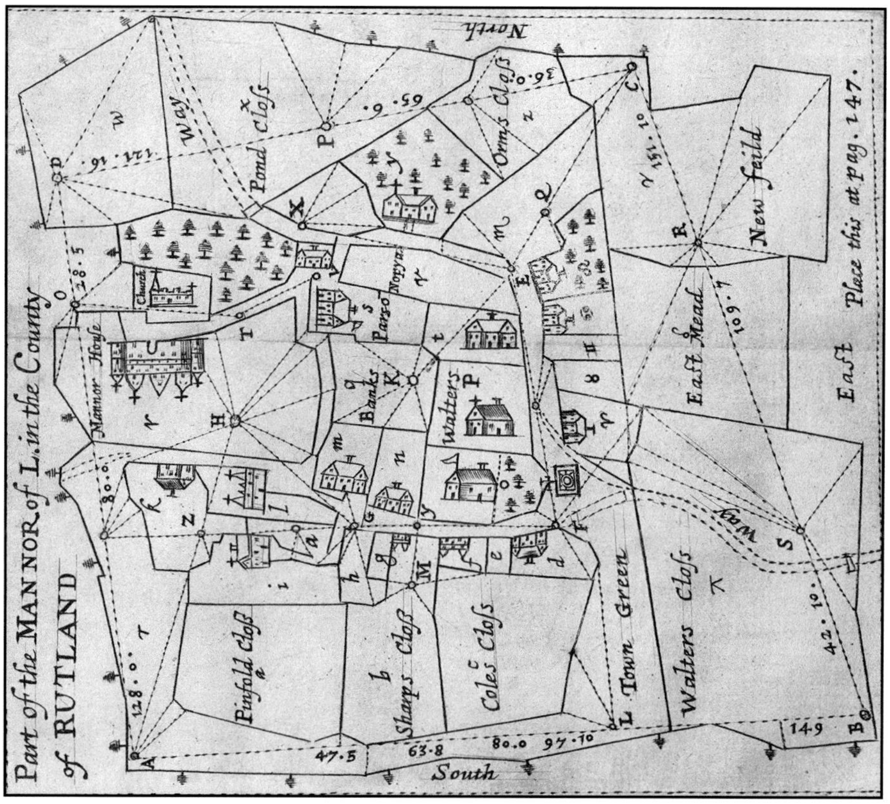

Figure 52: Lyndon

Vincent Wing's plan of Lyndon (rotated so north is at the top for comparison purposes with the plan above), from his book 'Geodaetes Practicus'. © Science Museum Group. (see also page vii, this volume, for a colour version, oriented correctly).

Figure 53: Market Overton village earthworks

photographs (RAF CPE/UK/1932 4042-5: 1925 4061-2) at SK910044 and SK907043 and Wing's plan calls this 'Banks' close. There may be a prospect mound at (d) belonging to the buildings to the east. Field/close (g) called 'Pinfold' by Wing has building foundations at (e) and (f) which may also be a building shown to the edge of this field by Wing. The area (h) is field 'T' on Wing's plan and seems to run around the closes as far as the Rectory and may be an area of common land.

MARKET OVERTON

Village Earthworks (fig 53) **SK886165**

Market Overton village shows signs of having shrunk in size, particularly in the north-west corner, where the parish church now stands in isolation. The Ordnance Survey recorded earthwork boundaries of old closes at (a, b, c, d, e). To the west is the boundary of the old village (f) beyond which was the open field with its ridge and furrow. To the south, the lane to Ashwell runs in a hollow way, and beyond it are two more old closes (g, h). To the east, near the centre of the village, is a substantial building platform.

A map made in the early 19th century shows former buildings at (j, k, l) and at (m) near the Rectory. Across the road from the sites of buildings at (k) and (l) the Ordnance Survey marks two wells (x), probably the sites of at least two more cottages. Numerous Roman artefacts were found during ironstone quarrying just north of Market Overton, leading theOrdnance Survey to conclude that the earthworks at the north end of the village were of Roman origin. On balance it seems more likely that they were medieval or post-medieval features as described above.

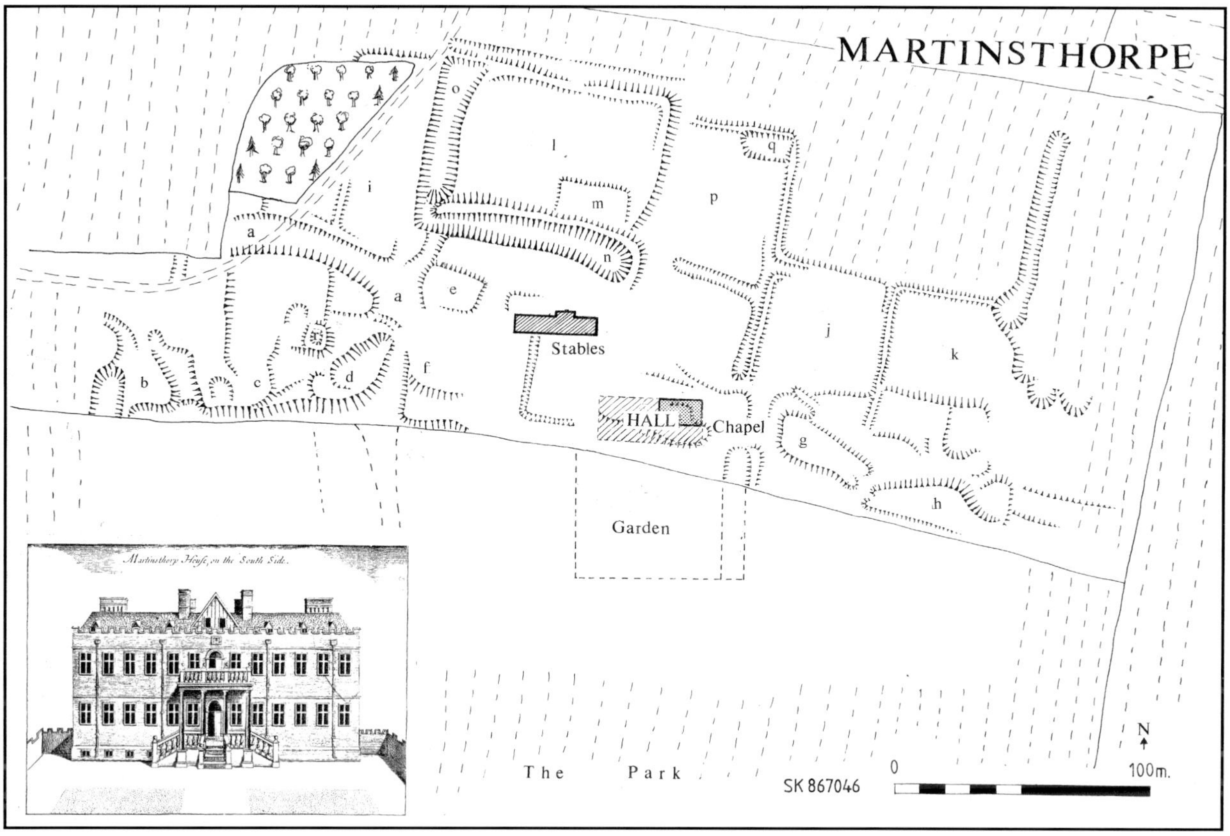

Figure 54: Martinsthorpe, Village and Mansion House
(inset view of Martinsthorpe House is from Wright's history of Rutland, 1684)

MARTINSTHORPE

Village and Mansion House (fig 54) **SK867046**

Both the village of Martinsthorpe, and the great house which replaced it, have vanished, with only slight ruins of the grand stable block to indicate the site. They lie on a trackway which follows the crest of a narrow ridge where the streams of the Gwash and Chater are only one kilometre apart, before diverging again to make their different courses to join the Welland.

There are traces of a hollow way (a-a), which may once have continued eastwards through the area where the Hall and its gardens were later laid out. There are mounds and platforms probably marking the sites of houses (b, c, d, e, f, g). Probably associated with these properties are several small enclosures or tofts (i, j, k).

The central area of the village was most affected by the development of Martinsthorpe House. There is a large terraced enclosure (l), bounded on two sides by fish pond (n, o), and containing

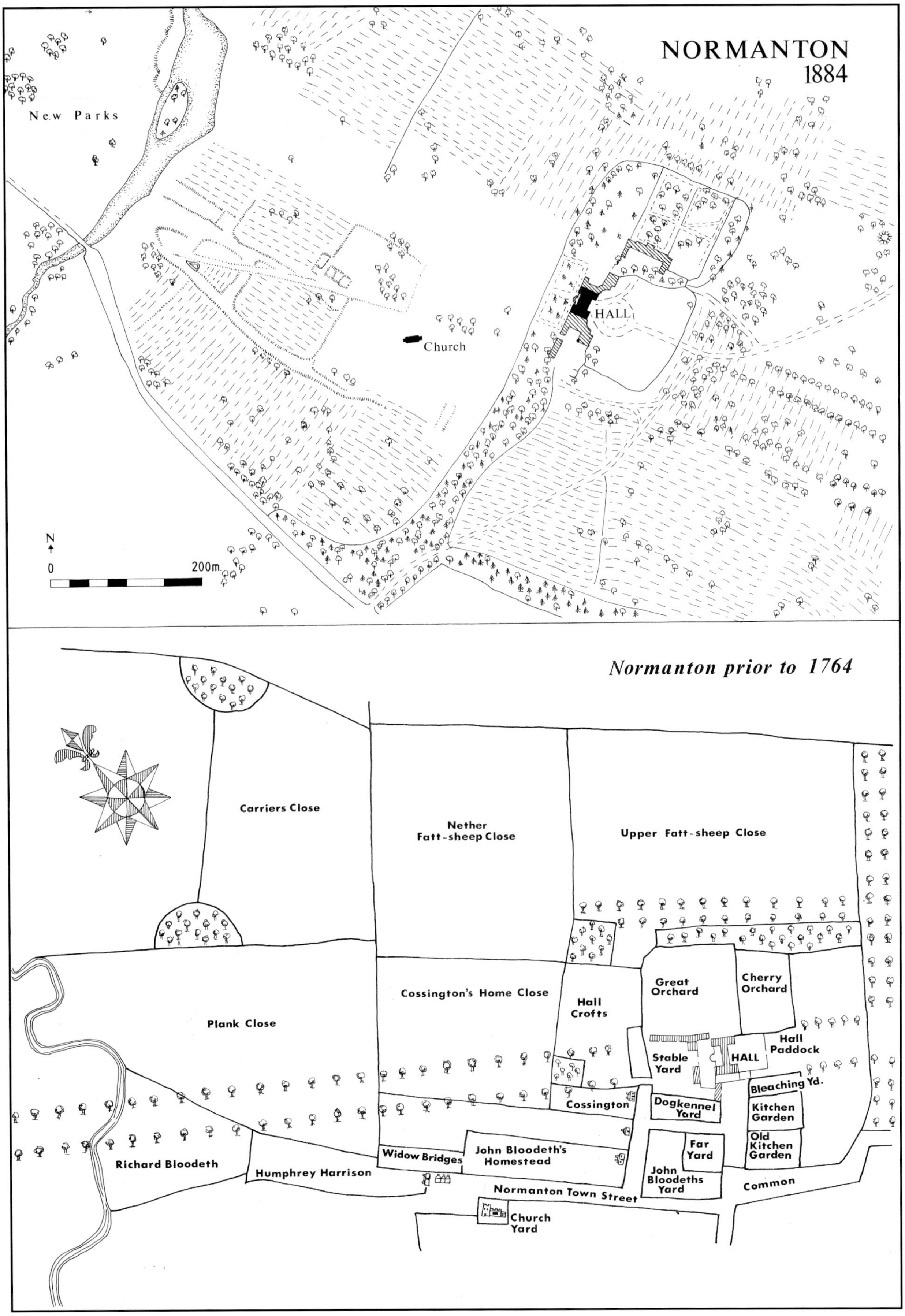

Figure 55: Normanton 1884 and prior to 1764

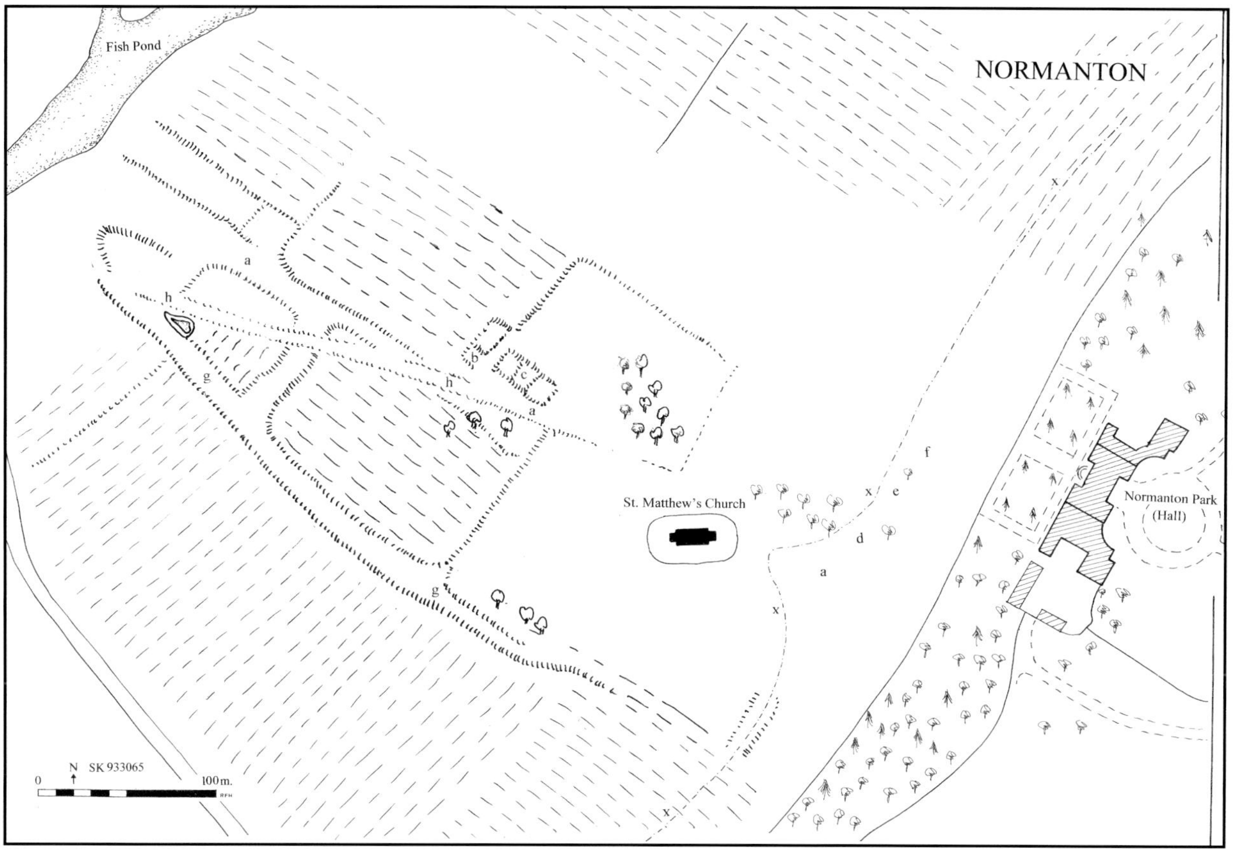

Figure 56: Normanton deserted village

a rectangular building platform (m). This may have been part of the gardens of the 17th century Hall, or possibly the site of an earlier manor house and garden which preceded it. To the east is another close (p), probably part of the medieval village, with a small fishpond (q) in the upper east corner. Excavations were carried out here by John Wacher in 1960 (TLAHS 39, 1963-4, 19).

MORCOTT

No specific earthwork sites are noted. The village had three open fields in 1702 - South, North and West. They were enclosed by an Act of 1836 (Ryder 2006, 66).

NORMANTON

Deserted Village of Normanton (figs 55, 56) **_SK933065_**

The Normanton Hall estate was purchased in 1729 by Sir Gilbert Heathcote MP (1652-1733), a merchant who had become immensely wealthy through trade with the West and East Indies, and was Lord Mayor of London in 1710-11. His son Sir John Heathcote (1689-1759) was a director of the Bank of England and the East India Company, and set about the rebuilding of Normanton Hall on a suitably grand scale. His grandson Sir Gilbert Heathcote (3rd Baronet, d1785) remodelled the surrounding parkland in the 1760s, and a map of 1764 shows how his plan for a grand avenue of trees required the clearance of the last surviving part of the village of Normanton.

Vertical aerial photographs taken in 1945 record some earthwork remains of the village in the parkland extending north-west from the hall (RAF CPE/UK/932, 2065-6). From the photographs, and referring to a plan of 1764, it is possible to identify the hollow way of "Normanton Town Street" (a-a-a). The aerial photographs show building foundations at (b) and (c), and the 1764 map confirms these, indicating two cottages at (b) and three at (c).

The 1764 map also shows houses roughly at (d), (e) and (f) on a side-street heading northwards, but nothing is visible on the aerial photographs. A back lane (g) bounded the village on its south side. The earthworks of the village around the Hall and church, if any, must have been levelled by landscaping in the late 18th century, but the village probably once extended across this area. On the aerial photos a straight track (h-h) cuts across the village earthworks. This may be the remains of an avenue of trees extending into the parkland.

On the 1764 map the medieval village church appears, but even this was to be replaced piecemeal - the tower being replaced in 1826-9 and the nave in 1911 (Pevsner & Williamson, 2003, 488). The great house of Normanton Park was demolished after the Second World War, but most of the outbuildings survive.

The construction of Rutland Water in the 1970s removed the last visible traces of Normanton village. The edge of the reservoir is marked by the dashed line (x-x-x), and everything to the west of this line was eradicated, except the church. This was slated for demolition, but a vociferous local campaign led to its retention. Its present appearance, rising out of the lake, is striking and rather odd, because the usual maximum water level is some way above the church's original floors. The graveyard was cleared away prior to the filling of the reservoir.

OAKHAM & BARLEYTHORPE

Oakham was a royal manor at the time of the conquest and remained as such until 1075. It was later divided into two manors, one (Lordshold) remaining in royal hands and the other beig granted to Westminster Abbey (Westminster Fee, later known as Deanshold, including Barleythorpe). Barleythorpe became a separate civil parish in 1874.

OAKHAM

Oakham Castle (fig 58 overleaf) *SK862089*

Oakham Castle must once have dominated the tiny market town outside its gates, and the earthworks are still impressive viewed from the east and the north. Secluded inside this area is the Norman castle hall (a) of *c.*1180, which has almost miraculously survived, thanks to its use from the 16th to the late 20th centuries as Rutland's court of justice. Built of Clipsham stone, it is one of the finest examples of late 12th century domestic architecture in England.

The defended area of the castle is roughly square, with sides extending approximately 140m. The walls are massive, and much of the material in the present earthwork banks (b-b-b-b) must represent collapsed masonry. The entrance seems always to have been on the south side (c), from the Market Place.

At their highest point, in the south-east corner, the ramparts broaden noticeably, and it is probable that this represents the remains of a motte (d). The walls are also strengthened by the presence of two towers (e, f) near the south-west corner, looking out towards the parish church. There were almost certainly other towers or bastions around the perimeter. The area inside the defences has a considerable amount of earthwork evidence. There are foundations of three or four buildings (around g), probably once linked to the Great Hall and including kitchens. Inside the eastern rampart are traces of several buildings or storage yards (h, i, j, k), and near to the western rampart are building foundations (l, m, n, o, p). Two areas appear to have been quarried (q, q), probably for material to make the ramparts. A bank (r-r-r) extends in an irregular line across the site from north to south, apparently indicating the site of a wall or fence which once divided the site into two. There is a small, probably recent mound (s) in front of the Great Hall. This was the site of a large horse-chestnut tree which flourished in the mid-20th century. The entire castle would probably once have been surrounded by a water-filled moat (t-t-t-t) which extended into two arms north of the castle. There would have been a bridge or drawbridge of some sort at (u).

Oakham Castle as it appeared in 1730 in an engraving by Samuel and Nathaniel Buck

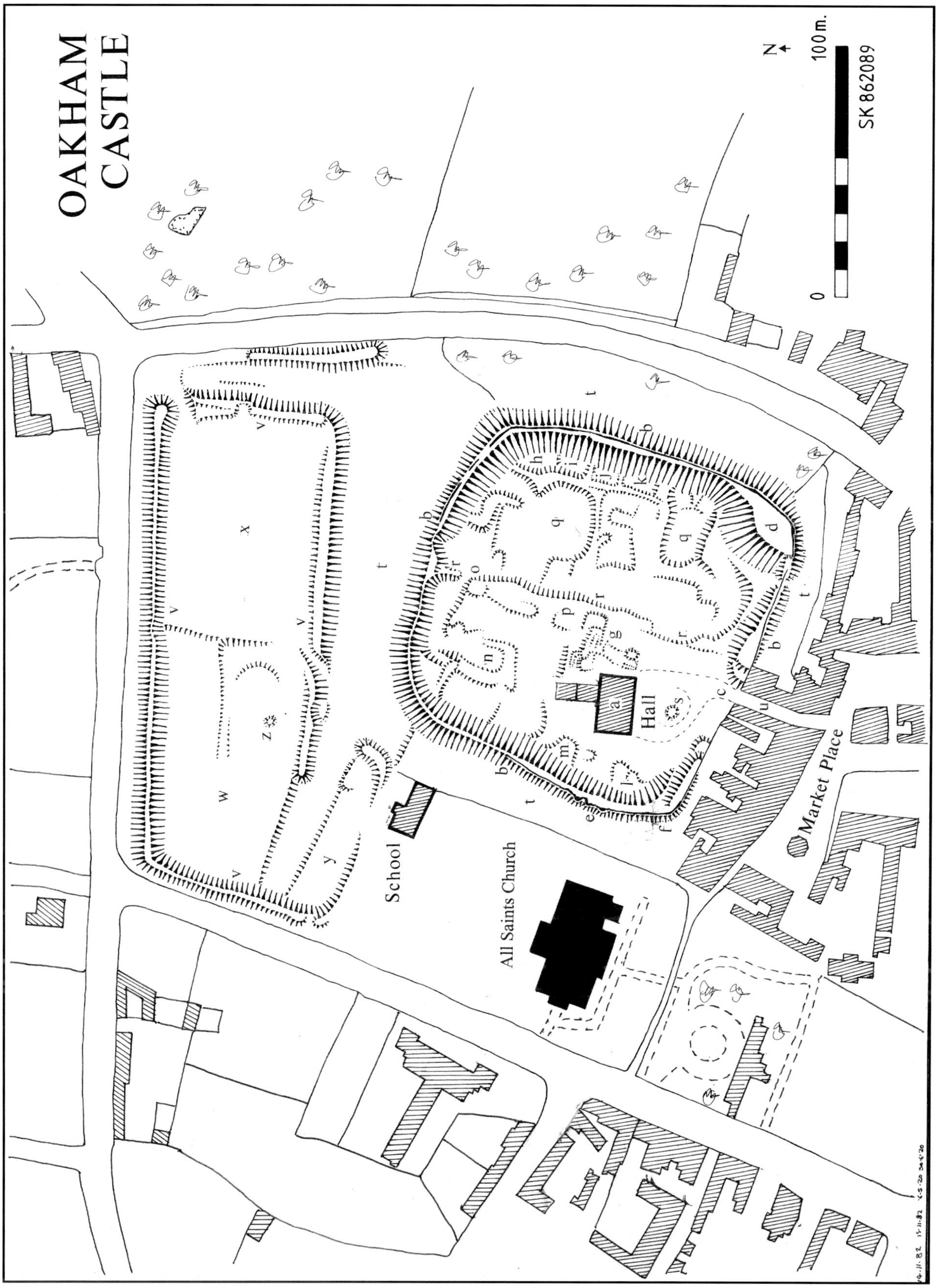

Figure 58: Oakham Castle

North of the moat is a large area enclosed by earthwork banks (v-v-v-v) which in their present form date to the 19th century. They enclose the area known as Cutts Close which is probably the site of fish ponds and the castle garden (Clough 2016), with three distinct areas (w, x, y) perhaps indicating where garden parterres and/or an orchard were located. In area (w) is a small mound of earth (z).

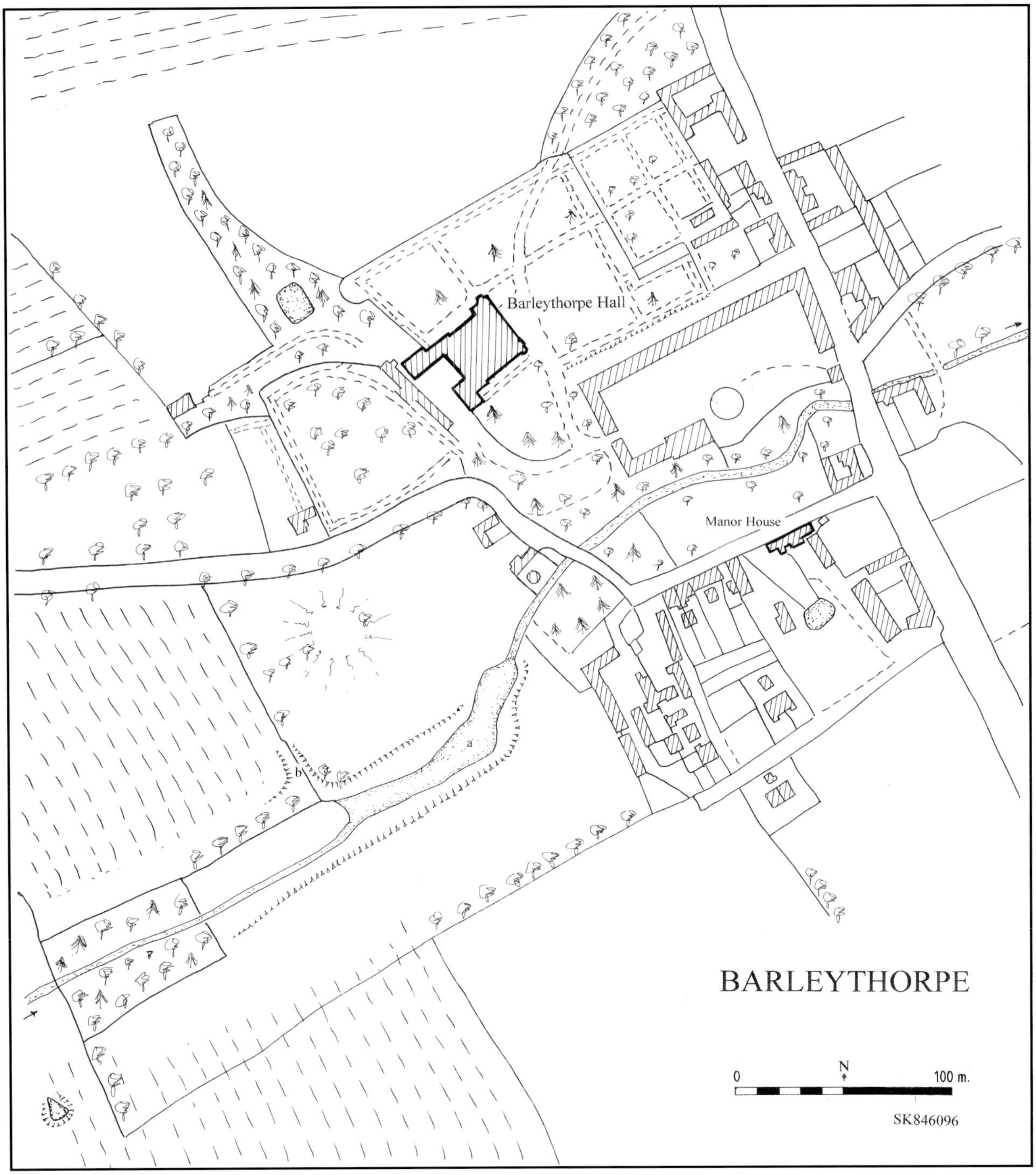

Figure 57: Oakham: Barleythorpe

Barleythorpe Ponds (fig 57) ***SK846096***

The stream through the village was dammed at some stage to form a long, narrow pond (a, b). The field to the north has indications of a low spreading mound. This hamlet was enclosed in 1772, prior to which there were three fields, West, South and Nether (Ryder 2006, 62).

The village was extensively modified by the creation of Barleythorpe Hall, a hunting lodge built for the Lowther family in the mid 1840s, with extensive additions to the stables and outbuildings in the 1880s (Crosby 2017, 302-314).

Catmose Water Mill (fig 59) **SK873089**

This water mill site was identified by local fieldworkers at a site one kilometre east of Oakham Castle, just below the confluence of two streams. The main feature is the leet or supply channel, (a-a-a), which would have conveyed water along the contour of the valley side for a distance of some 300m, before turning to reach the site of the water mill (b). The identification is confirmed by John Speed's county map of 1611, which marks "Catmouse Mill" at this location.

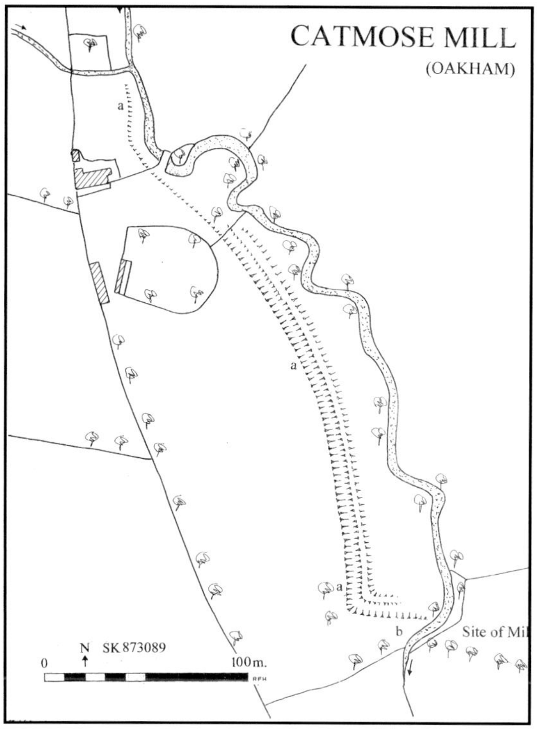

Figure 59: Oakham, Catmose Mill

Flitteris Park **SK820080**

As Lord of the Manor of Oakham, Richard, Earl of Cornwall obtained licence from King Henry III in 1250 to form a deer park in the Wood of Flitteris, on the western edge of the manor and the northern edge of Rutland Forest (Cal. Pat. R. 36, Hen III, 61. in: Cantor & Squires, 1997, 78). In the course of its creation, the earl of Cornwall had enclosed two roods of the King's highway. In 1300, the park was stocked with deer, in 1371 reference is made to a lodge in the park, and in 1372 William Flore of Oakham was allowed a sum of money by the Crown "for the palisades of 160 acres enclosed within the Park of Flyterys" (VCHR 1, 111).

In 1399 it belonged to Edward, duke of York, who bestowed the keepership on Roger Flore (Cantor 1976-7, 76), and in 1521 it was described as "a little park called Flitteris Park containing about a mile and a half and having in it 80 fallow deer". It is shown on Saxton's 1576 map of Leicestershire and on John Speed's 1610 map of the same county (Cantor 1976-7, 76).

In the Victoria County History of Rutland (1, 111) the park is described as being surrounded by a double vallum (or bank) and intermediate fosse (or ditch). Squires reviewed the historical and field evidence for the park in detail in 1992, noting that the probable line of the pale is three miles in length and encloses an area of about two hundred and twenty acres (Squires 1992, 50).

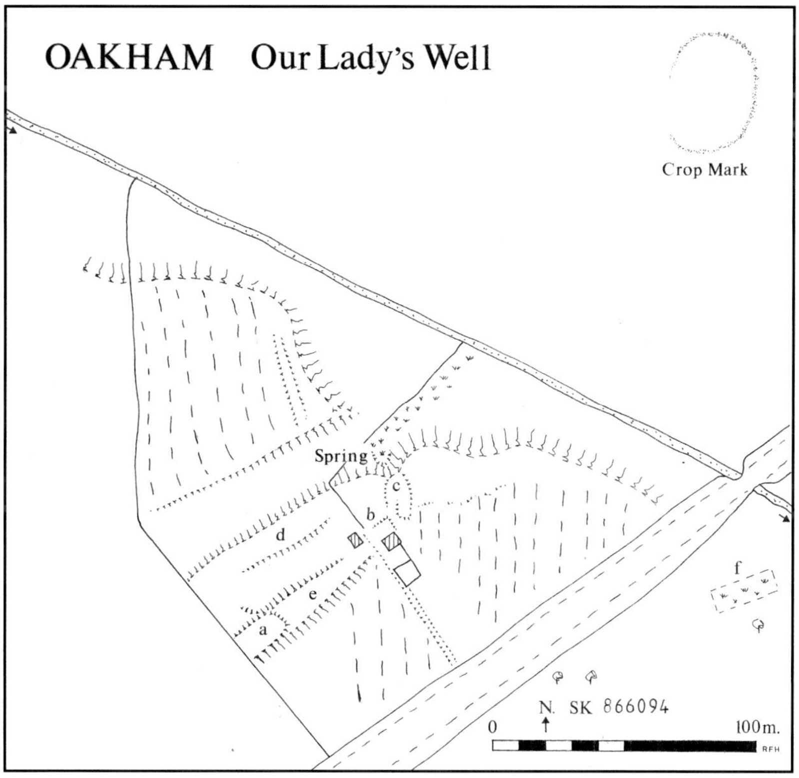

St Mary's Well/Our Lady's Well (fig 60) **SK866094**

East of Oakham, where the road to Burley crosses a stream, is the site of St. Mary's Well. There seems to have been a small settlement here over many years. Three platforms (a, b, c) show the former sites of buildings on a low ridge with two parallel banks (d, e). Across the road, to the east, the Ordnance Survey recorded what seems to be a small, silted-up pond of rectangular shape (f).

Figure 60 Oakham, Our Lady's Well

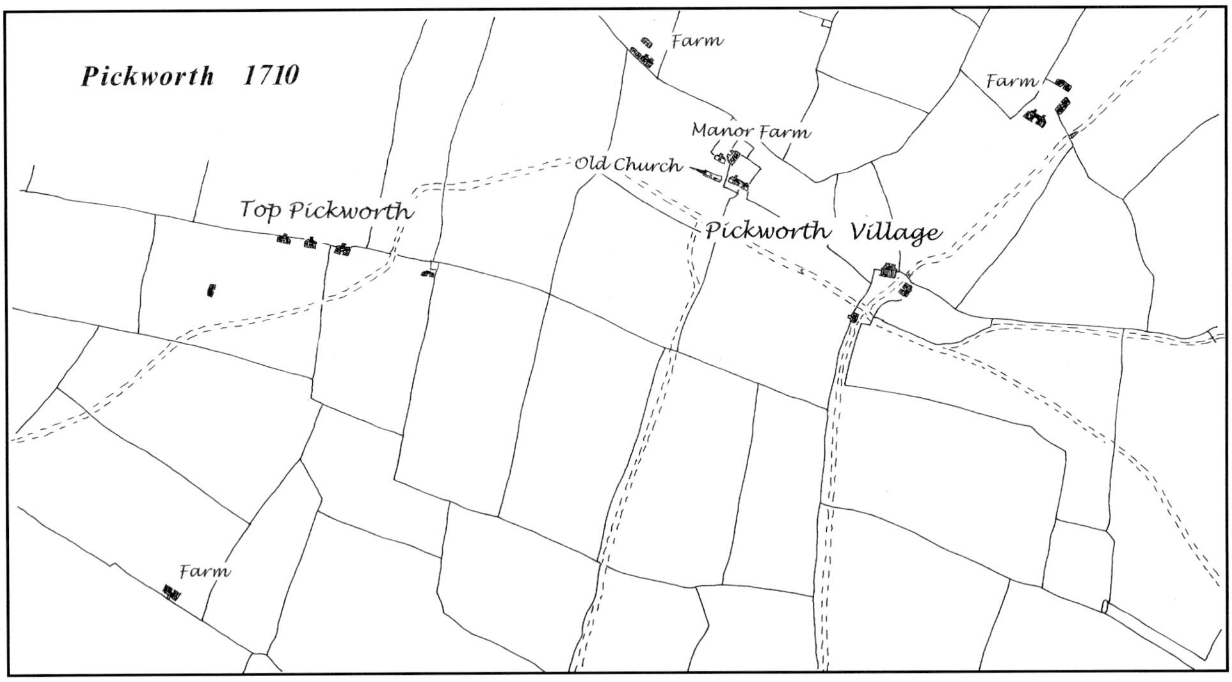

Figure 61: Pickworth 1710 (from a copy of John Wing's map of 1710, NRO Map/4372)

PICKWORTH

Manor House Site and Village Earthworks (figs 61, 62) *SK992138*

The farm buildings of Pickworth Manor Farm are surrounded by earthwork evidence of previous eras. To the north-west of the buildings at (a) are foundations of a large building, approximately 20m x 15m. This site lies within an enclosure defined by banks (b-b-b) which is itself inside another enclosure (c-c-c), with a possible small pond (d) on its north side.

East of the farm buildings is an archway, a fragmentary remnant of the old parish church. The nave and chancel were roofless by 1710, with just the steeple standing. It was named "mockbeggar" because any beggar walking to it in search of alms would have been disappointed. A replacement church, St. Luke's (now All Saints') was built in 1821, some 50m south-east of the old church. To the east of the old church is a platform (e), at a point where a building is shown on a copy of John Wing's map of 1710 (NRO Map/4372).

Between the two churches is a hollow (f) which appears to be an abandoned quarry, but which contained a pond at the time of the 1884 Ordnance Survey map. There is another flooded hollow further east. South of the Manor Farm buildings is a fairly level terrace (g) with a bank along part of its southern edge. To the west, near the Manor House, are garden terraces (h, i), probably created in the 19th century.

The main enclosures around the Manor Farm (within b and c above) seem to have been entered by means of a droveway (j, j) to bring livestock to and from the fields north of the village. In the area south-east of Manor Farm are levelled hollows (k, l) and platforms (m, n, o), which probably mark the site of more vanished buildings. Further east at (p) are footings of another small building.

To the west of the Manor House are foundations of several stone-built cottages (q, r, s, t, u). The remains at (s) and (t) indicate buildings with two rooms. A mound of rubble (v) may mark the site of another building. There are no buildings shown in this area on the 1710 map, or on the First EditionOrdnance Survey maps of 1884, and it appears to be a late 18th/early 19th century industrial settlement associated with the adjacent quarry and limekilns. The poet John Clare worked here at the limekiln in 1817.

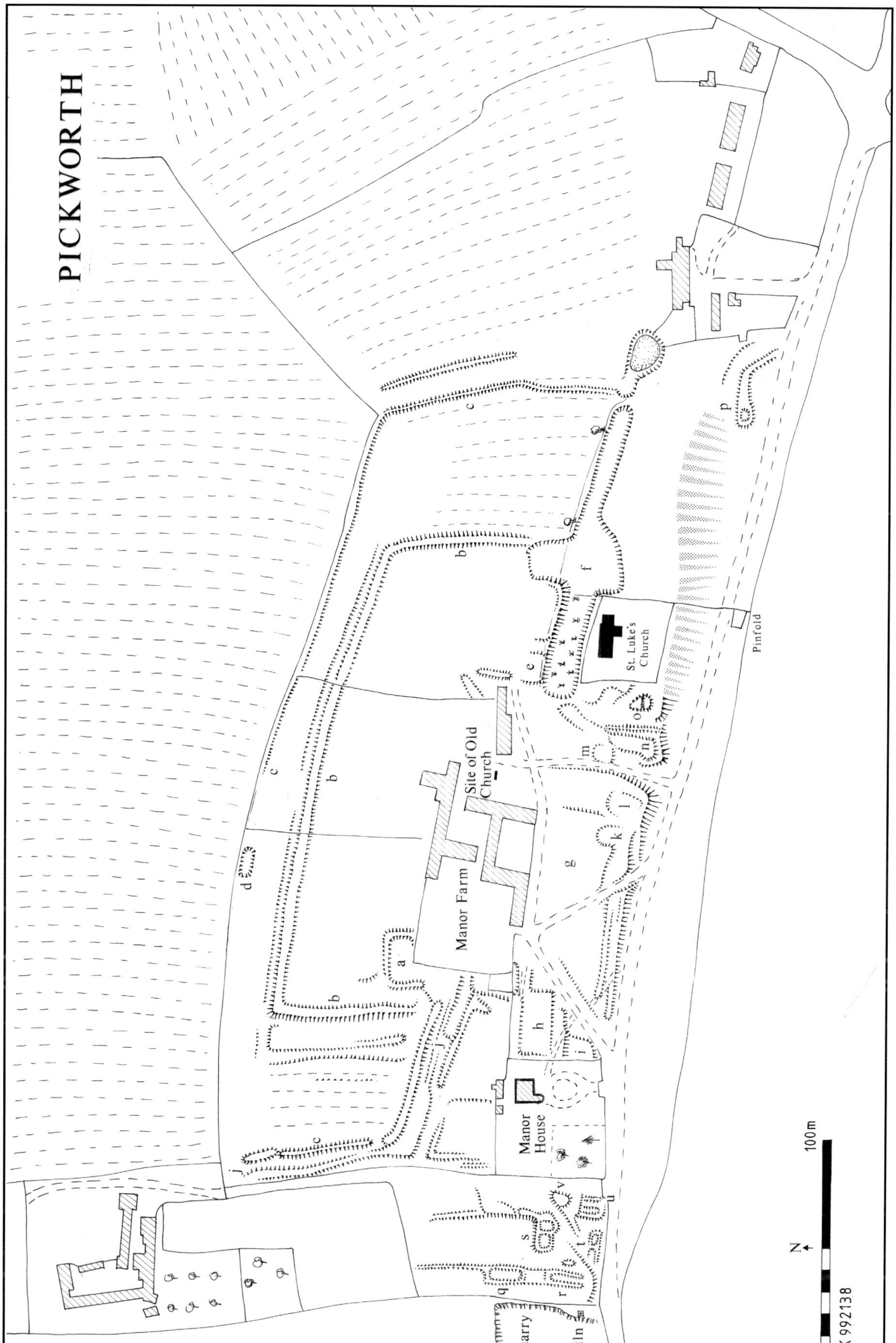

Figure 62: Pickworth, Manor House Site and Village Earthworks

Earthwork Pickworth Great Wood (fig 63)
SK978147

Near the centre of the wood is a ditch or moat which encloses three sides of a rectangular platform (b). The fourth, west side of the platform is defined by a slope (c). These features may be the site of a medieval lodge, or might perhaps be a much earlier enclosure, of 'Iron Age' origin.

Top Pickworth Village Earthworks (fig 64)
SK985136

Some way to the west of Pickworth Manor Farm was the outlying settlement of Top Pickworth. The Ordnance Survey First Edition 1:2500 map shows several cottages here, at (a, b, c, d). Traces of these still exist, with rubble at (c) and (d) and two more cottages, of which no trace remains, at (j) and (k). Another rectangular mound (e) probably represents the site of a cottage abandoned before 1885, with a pond nearby (f). A patch of nettles at (g) may indicate the site of a building, with another small mound (h) and a larger one (i) surrounded by a ditch.

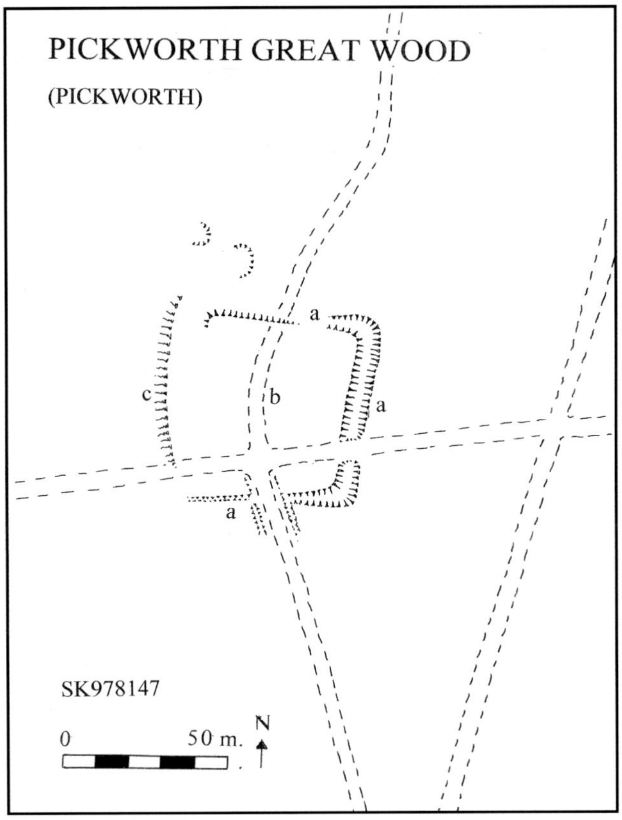

Figure 63: Pickworth Great Wood

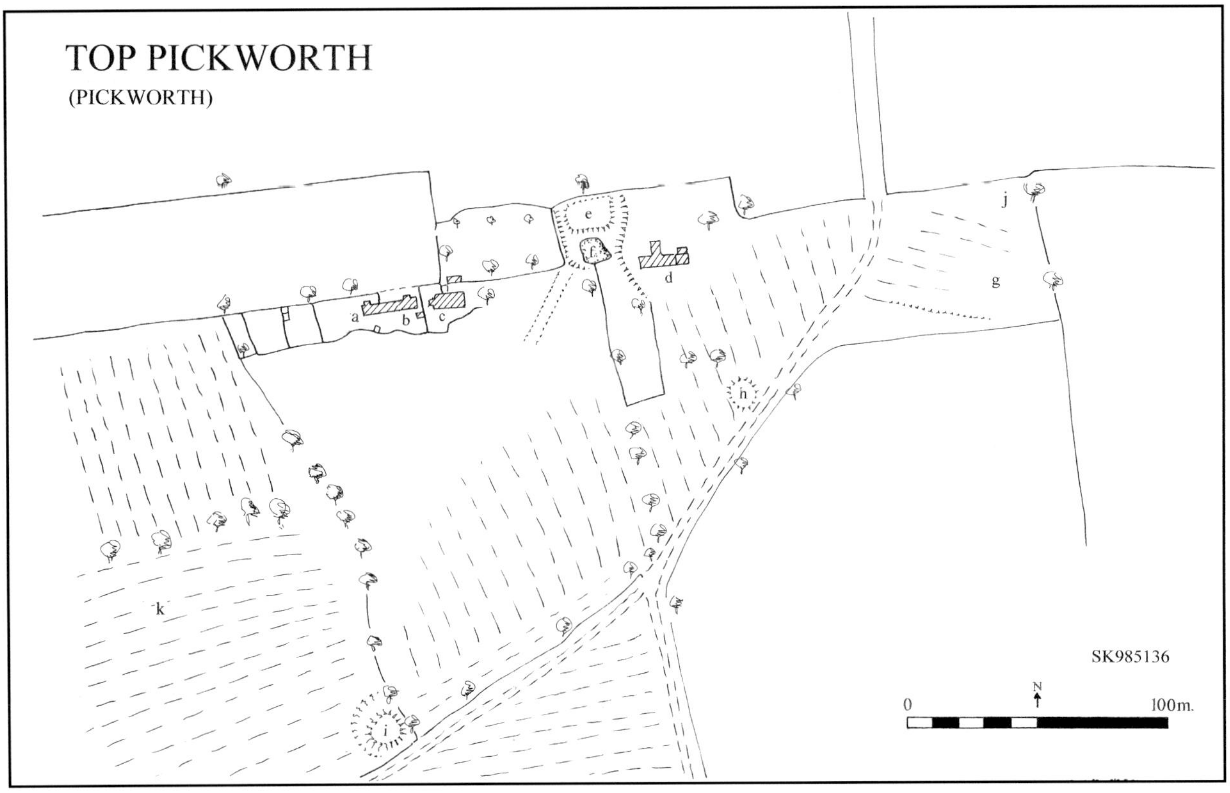

Figure 64: Pickworth, Top Pickworth Village Earthworks

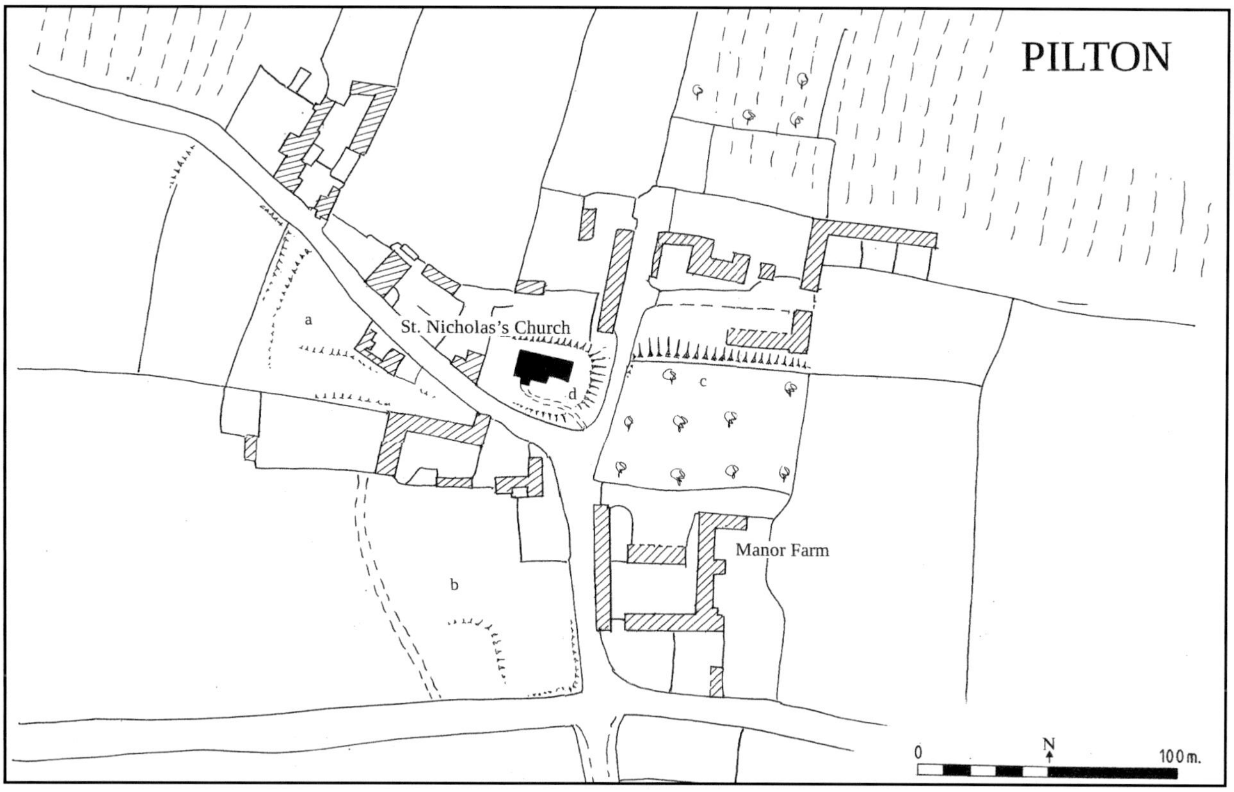

Figure 65: Pilton Village Earthworks

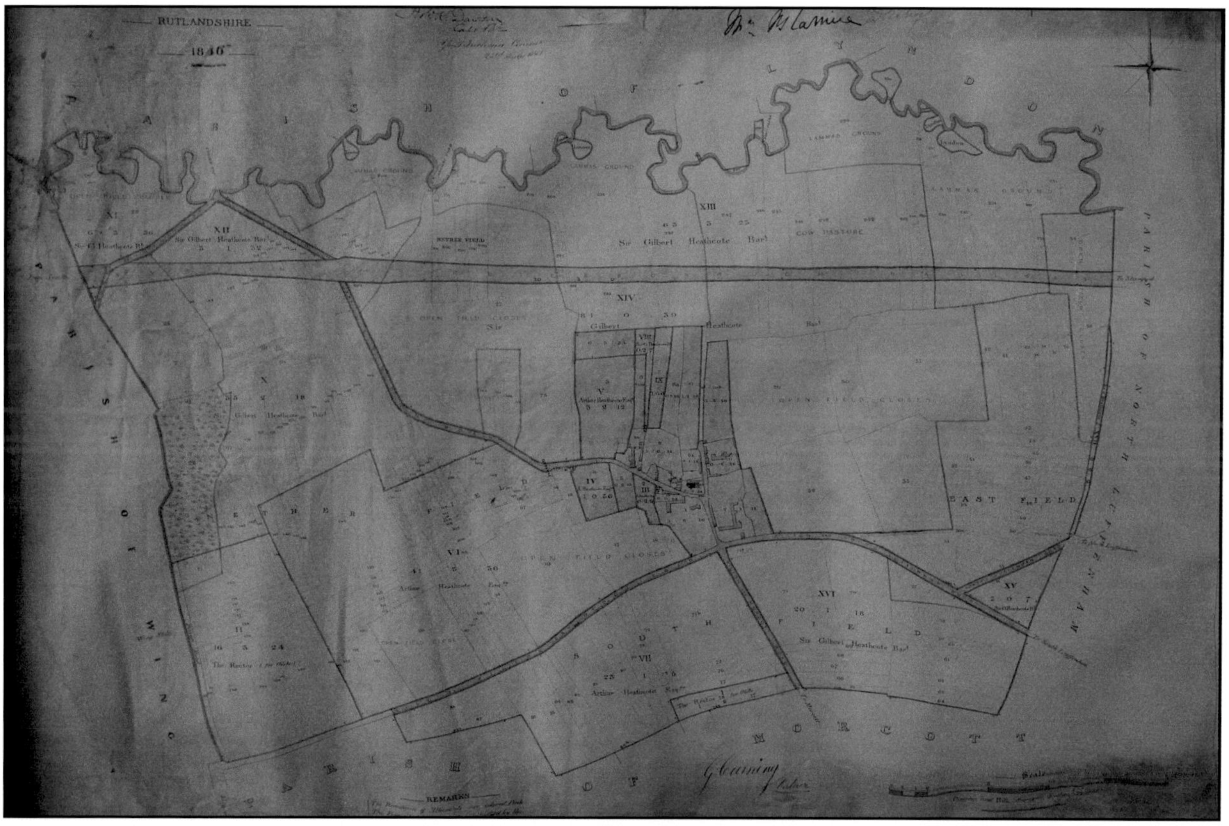

Pilton Enclosure Map 1846 © ROLLR DE1175 MA/EN/A/R37/1

PILTON

Village Earthworks (fig 65) ***SK914029/SK914031***

The small village of Pilton was enclosed in 1846, at which time there were three open fields - East Field, South Field and Nether Field (Ryder 2006, 66). RAF vertical photographs have indications of old closes at SK914031, which are shown on the enclosure map. There were traces of more old boundaries at SK914029, (a), including circular foundations of what might be a dovecote. Further south was more slight evidence of village earthworks (b). There is a levelled garden terrace of probably 17th or 18th century date (c), and across the road the churchyard (d) forms a conspicuous mound.

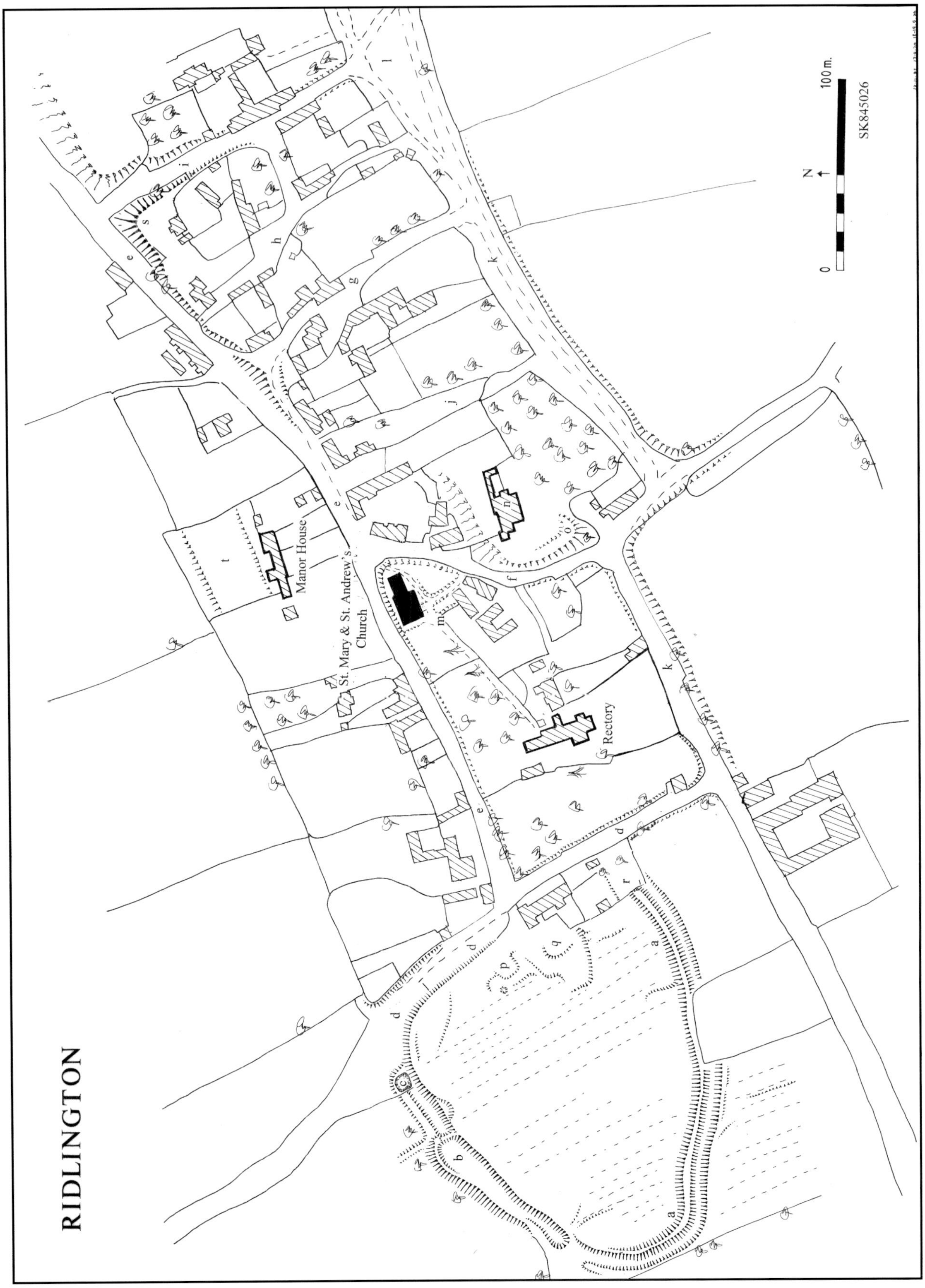

Figure 66: Ridlington Village Earthworks

PRESTON

No specific earthworks are noted in Preston. There were three open fields - North, South and East, prior to enclosure in 1773 (Ryder 2006, 66).

RIDLINGTON

Ridlington Village Earthworks (fig 66) **SK845026**

At the west end of Ridlington village is a sub-circular enclosure with an inner bank (a-a-a) and an outer ditch, which widens on the north side to contain the sites of two ponds (b, c). The east side of the enclosure is the hollow way (d-d) of a lane.

The enclosure has been interpreted as a possible Iron Age settlement site, and the size and location, on top of a ridge, tend to support this. Alternatively it might be related to Ridlington's importance in the management of the medieval hunting chase known as the Forest of Leicestershire and Rutland.

From the centre of the east side of the enclosure the main street of Ridlington extends to the east (e-e), forming a hollow way in places, and passing very close to the parish church. Smaller lanes lead off at right angles (f, g, h, i) and there was probably another at (j), all linking the main street to the back lane (k), along the south side of the village, which widens at the east end into a green (l).

There is a building platform just south of the church (m), and the old mansion house (n) has a garden with a raised screening bank (o), probably of 18th or 19th century date.

Returning to the large enclosure (a), inside the east side, near the probable entrance are the sites of three small buildings (p, q, r). These are presumably post-medieval, as they cut into the pattern of ridge and furrow cultivation strips within the large enclosure.

Deer Park **SK8301**

A royal deer park existed at Ridlington from about 1238 to 1623. In 1238 it was in the hands of the Crown as part of the Forest of Leicestershire and Rutland, and it remained so until sold in 1623. Squires reviewed the history and the landscape evidence for the park (Squires 2003, 105-110). The modern Park Farm is in the centre of the area, which broadly corresponded with the western end of Ridlington parish. The subsequent discovery of an 18th century map of the park, amongst the Exton Estate papers, confirmed his analysis (ROLLR DE3214/4606).

Fish Ponds **SK840015**

The large fishpond at this location formed part of the amenities of the post-Medieval park and is shown on the plan of 1624. The farm called The Lodge (VCHR 2, 102) was subsequently built nearby.

Water Mill **SK847037**

The online Mills Archive records a water powered corn mill at this location with no further documents or photographs. (https://new.millsarchive.org/mills/index/?which=4596)

RYHALL

Belmesthorpe Village Earthworks (fig 67 overleaf) **TF045103**

A hollow way (a-a-a) runs along the northern edge of the village, and near its east end is an old close (b). The south-eastern quarter of the village has been depopulated, leaving earthwork remains in a pasture field. There are probable sites of houses (c, d, e), and behind them are two building platforms (f, g) and mounds of material perhaps representing the sites of more buildings (h, i, j). Behind these again are the boundaries of old crofts (k, l).

All of these features were later incorporated into three closes of pasture land (m, n, o), with traces of two more closes further west (p, q). At the west end of the village a deep hollow way (r) leads in a south-easterly direction towards Uffington, in Lincolnshire.

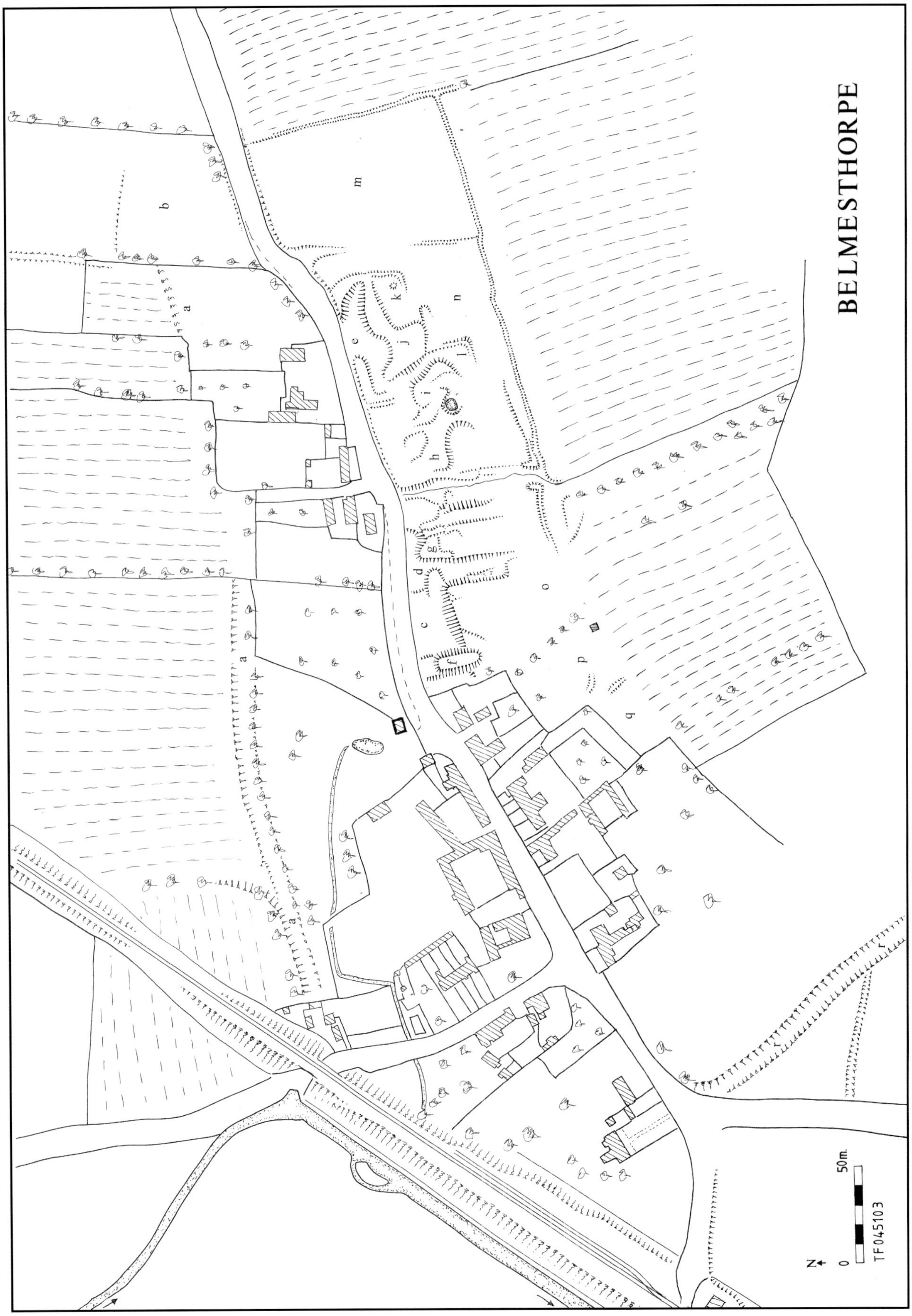

Figure 67: Ryhall, Belmesthorpe Village Earthworks

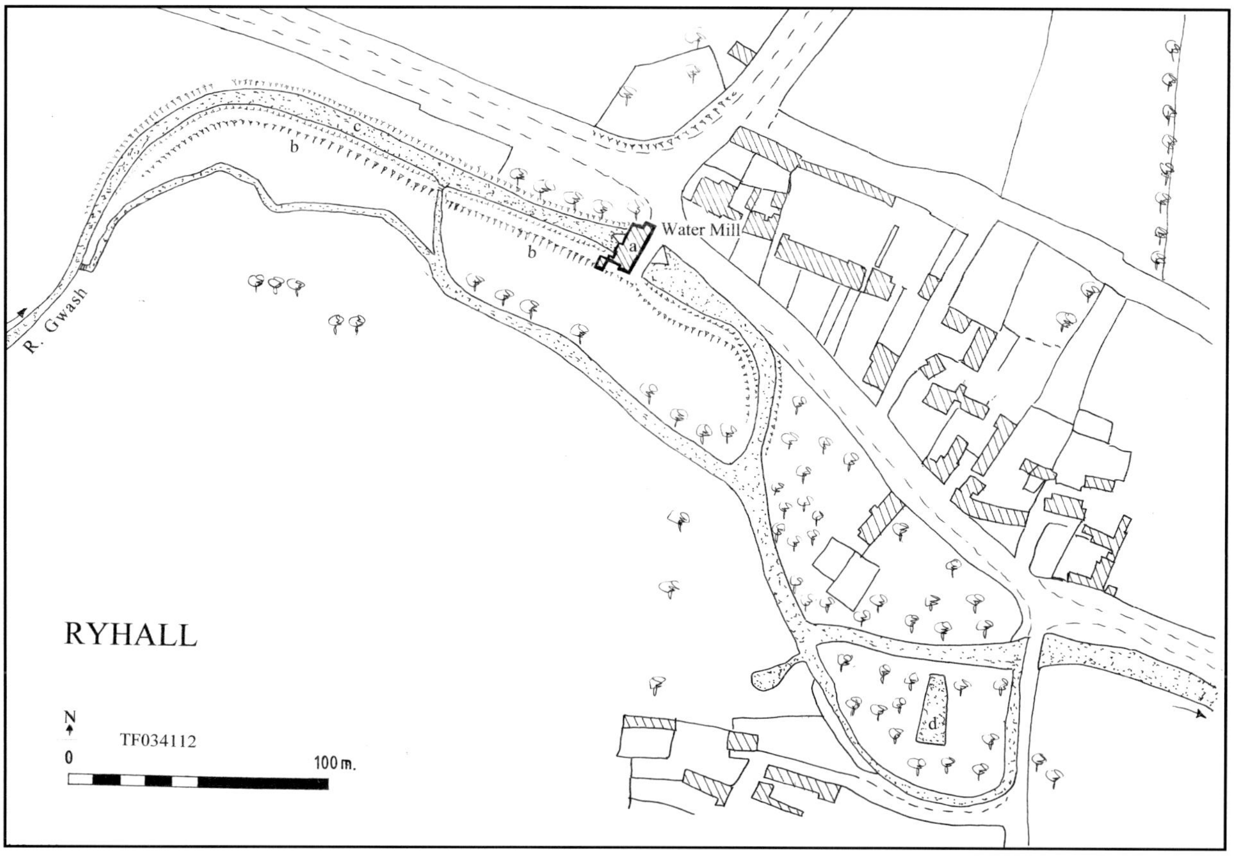

Figure 68: Ryhall Water Mill

Ryhall Water Mill (fig 68) ***TF034112***

North of the village is the site of the medieval water mill (a). A raised bank (b) would have retained water in the mill pond (c) fed from the River Gwash.

SEATON

Seaton was one of the last villages in Rutland to be enclosed. This took place in 1855-58, at about the same time as neighbouring Thorpe by Water. The common pasture land on Seaton Burrows, shared by Seaton, Thorpe and Lyddington, was enclosed at the same time. This event must have lived long in the memory, and even in the 1980s the farmers met here and still seemed to have an unusual awareness of history and tradition. Prior to enclosure there were three fields - North or Mill Field, West, Red or Uppingham Field, and South, Nether, or Harrington Field (Ryder 2006, 67).

Village Earthworks (fig 69) ***SP902983***

When surveys were carried out in 1982 Seaton had a remarkable amount of earthwork evidence of changes to the village layout. Most of these features appeared to survive in 2020.

At the west end of the village is a broad hollow way (a-a-a). This is shown and named on an 1727 map by Tycho Wing as "The Drifte Way" (NRO, Map/6322) and would have been the way that cattle and sheep from the village would have been taken each day to graze on the common pasture of Seaton Barrows. This area of pasture was shared with the villages of Thorpe and Lyddington.

Joining the Drift Way is another hollow way (b) of an old lane through the village. Between here and All Hallows' Church is a block of land enclosing the Manor House. This area is also largely surrounded by hollow ways, suggesting that its boundaries are ancient. North-east of the Manor House are several old closes (c, d, e, f) marked by the substantial rubble banks of

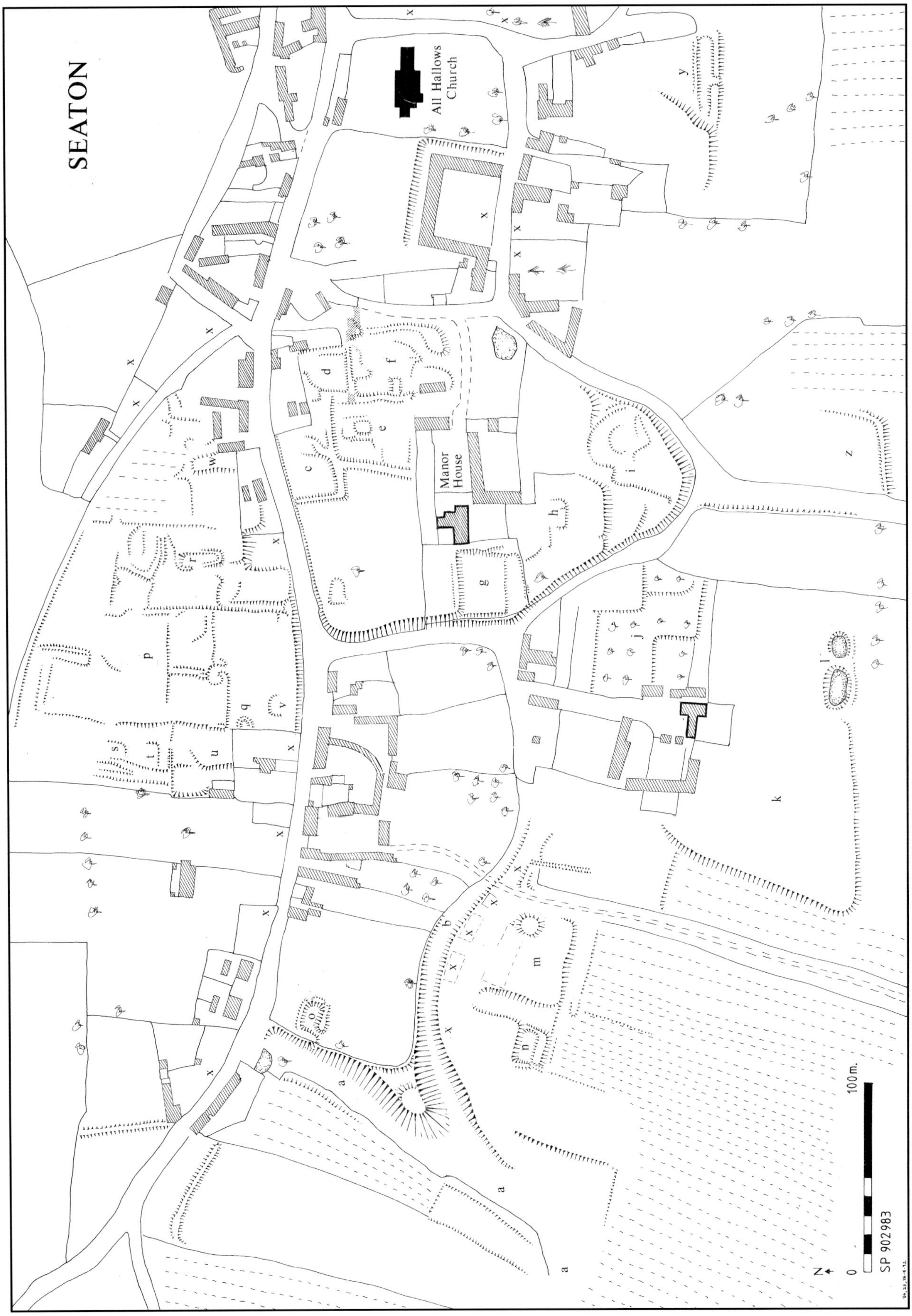

Figure 69: Seaton Village Earthworks

collapsed walls. Within enclosures (e) and (f) are three or four rectangular platforms where buildings probably stood.

The manor house has gardens on its west and south sides, with garden terraces (g) and below them another terrace with a building platform (h). The area to the south of (h) has earthworks which are difficult to interpret. There were probably buildings here at some time, but on the 17th century map this area is named "The Cunnygrey", showing that it was then, or had previously been, a rabbit warren.

Across the lane, to the south-west, is another substantial farm house, named as "Mr. Broughton's" on the early 17th century map. This house also has garden terraces (j), and south of the houses are the boundary banks of an ancient close (k), which contained two ponds (l). Further west is another old close or croft (m), containing a low circular mound and a pond (n). To the north of this is another embanked pond (o).

The northern edge of the village has another area, around (p), full of complex earthwork evidence. There is a rectilinear pattern of terraces and tumbled walls, with footings of a small circular building (q), perhaps a dovecote, and foundations of a large stone building (r), some 25m long with an entrance in the long west side. This is likely to have been a threshing barn. There are more sites of buildings, with platforms or hollows at (s, t, u, v, w). On the early 17th century map this area is shown as a large close, with one big building "Marshall's Farm" sited approximately at (u). The farm had gone by the time of the 1727 map.

The 1727 map shows at least 18 houses in the village which had been abandoned by the late 19th century, and of which little trace exists in the form of earthworks. Their approximate sites are marked (x). South of the church was another embanked pond (y), a 'perched pond' probably built on the spring line. To the south-west of this pond is the bank of an ancient close (z) which is marked on the 1727 map.

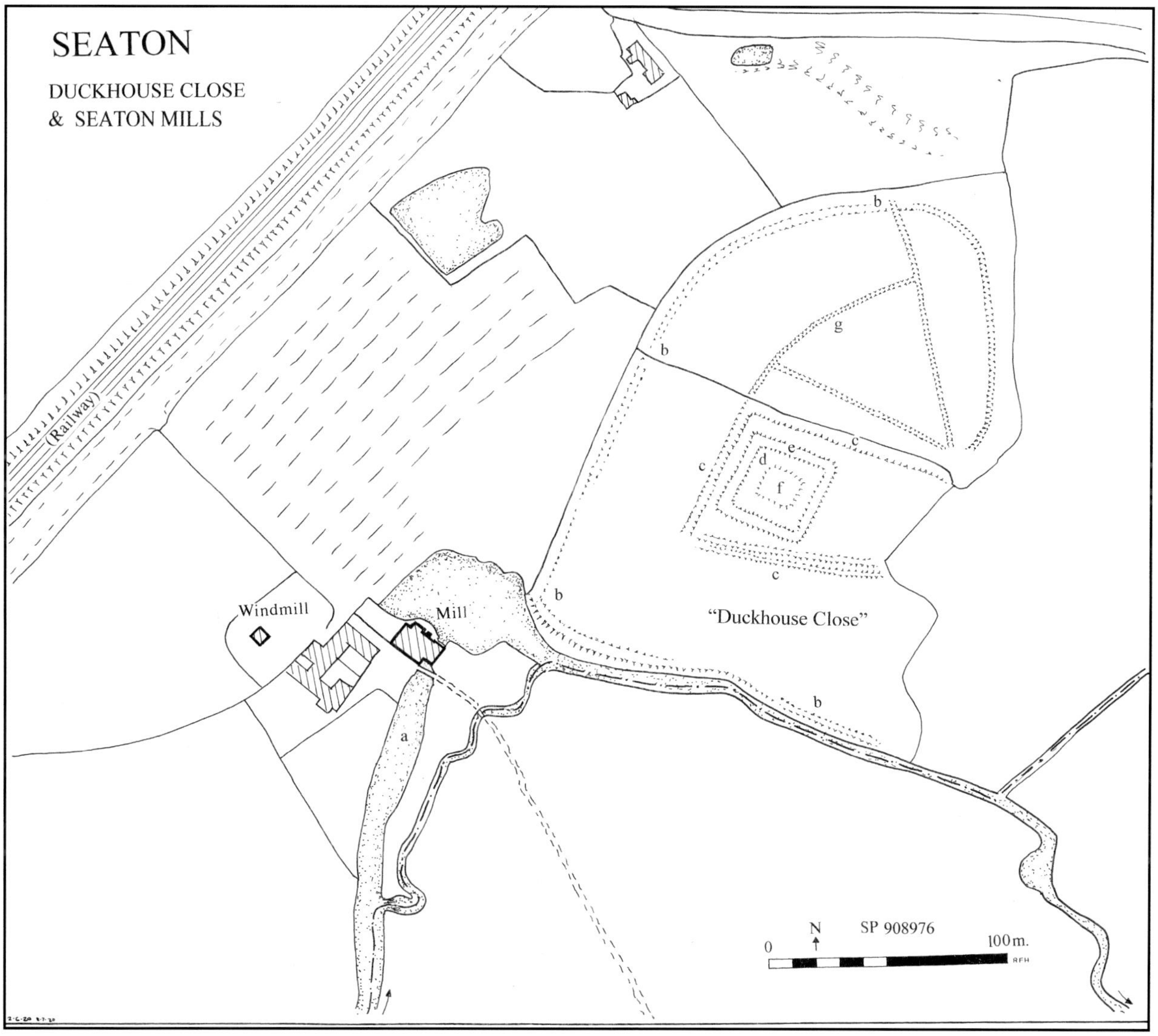

Figure 70: Seaton Watermill and Windmill, Earthwork "Duckhouse Close"

Water Mill and Windmill (fig 70) **SK907976**

Seaton Water Mill probably occupies a site which has been used for centuries, with the supply channel (a) diverting water from the River Welland to power the mill. Unusually a windmill was also built here. It was a post mill and the online Mills Archive has a drawing made by James Venn in 1944 (https://new.millsarchive.org/mills/index/?which=1708).

Earthwork, "Duckhouse Close" (fig 70) **SK909976**

To the east of the water mill is an area of low-lying land near the River Welland, largely enclosed by a bank and ditch (b-b-b). In the centre of this are more ditches and banks (c-c-c) around a rectangular area, within which is a drained moat (d), surrounded by a bank (e) and containing a rectangular platform (f). Brown notes that it existed at the time of the tithe map, when it was called Duckhouse Close, and considered that it was probably a duck decoy (Brown 1975 p23). While this seems likely, it is worth noting that the earthworks seem more substantial than would be needed just to create a decoy pond. There was a manor of "Down Hall" in Seaton, and this could conceivably have been the site of the manor house.

STOKE DRY

Village Earthworks (fig 71) **SK855967**

The main street of this small and secluded village is in a hollow way (a-a-a) which follows the crest of a ridge, descending from east to west. Aerial photographs show earthwork remains of three old closes (b, c, d) on the north side of the street, with a smaller hollow way (e), where a lane used to lead northwards into the fields.

The Rectory has extensive garden terraces (f, g) with a semi-circular projection (h) giving views to the south and west. The Rectory stands on the site of the manor house of the Digbys, whose chief seat it was from about 1450 to 1649. The most prominent member of the family was perhaps Sir Kenelm Digby, Gentleman of the Bedchamber to King Charles I, Commissioner of the Navy, and Governor of Trinity House. His support for the Royalist cause led to him being banished in 1649 and his estates sequestrated. It would seem at least possible that the Rectory garden terraces were created for the manor house in the early 17th century (VCHR 2, 223).

Across the street from St. Andrew's Church is a house named "The Grange" which has earthworks of a sunken garden (h), probably created in the 19th century.

STRETTON

Village Earthworks (fig 72 overleaf) **SK949157**

In the pasture field south of St. Nicholas's Church are earthwork banks indicating the former boundaries of three old closes (a, b, c). Within (c) , are well-preserved remains of what would appear to be a manorial site. There are footings of a large stone building (d), with a smaller building (e) attached, and a similar arrangement nearby with (f) and (g). The large buildings (d) and (f) are likely to have been barns, and each measure approximately 25m x 15m. Near to (d) are foundations of a square building (h). Several mounds of rubble nearby probably mark the site of outbuildings (i). On the southern edge of close (c) are foundations of two more buildings - one circular (j) and one square (k). These may have been dovecotes.

Towards the west side of the village are a garden terrace (l), probably 19th century, and a raised trackway (m). The First Edition Ordnance Survey 1:2500 map shows an earthwork bank (n) running parallel with Ermine Street (Great North Road) and forming the western edge of the village for a distance of some 350m, between the two road junctions. North of St. Nicholas's Church is a block of land which is noticeably higher than the surrounding lanes and hollow ways, with a particularly marked scarp slope on the northern boundaries (o-o-o-o). The layout of this part of the village would appear to be ancient.

Further north is a pond (p), while north-west of the village centre there used to be quarries (q) and limekilns in the 19th century. Terraces on the north side of the village (r) may have been caused by quarrying for limestone.

Figure 71: Stoke Dry Village Earthworks

Stocken Hall (fig 73, page 73) ***SK956182***

"Tenements in Stocken are once called a manor" (VCHR 2,148) suggesting the existence of a settlement here. At the time of the First Edition Ordnance Survey maps there was just Stocken Hall, with garden terraces (a) of probable 18th or 19th century origin. There is now no trace of a village, but its existence is demonstrated by the ridge and furrow its farmers laboured to create. If any remains are to be found it will probably be in the area of (b) in the valley bottom where there is no ridge and furrow in evidence. To the south are two fish ponds (c, d), probably

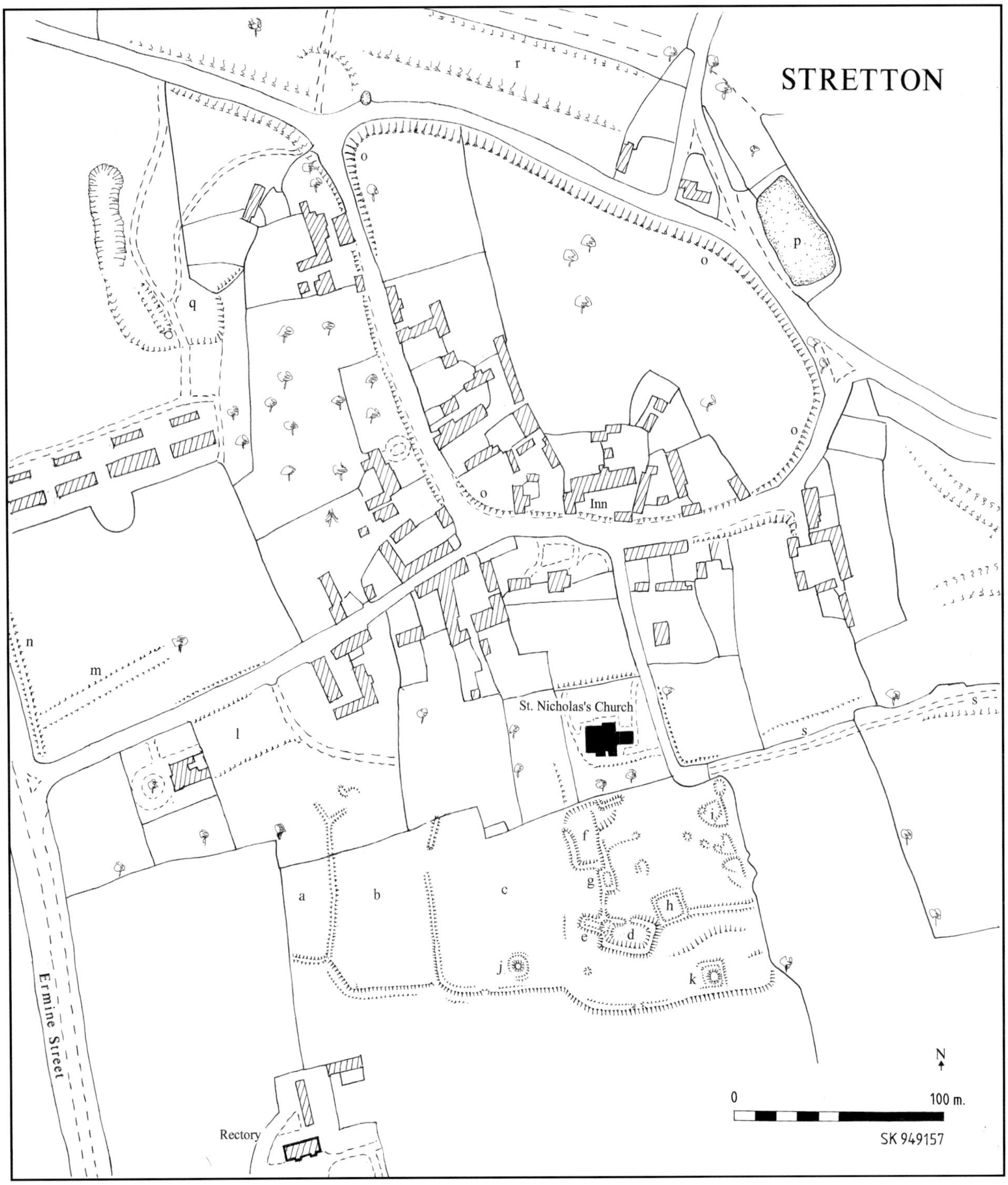

Figure 72: Stretton Village Earthworks

post-medieval. A cottage and outbuildings used to exist at SK955179 (e).
Stocken Hall was probably built by John Brown in the early 17th century. The buildings were modified in about 1774 and in 1877 (VCHR 2, 148). It has subsequently been in use as a prison.

Stocken Park

The Victoria County History notes a reference to a deer park in Stretton in 1291, when it was in the hands of the King, who gave custody of it to Ralph de Rede for life, but it seems to be otherwise undocumented (*ibid* 145).

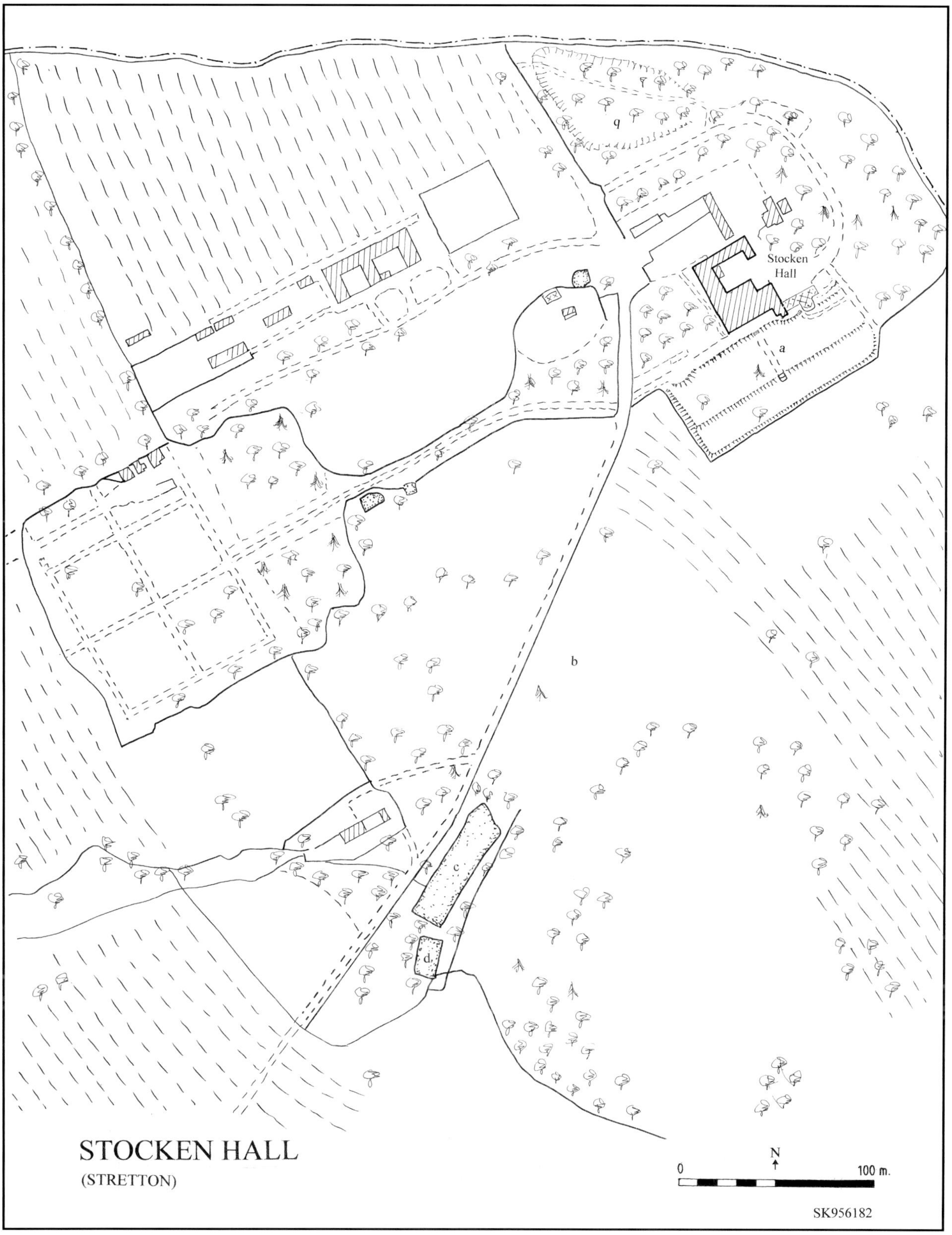

Figure 73: Stretton, Stocken Hall

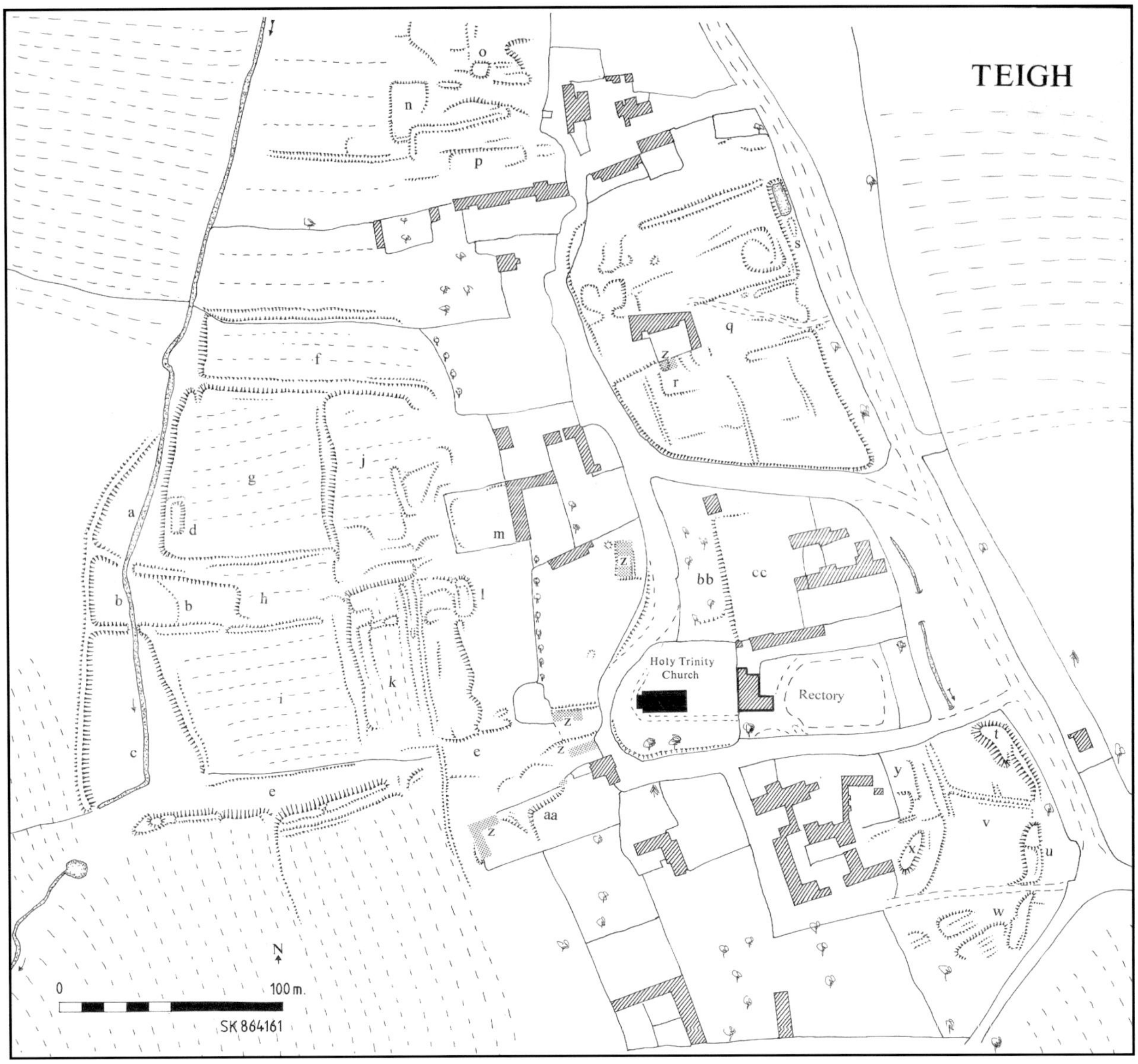

Figure 74: Teigh Village Earthworks

TEIGH

Village Earthworks (fig 74) ***SK864161***

The village of Teigh is full of earthwork evidence. The largest elements are a series of fish ponds (a, b, c). The dam which would have retained water in (c) has been largely removed. There is another, much smaller pond at (d). The three large ponds form the western boundary of a medieval manorial site. The southern boundary is an old lane (e, e) partly surviving as a hollow way. Within the manorial site are six old enclosures (f, g, h, i, j, k). Area (k) contains various smaller earthwork features, perhaps the remains of gardens or outbuildings of the manor house, and there are foundations of a stone building (l). The site of the manor house was probably somewhere in the vicinity of (m). To the north is another area of earthworks with a large building platform (n) and a small one (o). Amongst other features is a rectangular hollow (p) which may indicate where another building has been cleared away.

To the east, the field around (q) contains evidence of the boundaries of at least six old closes, and a building platform at (r). The lanes encircling this area are all in slight hollow ways, especially on the east side where a pond (s) has been excavated at some time.

The Ordnance Survey 25 inch First Edition map of 1885 shows a stream apparently commencing from this area and flowing southwards to a small field with a flat area (v) where there may perhaps once have been a pond, retained by a bank which survives as two mounds (t, u). At the time of the survey there was no longer any sign of the stream. There are four more low mounds around (w), and two platforms (x, y) which may mark the site of old outbuildings of the adjacent farm. The First Edition map also shows several buildings, mainly small cottages (z) which no longer exist. South-west of Holy Trinity Church is another possible building platform (aa) by the old lane which led west. To the north of the church is a sunken area (bb) - perhaps once a pond or small quarry - and immediately to the east of it is a levelled terrace (cc).

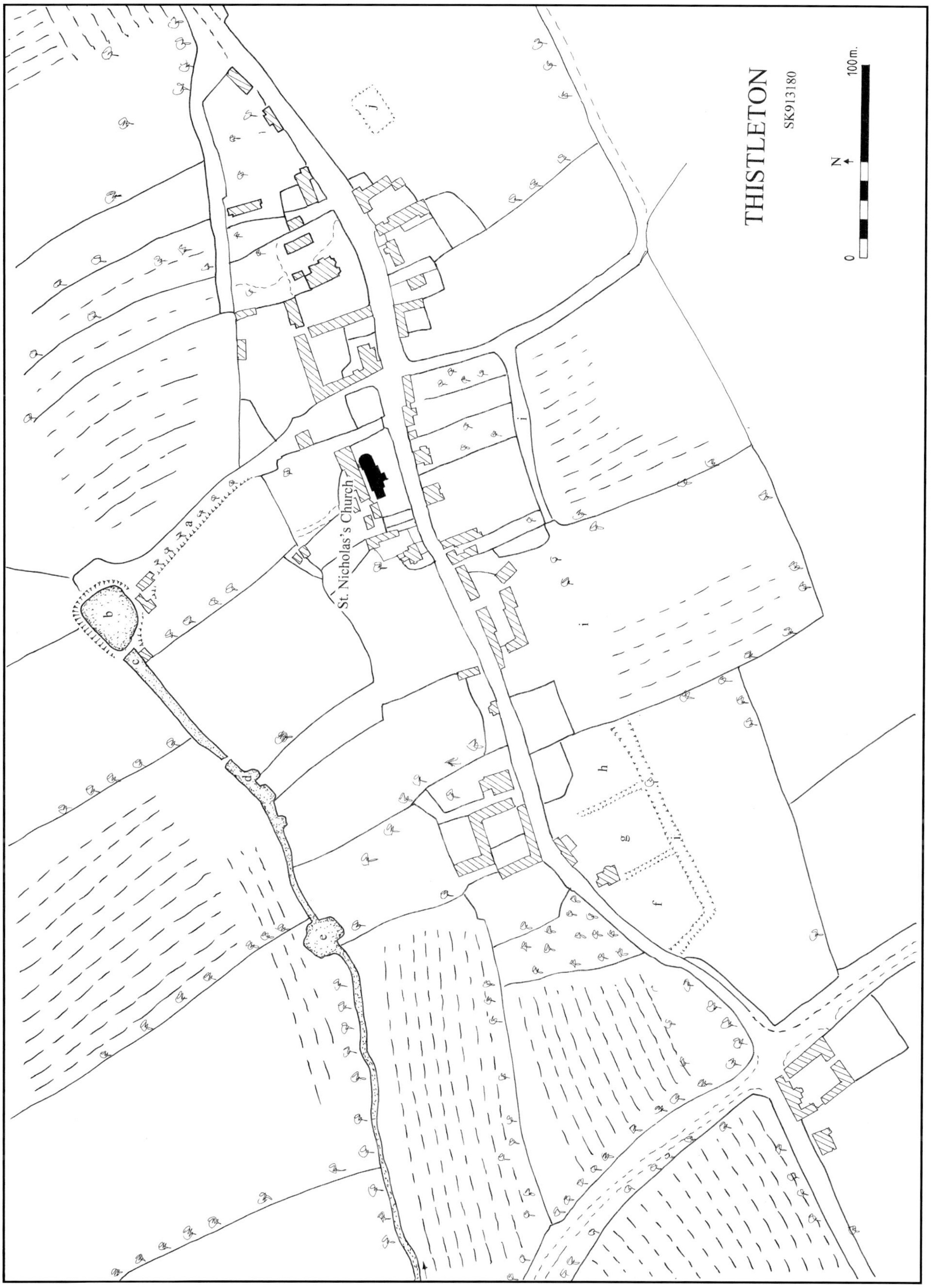

Figure 75: Thistleton Ponds and Village Earthworks

THISTLETON

Ponds and Village Earthworks (fig 75 previous page) **SK913180**

To the east of St. Nicholas's Church is a lane which runs northwards as a slight hollow way (a) to the stream. Earthworks of a square pond (b) exist here. The course of the stream is now overgrown, but the Ordnance Survey First Edition map shows three more ponds (c, d, e) in line upstream. These look like fish ponds, perhaps belonging to a now vanished manor house in the area of the church. The presence of the hollow way leading to the lowest pond (b) suggests that there may have been a water mill here. There can hardly ever have been a great flow of water, but it was still important in medieval and post-medieval times. The square pond is marked on a map of 1635 (NRO Map/1352), and the adjacent field is named "Dam Wounges Field".

Further south, aerial photographs show old closes (f, g, h), bounded by the hollow way of an old back lane (i, i, i). They also show indications of a possible building platform further east (j).

THORPE BY WATER

Water Mill and Village Earthworks (fig 76) **SP893964**

Thorpe is an outlying hamlet of Seaton. To the west of the little village is a hollow way (a) leading to the site of the water mill. The mill leet (b) channelled water from the River Welland through the mill. The railway from Rugby to Stamford, planned by Robert Stephenson, cut across the site in the late 1840s.

There are slight earthworks at the north end of the village, with a raised platform (c) and an old close (d). Behind the handsome old manor house (e) is a walled garden (f), flanked on its eastern side by a terrace or avenue (g) separated by a bank and ditch from the ridge and furrow field to the east.

TICKENCOTE

Hall Gardens and Water Mill (fig 77) **SK990095**

Tickencote Hall was built in *c.*1703 in the valley bottom alongside the River Gwash, and considerable work seems to have been done landscaping the area. A channel (a) to bring water to the site, follows the contour along the hillside. In the immediate vicinity of the Hall the water was piped under the parkland, before supplying the raised pond (b), which fed the water mill by the river. The mill building has a date of 1731.

North of the pond is a terrace (c), with two more slightly raised areas (d, e). A hollow way (f) leads northwards over the crest of the valley side. The Hall was surrounded by gardens with a parterre (g), and an earthwork bank (h) between the gardens and the river.

Village Earthworks (fig 77) **SK992094**

North of St. Peter's Church another lane in a hollow way leads to the Rectory. On either side of it are old terraces (i, j, k) probably once village closes. The church is unusual in having a remarkable Norman chancel arch. Nearby at the east end of the village are the most well-defined remains. A slight hollow way (l) runs north-south, and along it are hollowed out areas (m, n) where buildings have probably been demolished and the materials removed.

Elsewhere in the field walls and buildings have simply been abandoned, leaving very clear remains of stone walls. There are remains of two or three small buildings at (o), and a longer building with two internal walls (p). There is another small building of sub-circular plan (q), perhaps a dovecote, and a mound of rubble (r) probably indicating the site of another building. These features are surrounded by remains of five or six old closes, with the wall footings particularly clear in the south east corner (s). The field to the west has traces of another building (t), and two small terraced platforms (u, v), probably the sites of two more buildings.

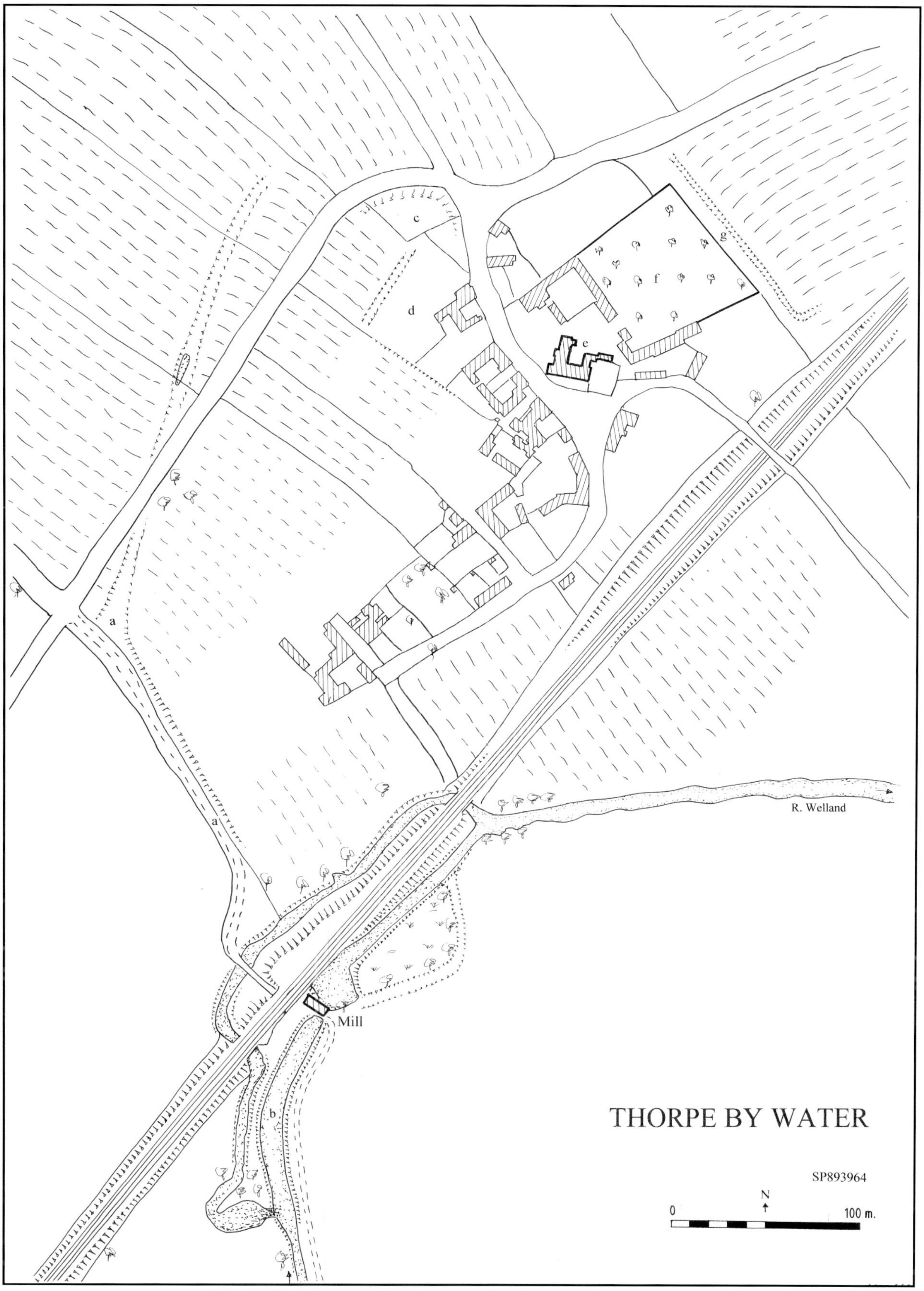

Figure 76: Thorpe by Water, Water Mill and Village Earthworks

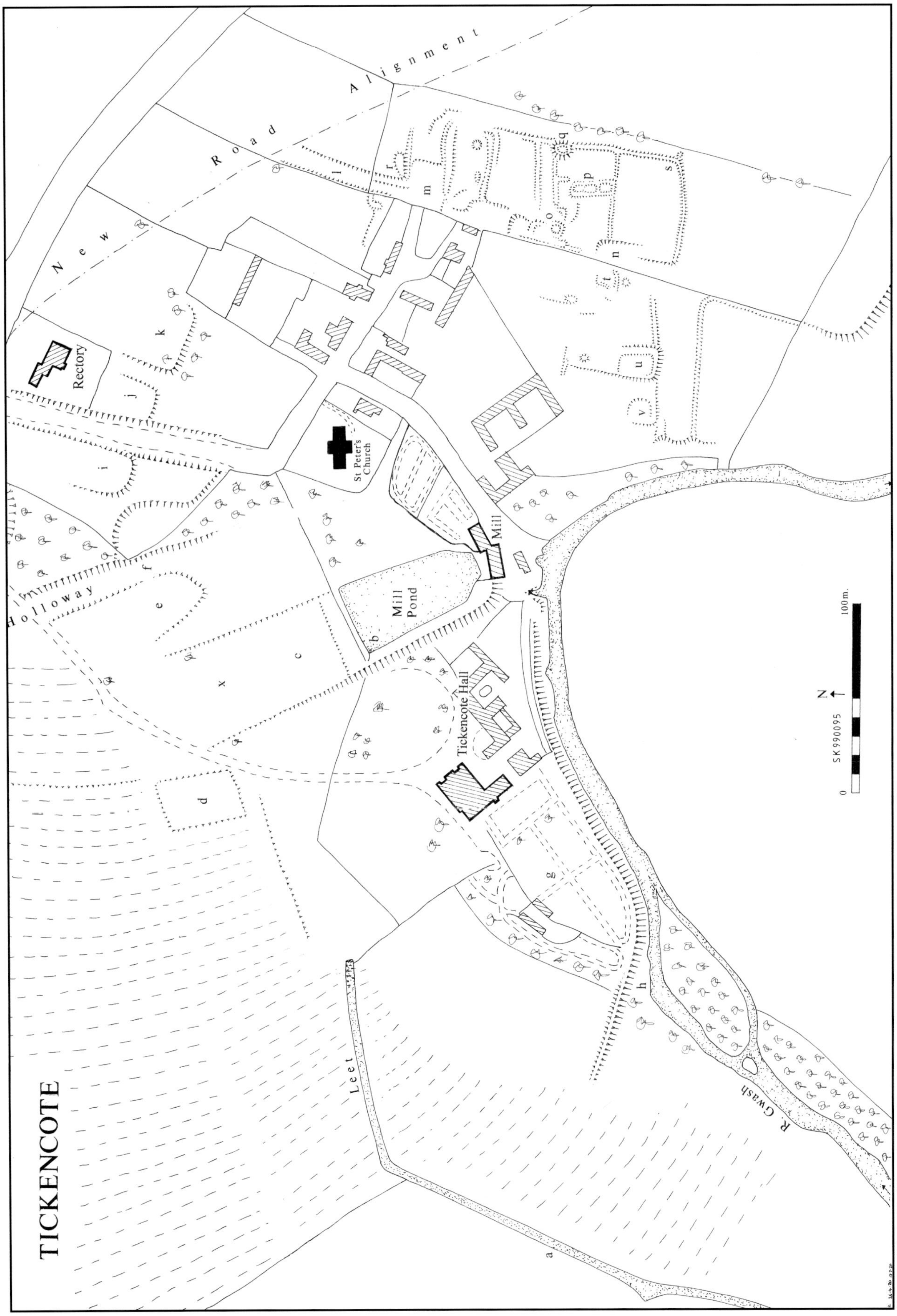

Figure 77: Tickencote Hall Gardens and Water Mill

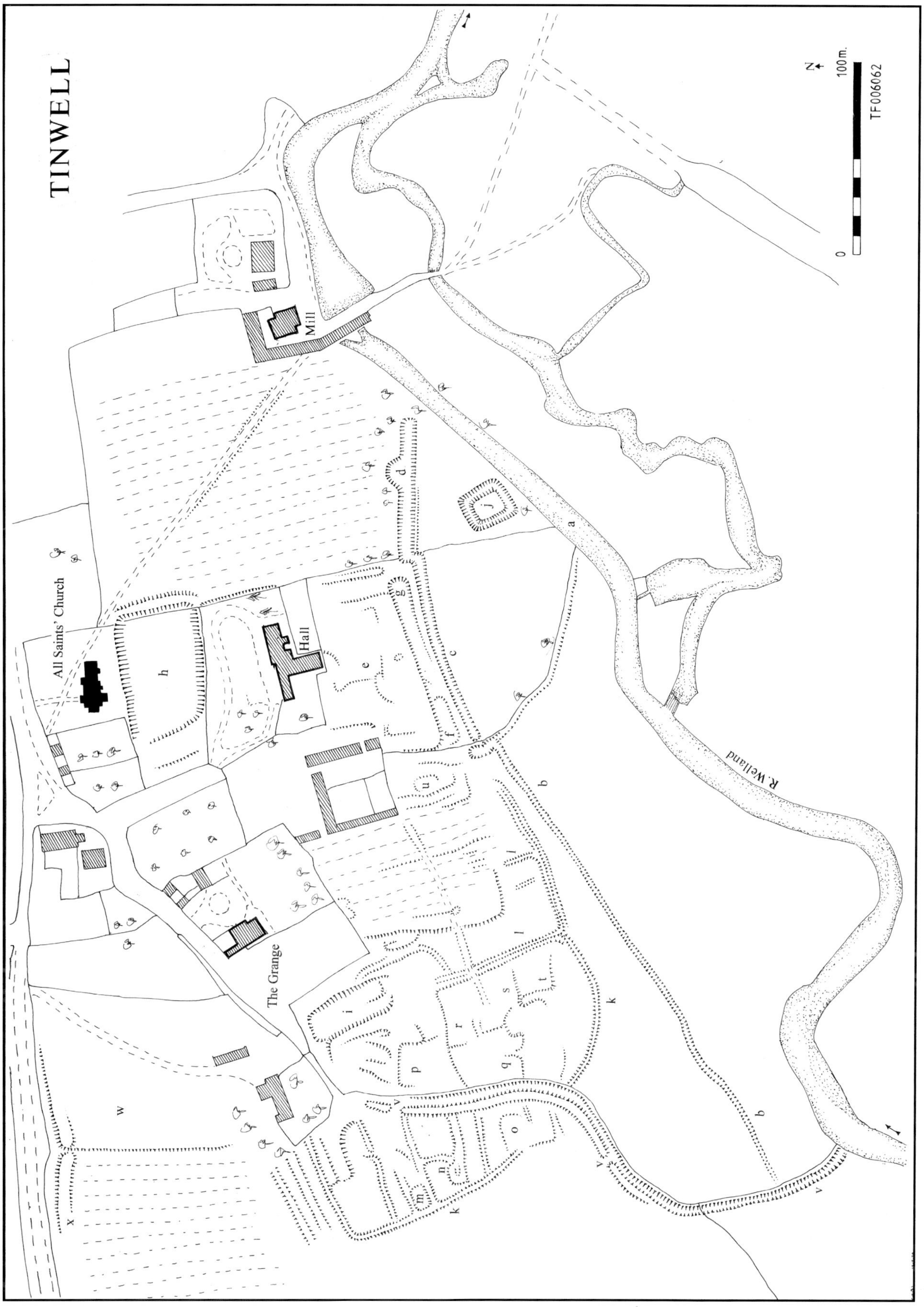

Figure 78: Tinwell Village Earthworks

TINWELL

Village Earthworks (fig 78 previous page) **TF006062**

The most prominent earthwork feature at Tinwell is the supply channel (a) taking water from the Welland to Tinwell Mill. To the north of it another, much narrower channel (b) seems to have supplied water to two ponds (c, d) in front of Tinwell Hall. Between the ponds and the Hall is an area (e) which has some earthwork evidence and was presumably once a garden, with two more possible ponds (f, g). Between the Hall and All Saints' Church is a rectangular hollow (h), probably the site of another ornamental pond. A smaller but similar rectangular hollow (i) further west, may also have been a pond. Between the Hall gardens and the mill channel was a small moat (j), probably a garden feature or a duck decoy. This was plotted from aerial photographs (RAF CPE/UK/1932, 2059-60).

To the west of the Hall and the house called The Grange an area of former village seems to have been cleared away. Within two old closes defined by banks (k, k) and (l, l) are numerous earthwork features, with sites of possible buildings at (m, n, p, q, r, s, t), and another near the farm buildings at (u). Perhaps related to the old ponds at (n) and (i) is a water channel or drain (v), which cuts through the village earthworks. To the north is another old close, marking the edge of the village, with an adjacent field of ridge and furrow and a plough headland (x).

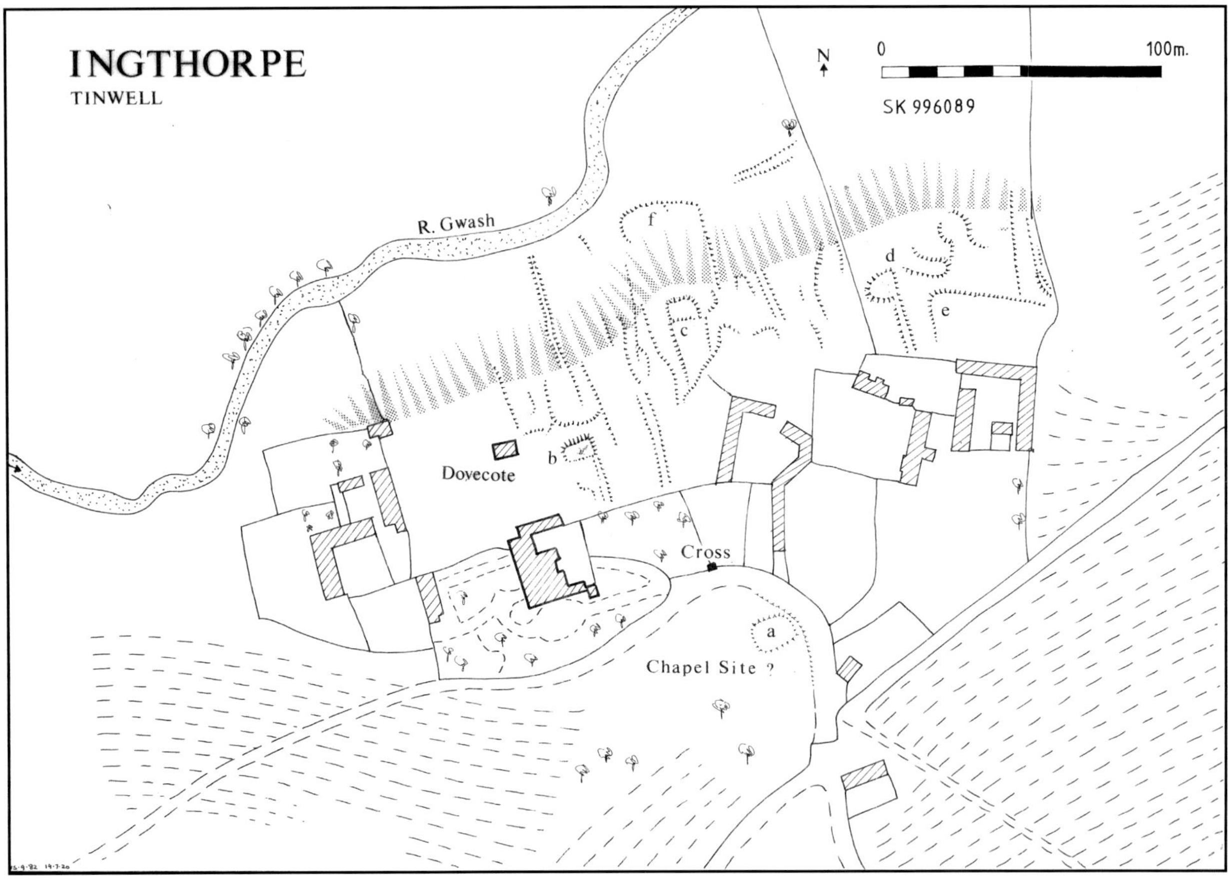

Figure 79: Tinwell, Ingthorpe Village Earthworks

Ingthorpe Village Earthworks (fig 79) **SK996089**

The hamlet of Ingthorpe is close to the river Gwash, and looks across to Great Casterton. The settlement is essentially one farm, but there is evidence of it once having been a village. East of the farm is a slight building platform (a) ploughed almost level, believed to be the site of a chapel, last mentioned in 1366 (VCH 1, 146; Brown 1975, 26). Nearby a cross shaft has been built into a wall. The field north of the farm has a dovecote, and evidence of old close boundaries. There are house platforms at (b, c) and further east at (d). At the time of the survey a walnut tree was growing in the middle of (b). Slight terraces at (e) and (f) indicate the boundaries of two more old closes.

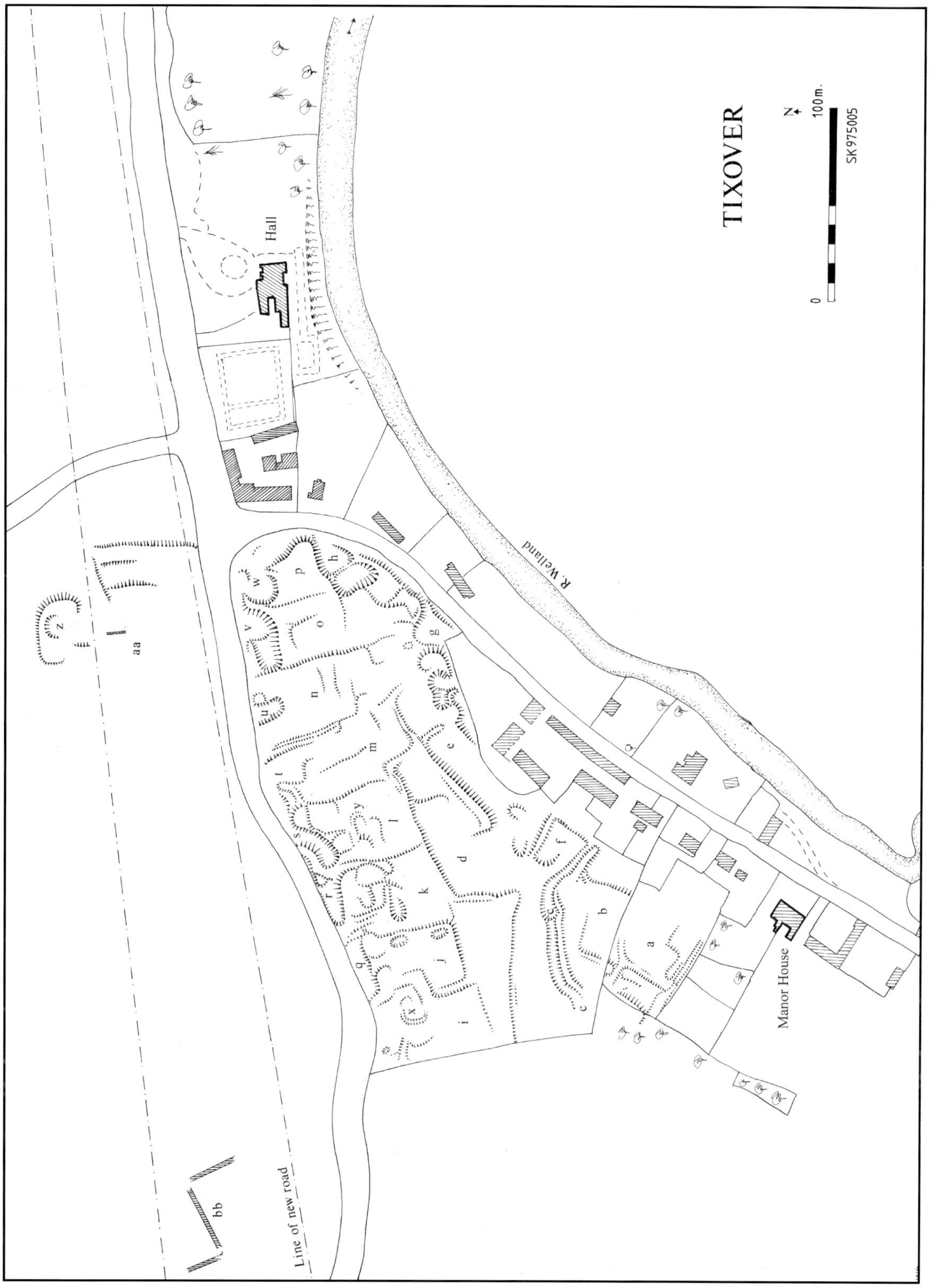

Figure 80: Tixover Village Earthworks

TIXOVER

Village Earthworks (fig 80) **SK 975005**

A complex of earthworks lies alongside the main Leicester to Stamford road where it descends to run along the River Welland. North of the Manor House are two old crofts (a, b), with terraces and platforms indicating the former sites of buildings. These are bounded on the north by what appears to be an old hollow way (c, c). To the north again are two levelled terraces (d, e), where buildings formerly stood, and another building platform (f). Adjoining the village street are more levelled areas representing the sites of former cottages, for example (g) and (h). Aligned with the main road is a series of crofts (i, j, k, l, m, n, o, p), with hollows and platforms where houses have stood (q, r, s, t, u, v, w, x, y). The village probably once extended into the ploughed field north of the main road, with a possible building platform (z). When the main road was re-aligned, wall footings were recorded at (a-a) and (b-b).

UPPINGHAM

No specific earthworks are recorded in Uppingham. The town fields were enclosed in the late 18th century, prior to which there were three open fields - Wood (or West), Brand (or South) and Lound (North or Mill) (Ryder 2006, 68).

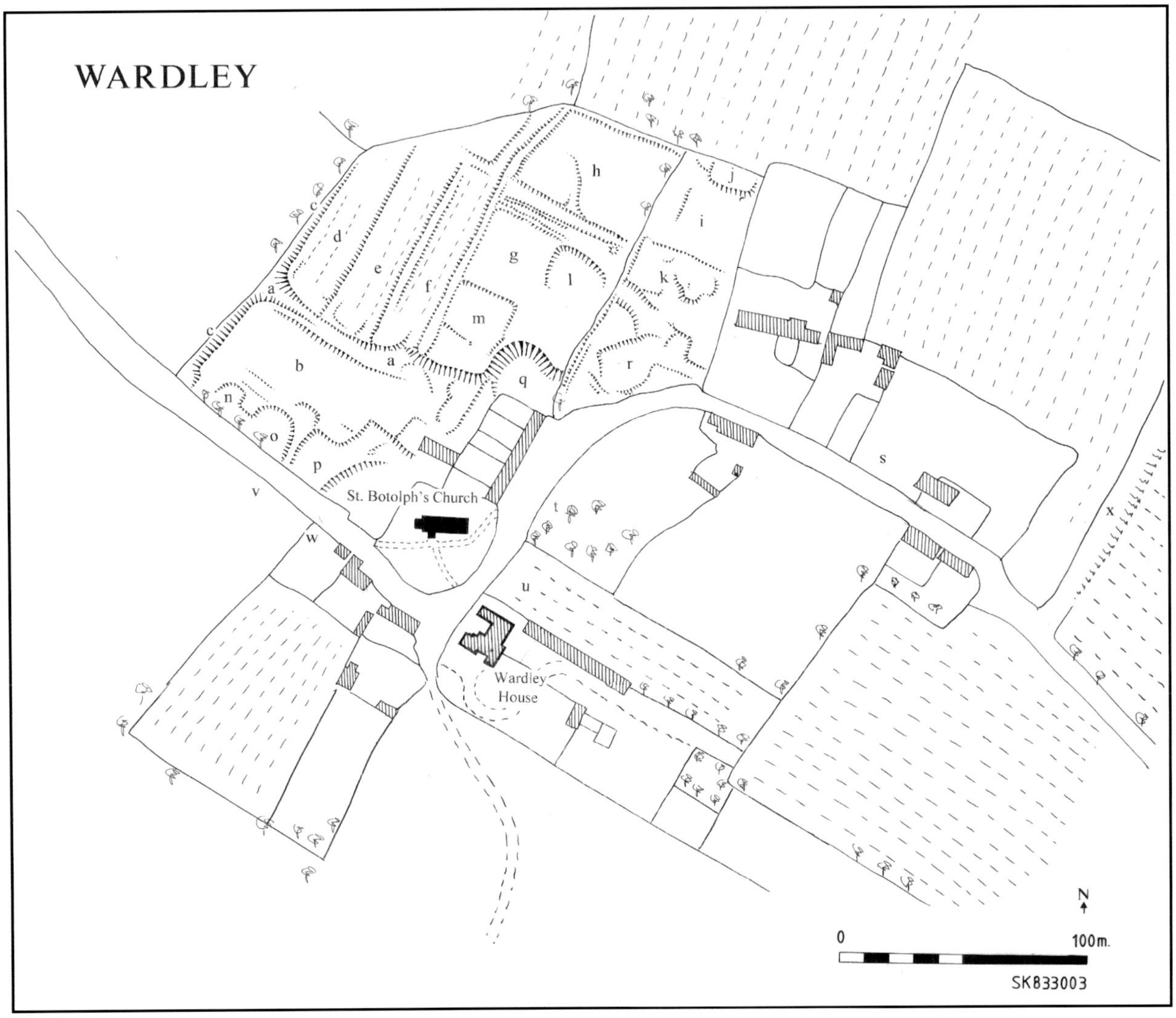

Figure 81: Wardley Village Earthworks

WARDLEY

Village Earthworks (fig 81) **SK833033**

There are two fields of earthworks west and north of St. Botolph's Church. The area is divided by a hollow way (a, a), to the south of which is a close (b). A slope on the west side marks the probable line of a back lane (c) which extends north, bounding another area which has been taken out of the ridge and furrow open field at some time, to create three

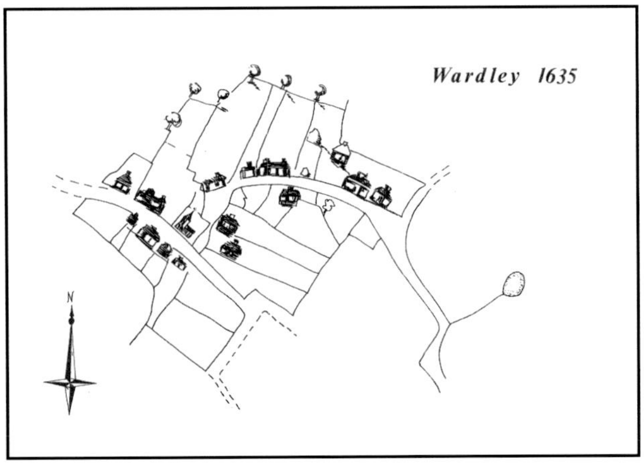

closes (d, e, f). To the east are more old closes (g, h) with platforms and terraces perhaps marking the sites of vanished buildings (j, k, l, m). A plan of the village dated 1635 (NRO Map/ 2991, The Brudenell Estate) shows houses at several locations (n, o, p, q and r) in the fields just noted, and also elsewhere (s, t, u, v and w), where evidence does not seem to survive. Further east is another hollow way (x) of the lane leading north out of the village.

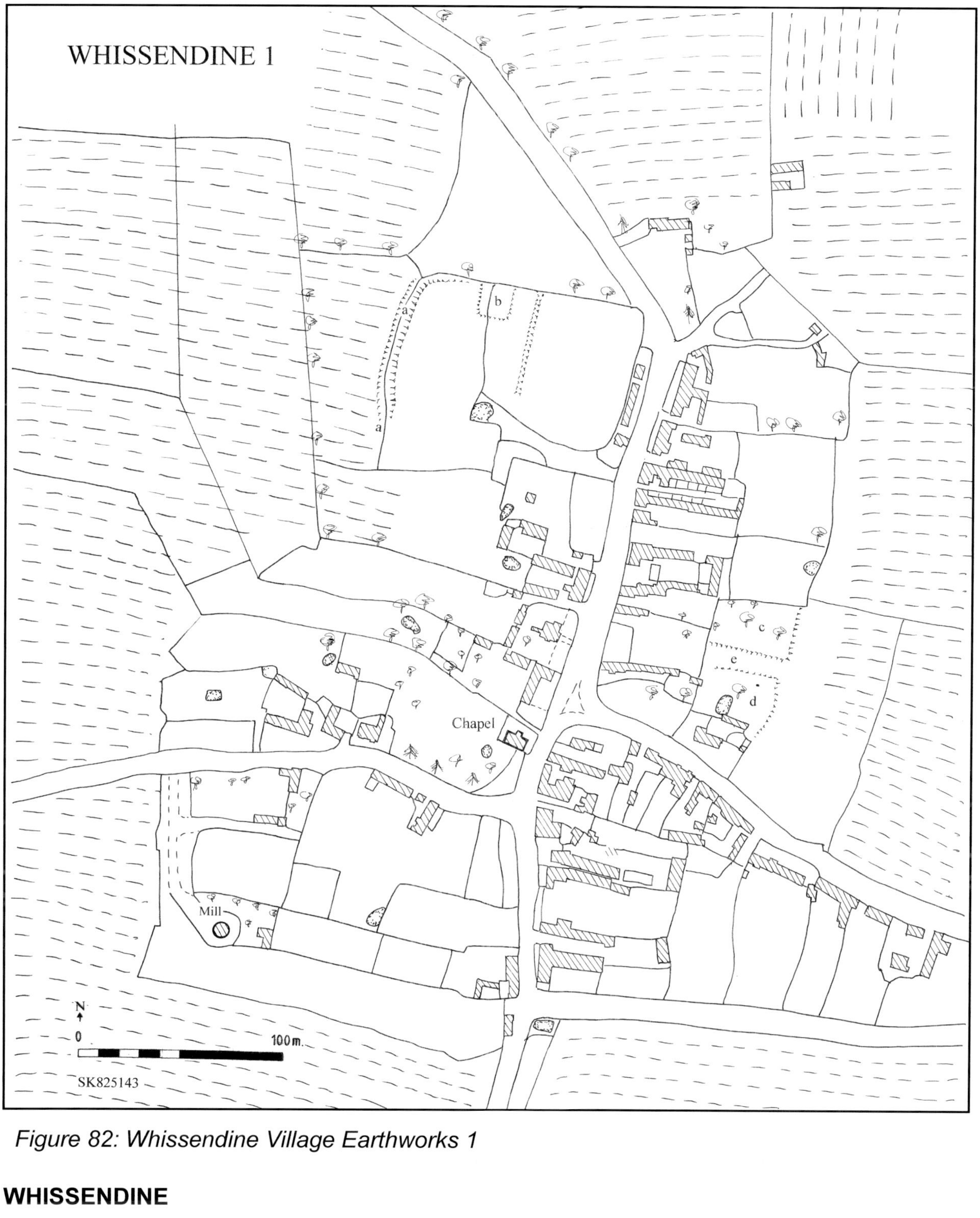

Figure 82: Whissendine Village Earthworks 1

WHISSENDINE

Village Earthworks 1 (fig 82) ***SK825143***

RAF vertical photographs record a great deal of earthwork evidence in Whissendine village, much of which has subsequently gone to make way for modern houses. The evidence plotted on these three plans of the village is mainly drawn from the aerial photos, and a walk around the village in 2018.

At the west end of the village there was an old close with a slight hollow way (a) defining its west side, and a possible house platform (b). To the south-east were traces of two more closes (c, d), separated by the slight hollow way of an old lane (e), heads south and east out of the village. .

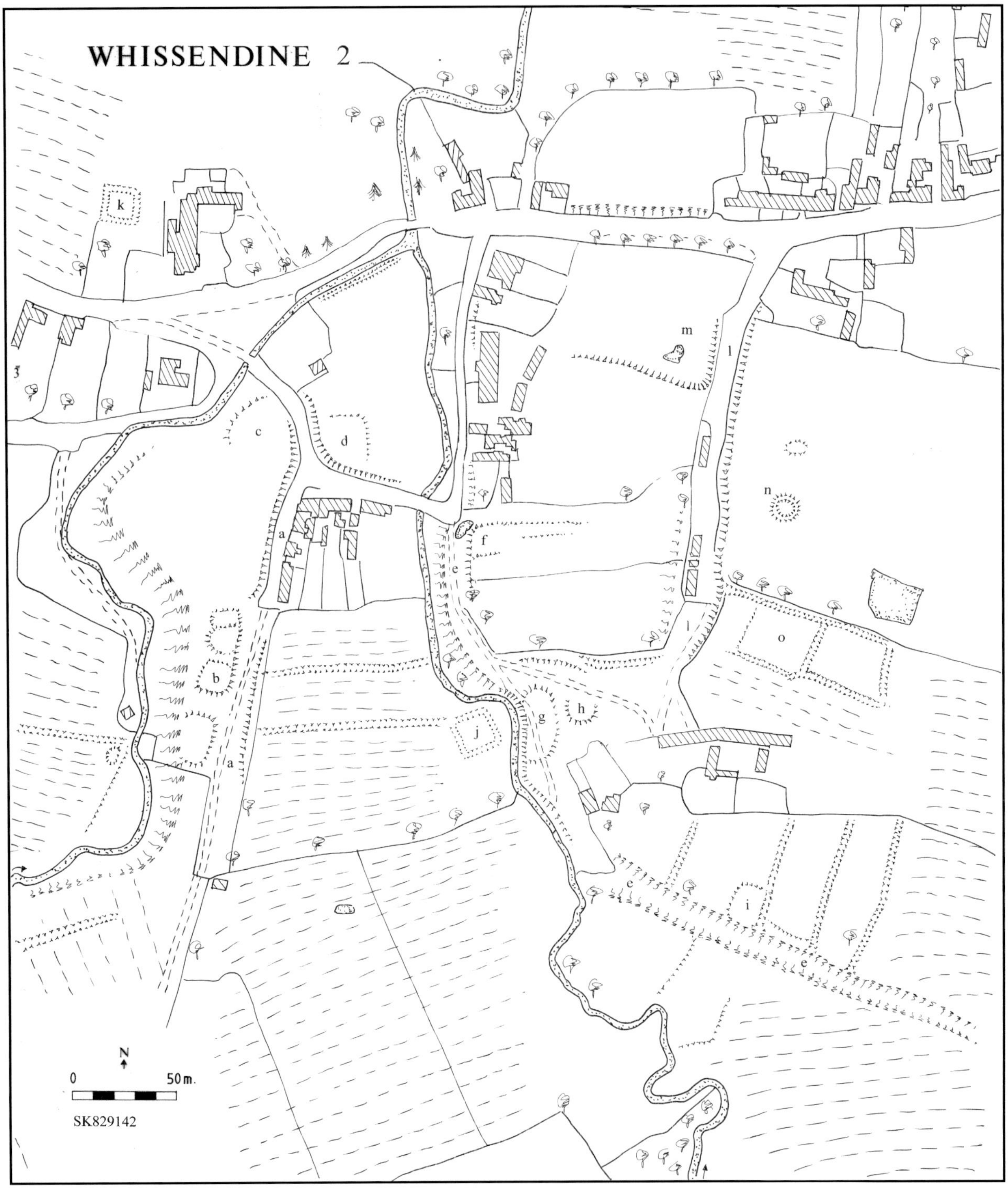

Figure 83: Whissendine Village Earthworks 2

Village Earthworks 2 (fig 83) ***SK829142***

From the middle of the village an old lane runs southwards as a hollow way (a, a) passing some mounds (b) which may mark the sites of old buildings. There are also faint traces of old closes (c, d). Another old lane is at (e, e). Above the stream in the centre of this plan area are three possible building platforms (f, g, h), with another (i) facing onto the hollow way (e, e). On the west side of the main stream is a small rectangular platform (j) surrounded by a ditch,

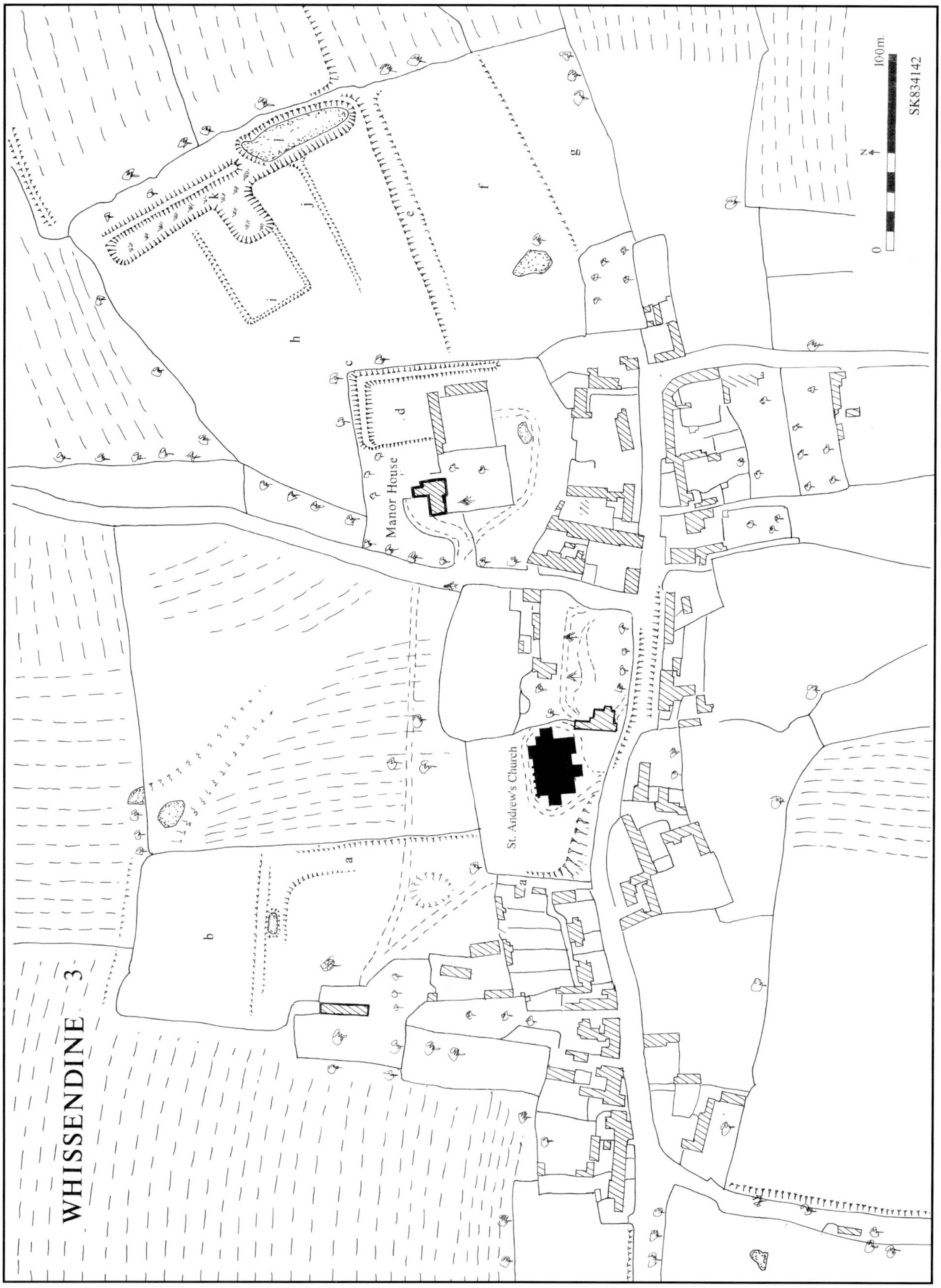

Figure 84: Whissendine Village Earthworks 3

to form a kind of small moat. There is a similar feature (k) near the large house in the upper left-hand corner of the plan. it seems likely that (j) was an enclosure for livestock while (k) was a more decorative garden feature. The lane on the east side of this plan runs in a hollow way (l), and there used to be a levelled area with traces of old buildings at (m). On the east side of the lane were the foundations of a circular building (n), probably a dovecote. There were

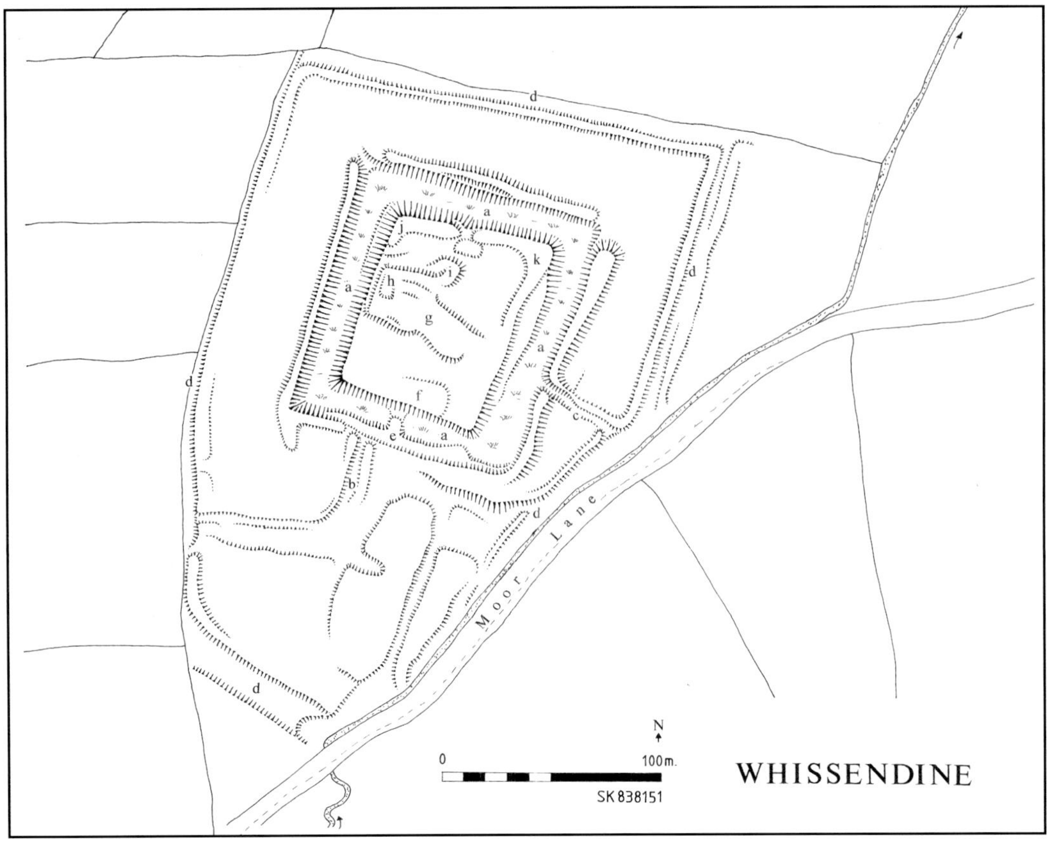

Figure 85: Whissendine Moor Lane Moated site

remains of more old enclosures to the south at (o). The windmill, built in 1809, was restored and began milling agin in 2009.

Village Earthworks 3 (fig 84) **SK834142**

West of St. Andrew's Church is some evidence of an old lane (a), partly in a hollow way, leading north to an old close (b) where there may formerly have been a building. The Manor House gardens include a terrace walkway (c) enclosing the site of a parterre (d). These features may date from the 16th century. To the east is evidence of more features of the manorial gardens, perhaps earlier in date. A hollow way (e) gave access through this area. To the south are the boundaries of two old closes (f, g) and to the north another one (h), which at some time has been subdivided by ditches (i) and (j) defining smaller areas. These were probably used for gardens or orchards, leading down to two fish ponds (k, l). All these features around the Manor House have been drawn from the Ordnance Survey 1:2500 maps or plotted from vertical air photos. All the features north and east of the terrace walk (c) were levelled by ploughing in the post-World War 2 period.

Moor Lane Moated Site (fig 85) ***SK838151***

At an isolated location in a low-lying area of the parish is a large rectangular moat (a, a, a, a). The moat seems originally to have been supplied by an inlet channel (b), with the water flowing out by way of a drainage channel (c). The moat lies in the middle of an area enclosed by a bank and ditch (d), and the space between the moat and this outer ditch probably contained an orchard, gardens and some farm buildings. The original entrance to the moat was probably near (e), with a gatehouse (f) inside the moat. There are foundations of substantial buildings at (g), (h) and (i), and there may have been more buildings along the edge of the moat platform at (j) and (k). This moat is likely to be the site of the manor house of Moorhall, referred to in documents from 1306 onwards (VCHR 2, 159-60).

Deer Park

Cantor notes a reference of about 1212, when David, Earl of Huntingdon is recorded as taking from

Richard de Morville 123 acres of land "outside the park" (Cantor 1980, 17). This may have been at the time the park ceased to be a hunting enclosure, and there seem to be no more references to it.

WHITWELL

Village Earthworks and Hall Gardens (fig 86) **SK925085**

The main road from Oakham to Stamford runs through the village and its course was marked as a hollow way on the 1st Edition Ordnance Survey 1:2500 maps (a, a). St. Michael's Church stands at a crossroads with the old lane from Exton to Normanton which runs southwards in a hollow way (b, b). From this lane another hollow way (c) led east, and branched, with another hollow way (d) leading back to the centre of the village.

Figure 86: Whitwell Village Earthworks and Hall Gardens

Between the old lanes (b) and (d) are remains of three old closes (e, f, g). In close (e) is at least one possible house platform (h), and there are two more (i, j) in close (f). Close (g) has remains of a much larger stone building (k), measuring some 30m x 10m, probably a barn. South of the Hall are remains of another old close (l), which probably once contained part of the Hall gardens, and adjacent to it is an ornamental pond (m). To the south, down the stream, are remains of a dam (n), which would have retained a larger pond, marked on a 17th century map. There is slight evidence of three more old village closes at (o) (p) and (q).

WING

Village Earthworks ***SK891029***

Brown mentions the existence of the site of a former building at SK89100295. Much of this field has been quarried (Brown 1975, 28).

Windmill Mound (fig 87) ***SK895027***

A windmill mound survives in part in the hedge line at SK89510274 at (b). There was another windmill, in use more recently, across the road at SK89580274 (c).

Turf Maze (fig 87) ***SK895028***

A small turf maze is preserved by the roadside at SK89550283. Little seems to be known of its origins. There is a possibility that it was once enclosed by an outer bank. The maze is 13m (40ft) in diameter, and a plan was published in the Archaeological Journal of 1858 (Trollope 1858, 255 & fig 6).

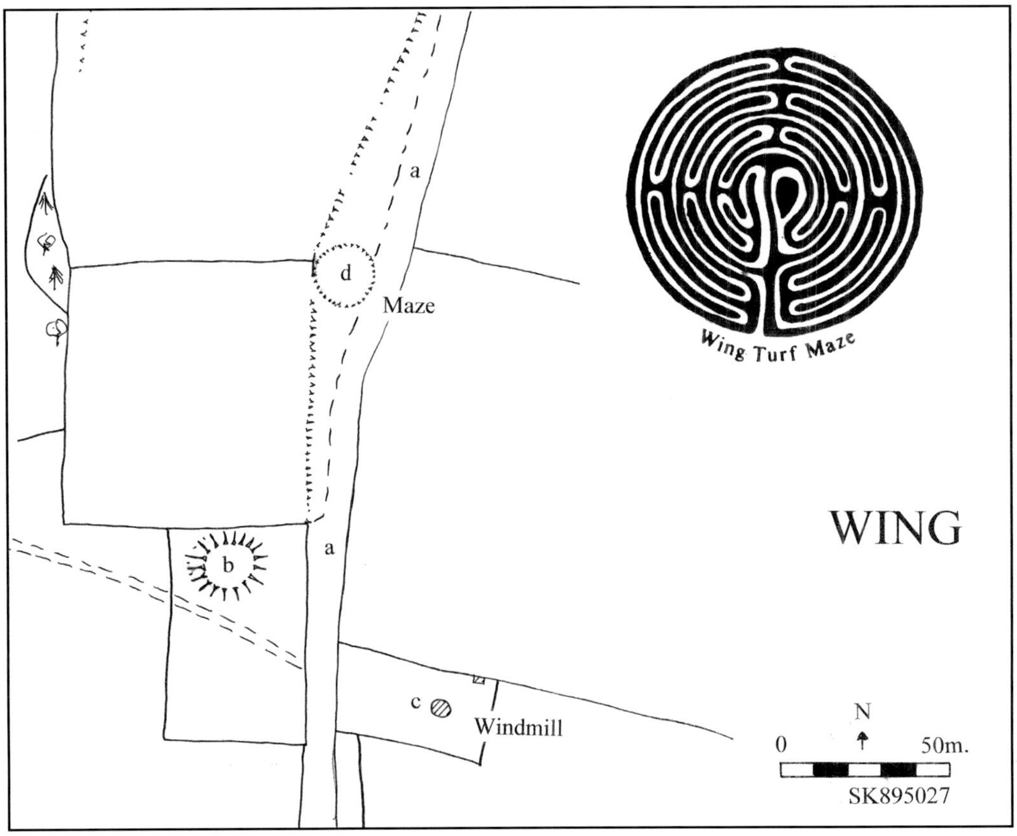

Figure 87: Wing Windmill Mound and Turf Maze

THE LANDSCAPE MAPS

SYMBOLS

- = Parish Boundary } c.1885 Civil Parishes
- *WING* = " Name
- = Roads & Tracks
- = Streams
- = Minor Settlement NEWBOLD
- = Ridge & Furrow
- = Woodland
- = Ponds

MEASUREMENTS

- One Mile
- 1000 Feet
- One Kilometre
- One Hectare
- One Acre
- Ten Acres

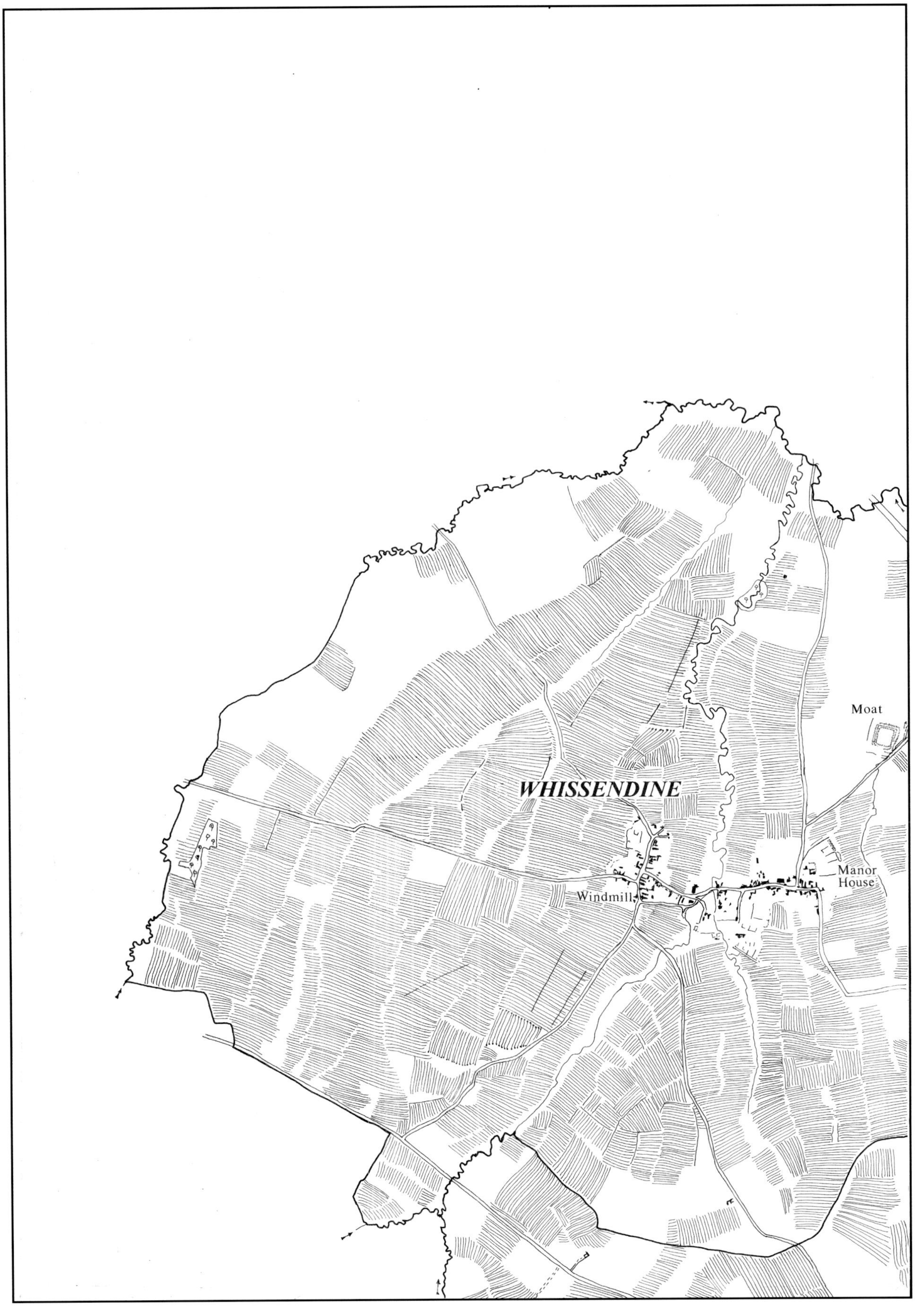

Landscape Map 1: Whissendine

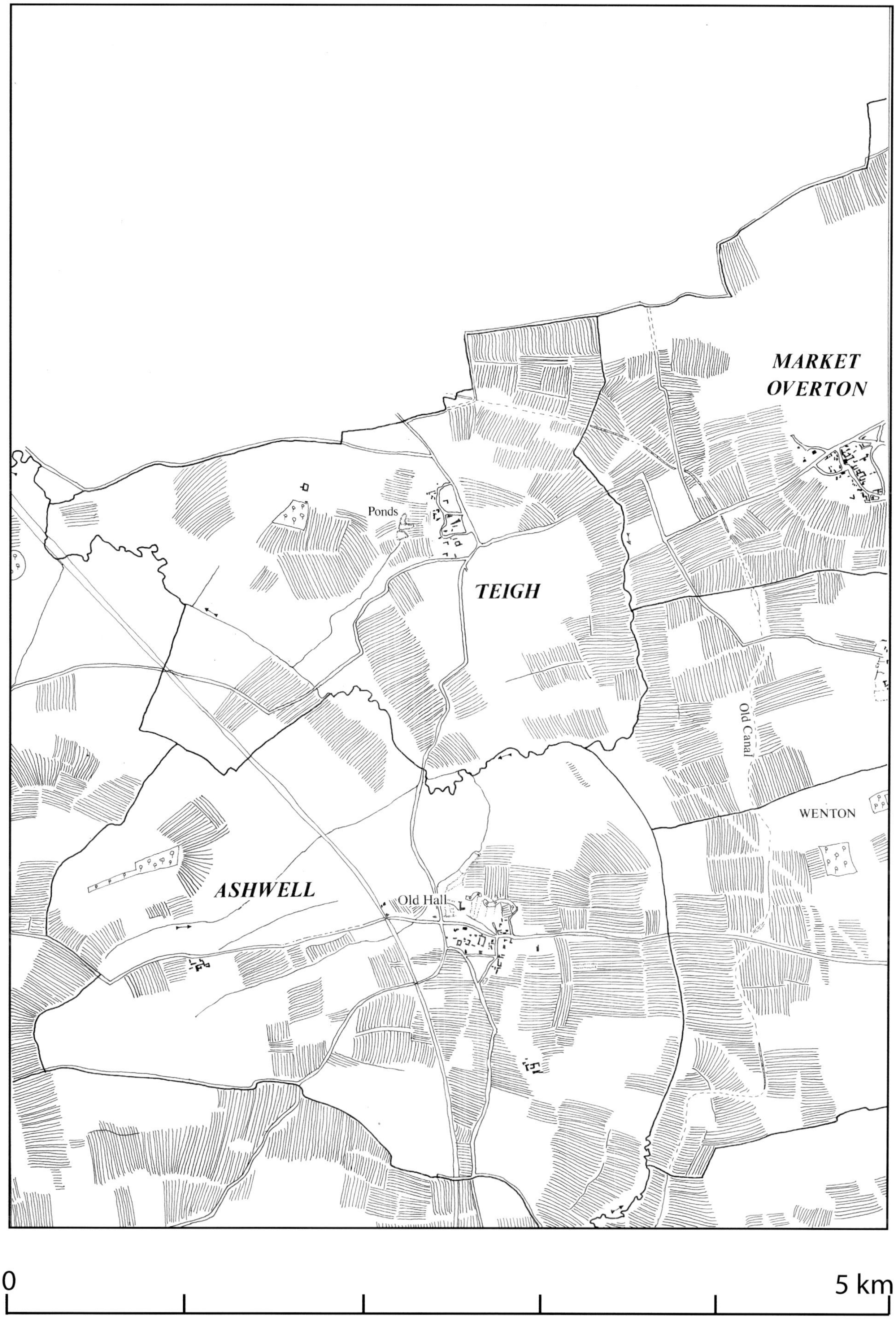

Landscape Map 2: Ashwell, Market Overton

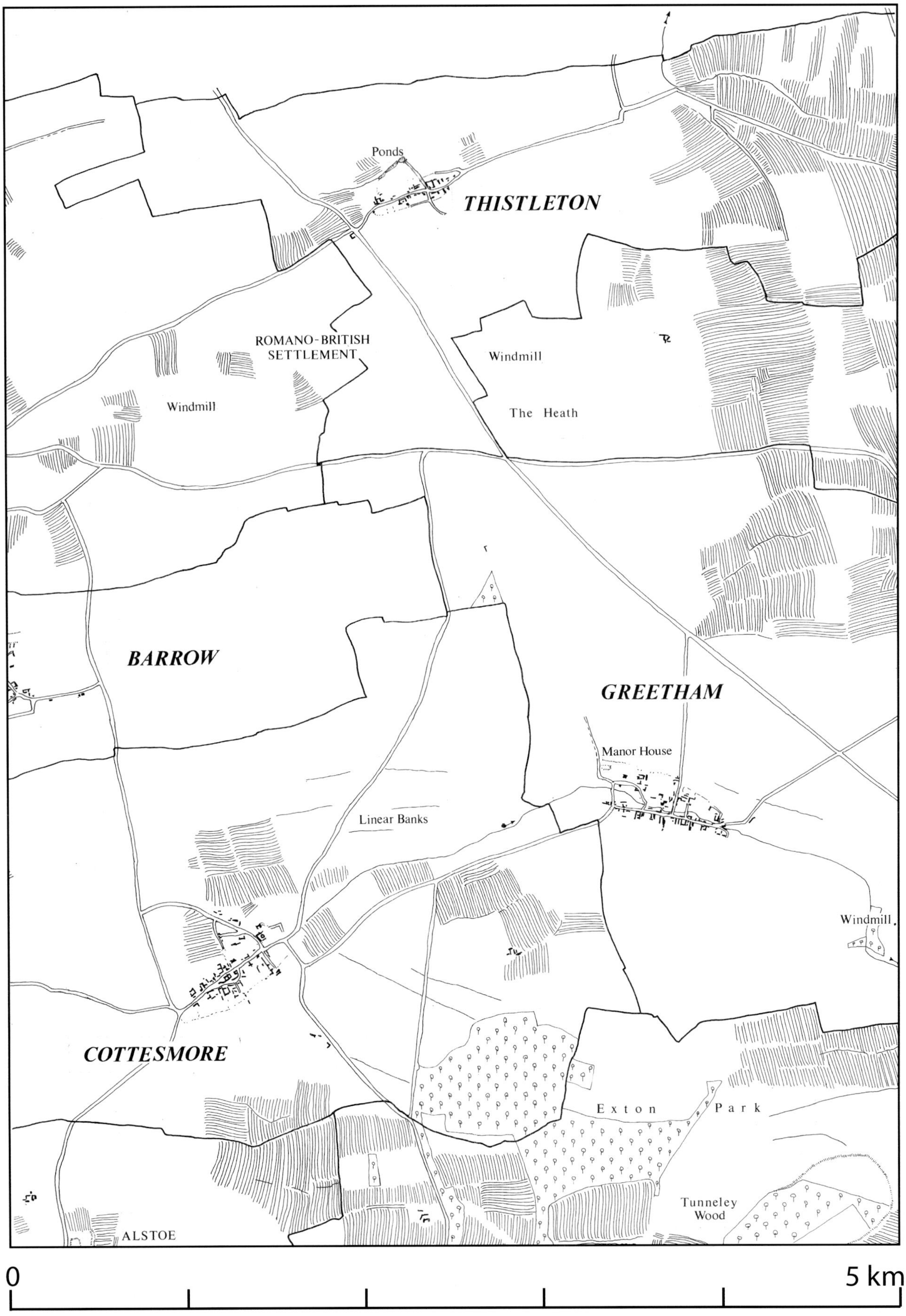

Landscape Map 3: Cottesmore, Thistleton

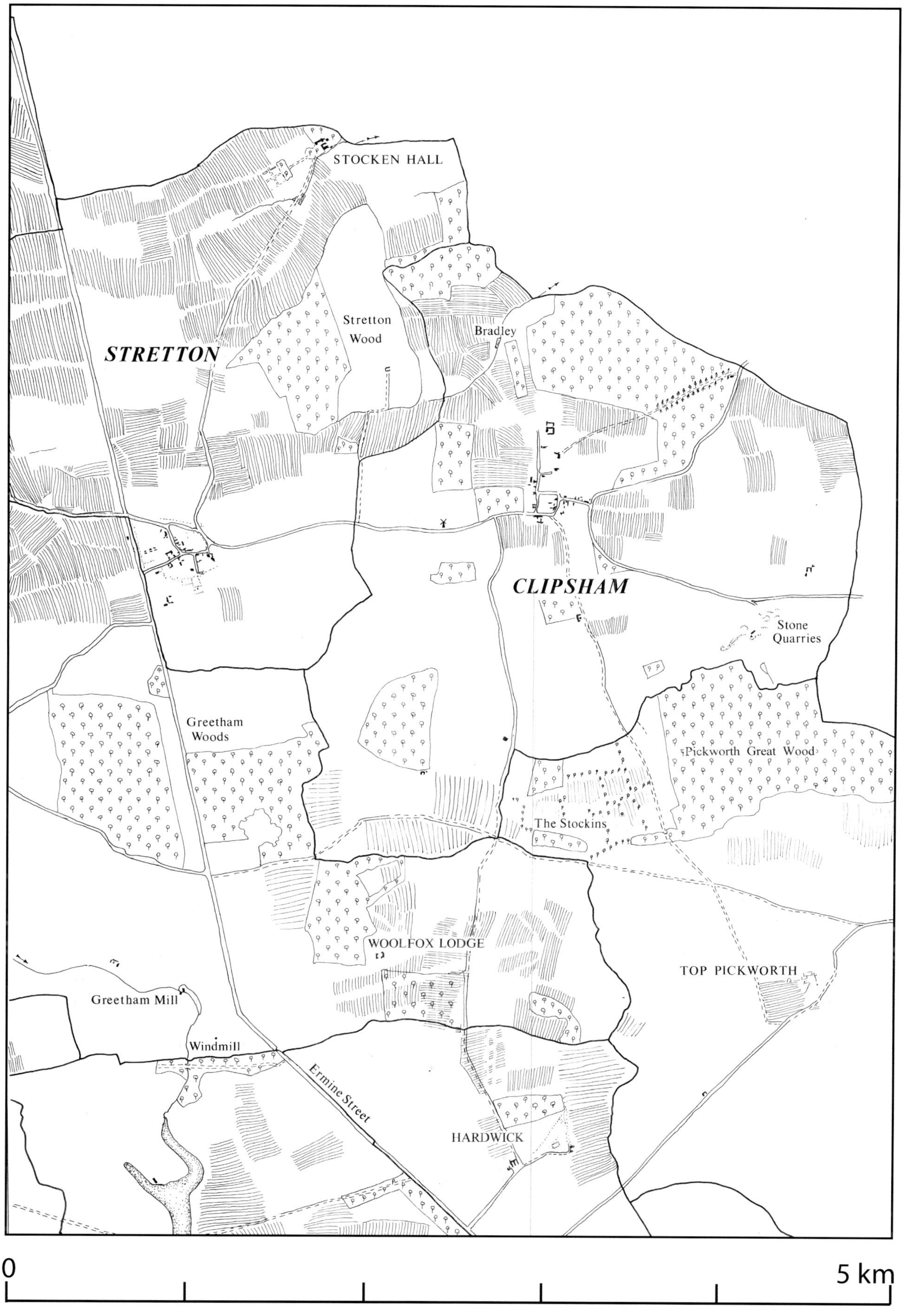

Landscape Map 4: Clipsham

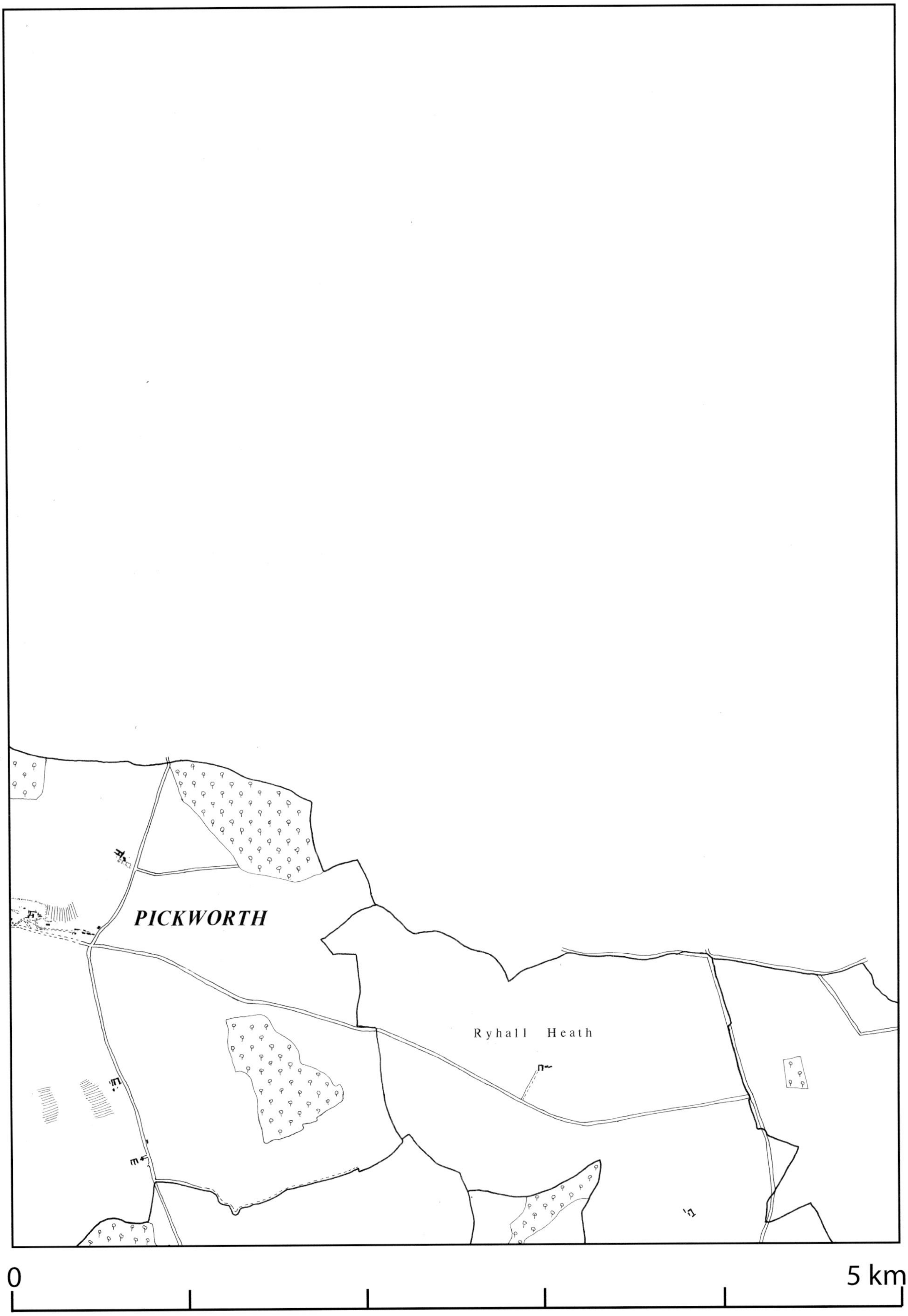

Landscape Map 5: Pickworth

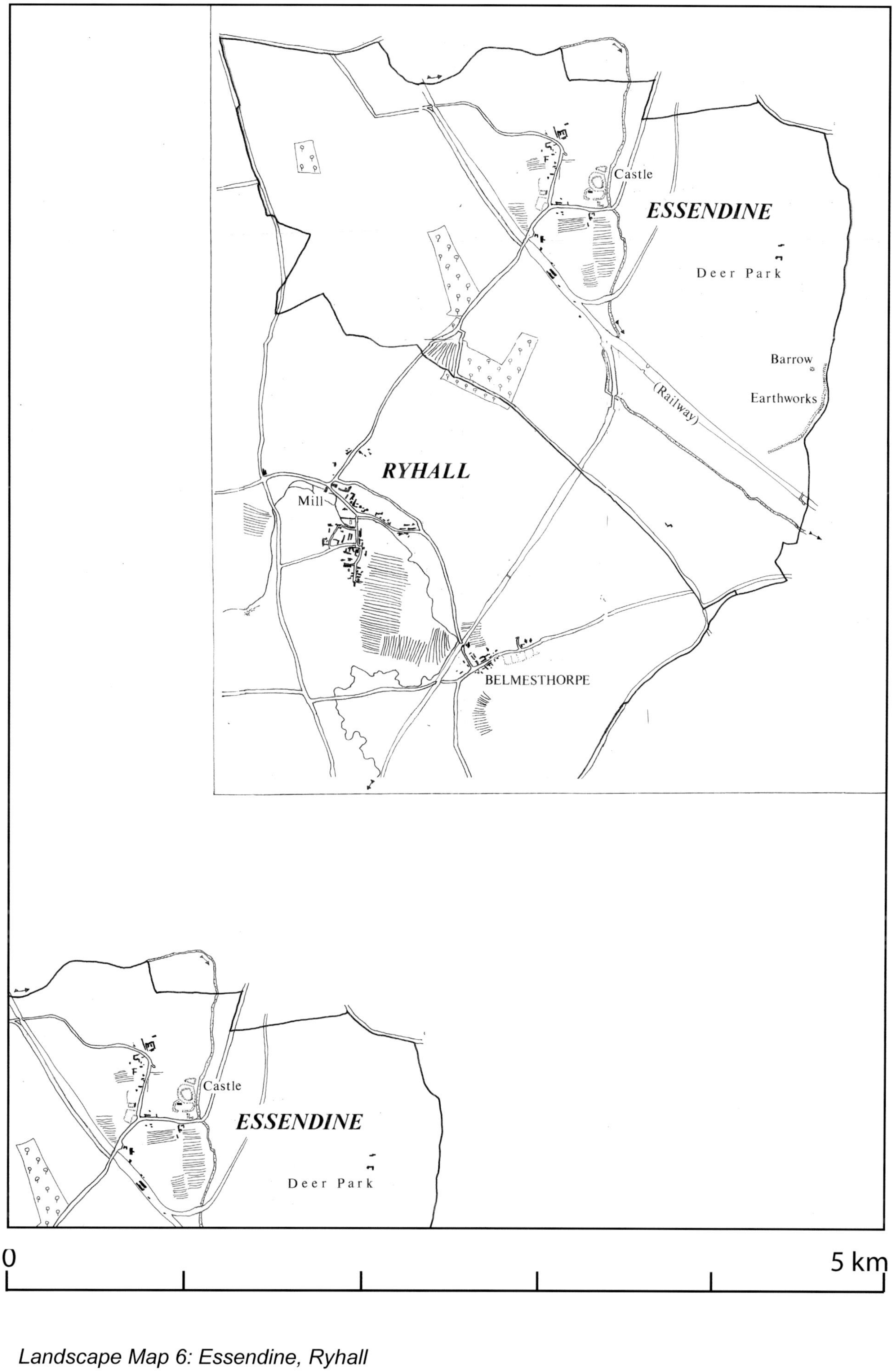

Landscape Map 6: Essendine, Ryhall

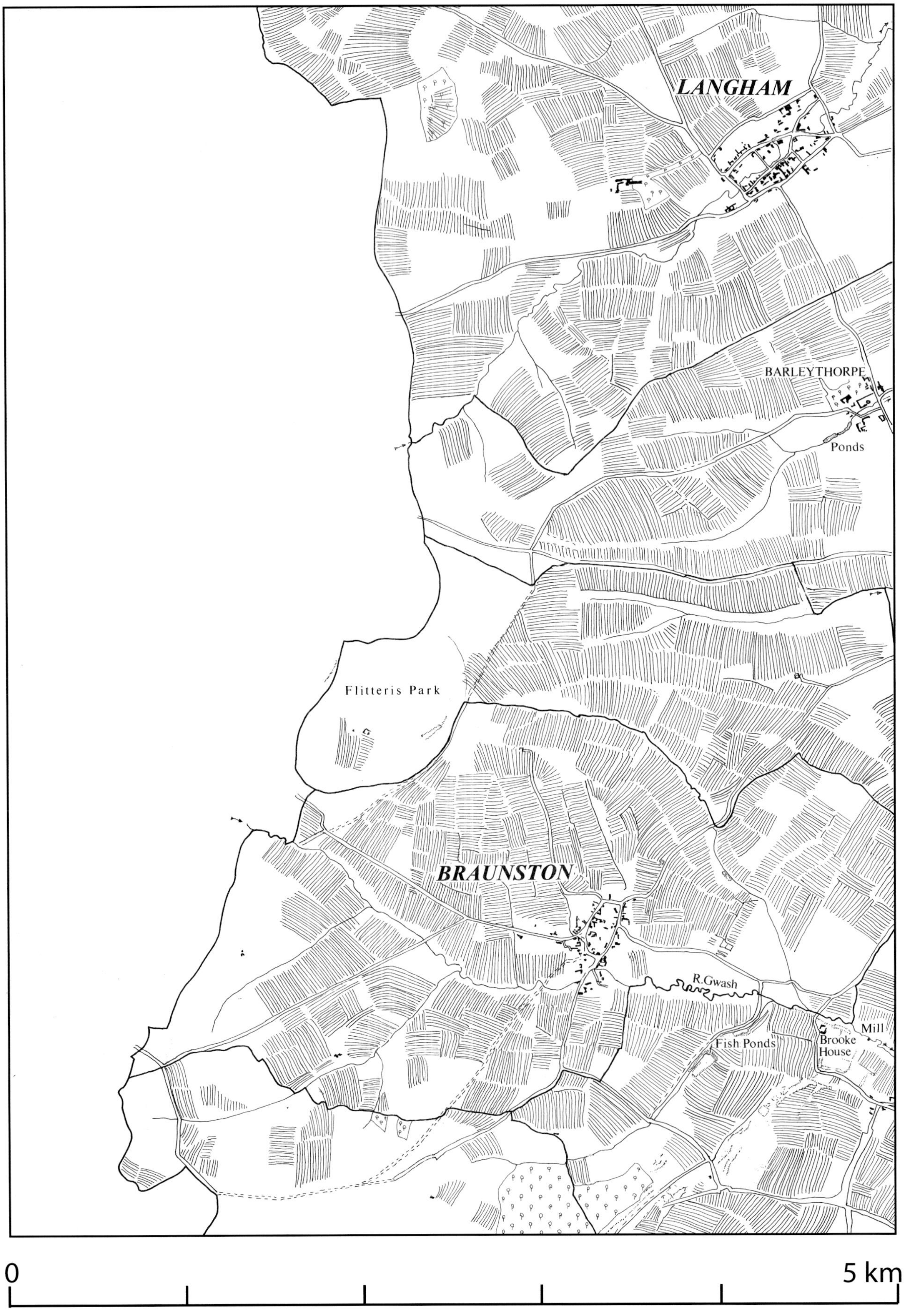

Landscape Map 7: Braunston, Langham

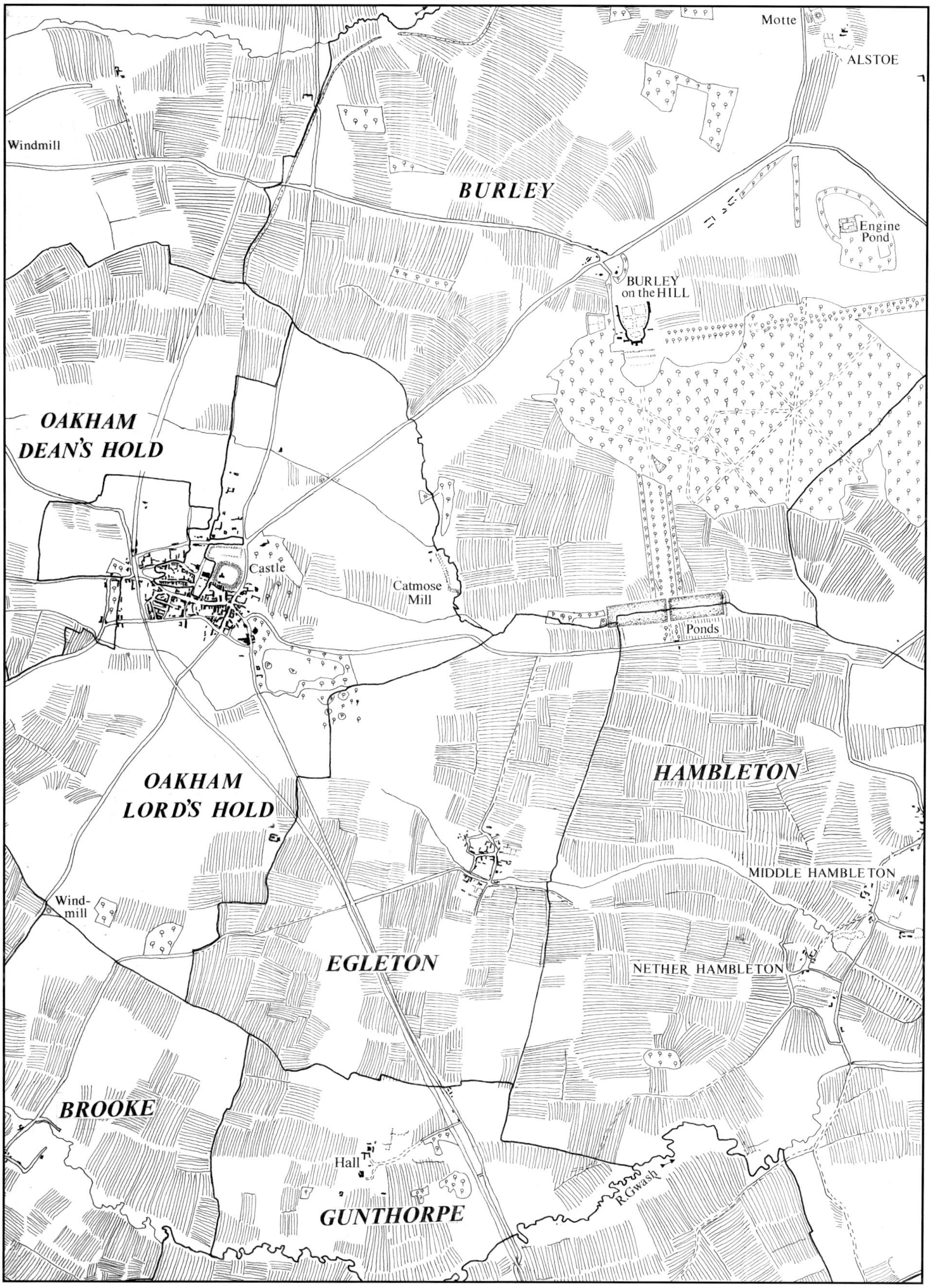

Landscape Map 8: Oakham, Hambleton

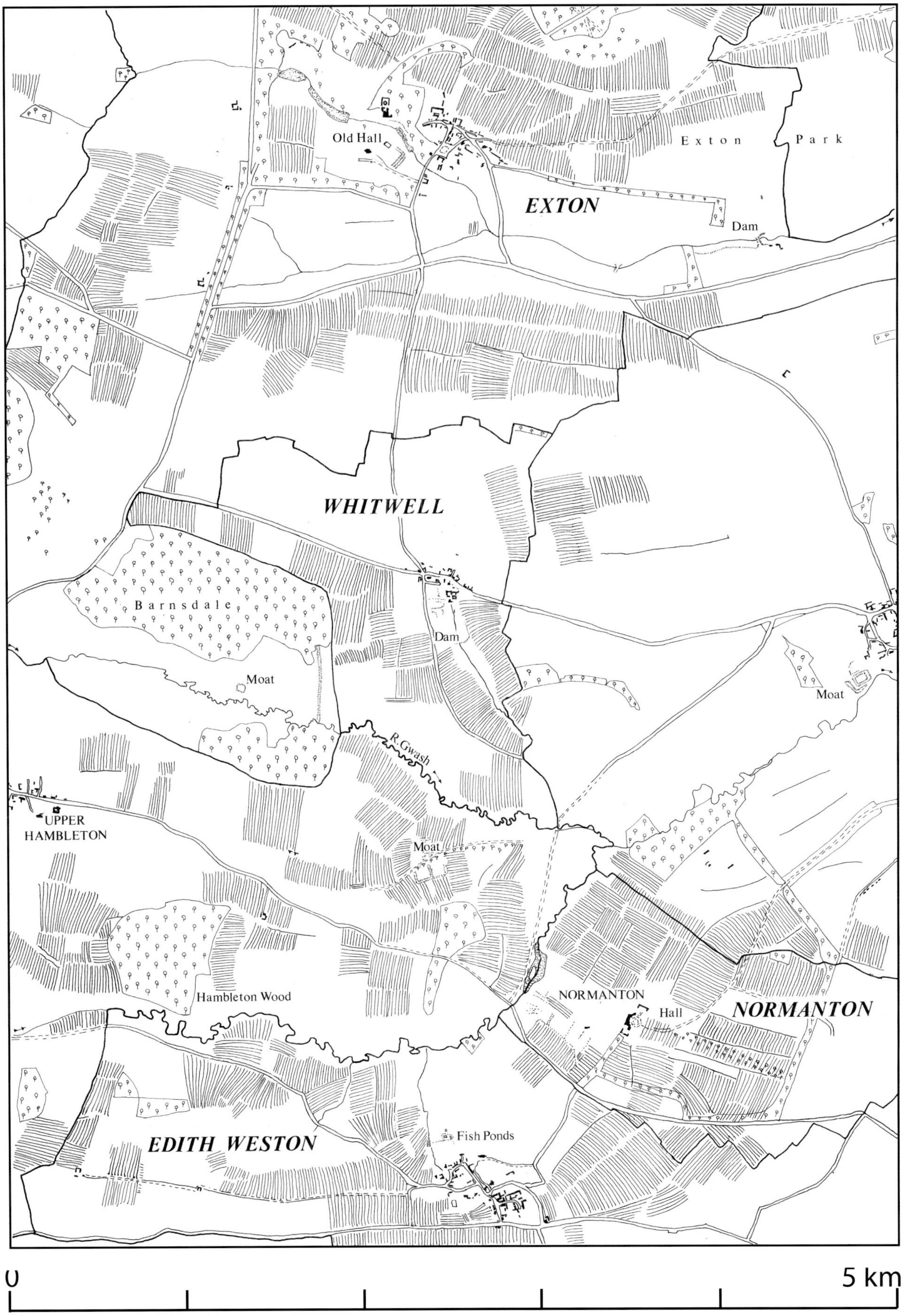

Landscape Map 9: Exton, Whitwell

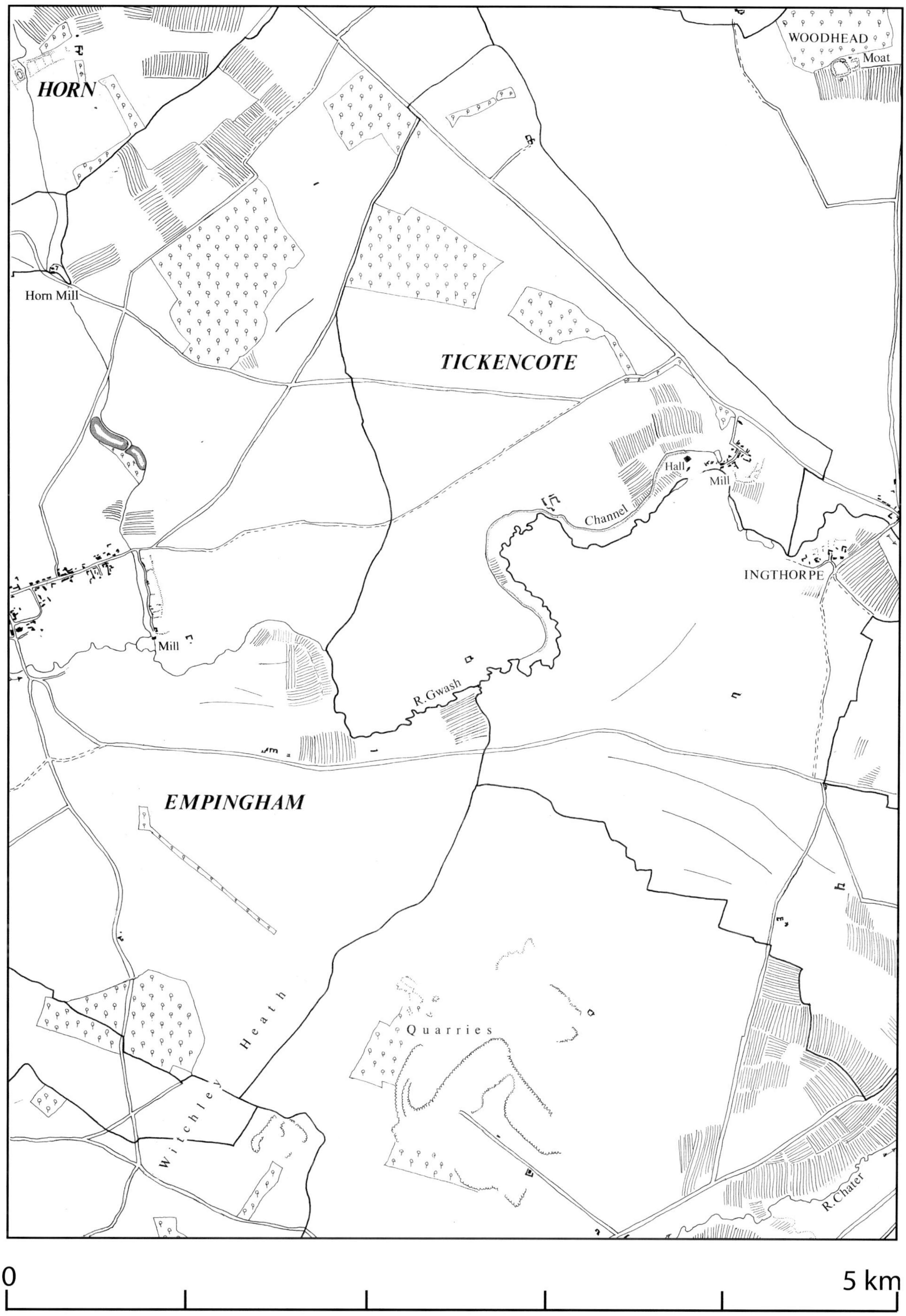

Landscape Map 10: Empingham, Tickencote

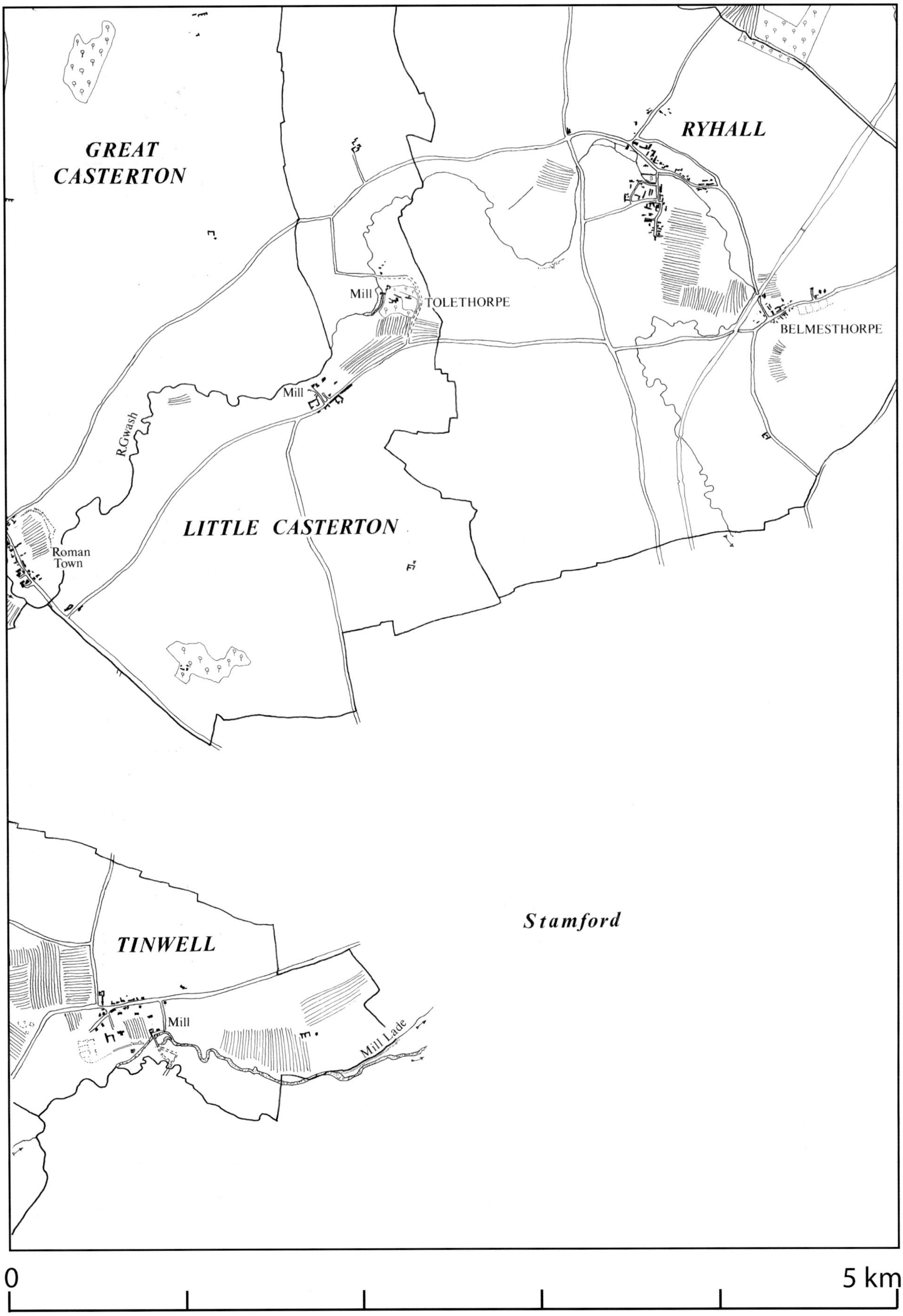

Landscape Map 11: Ryhall, Tinwell, Casterton

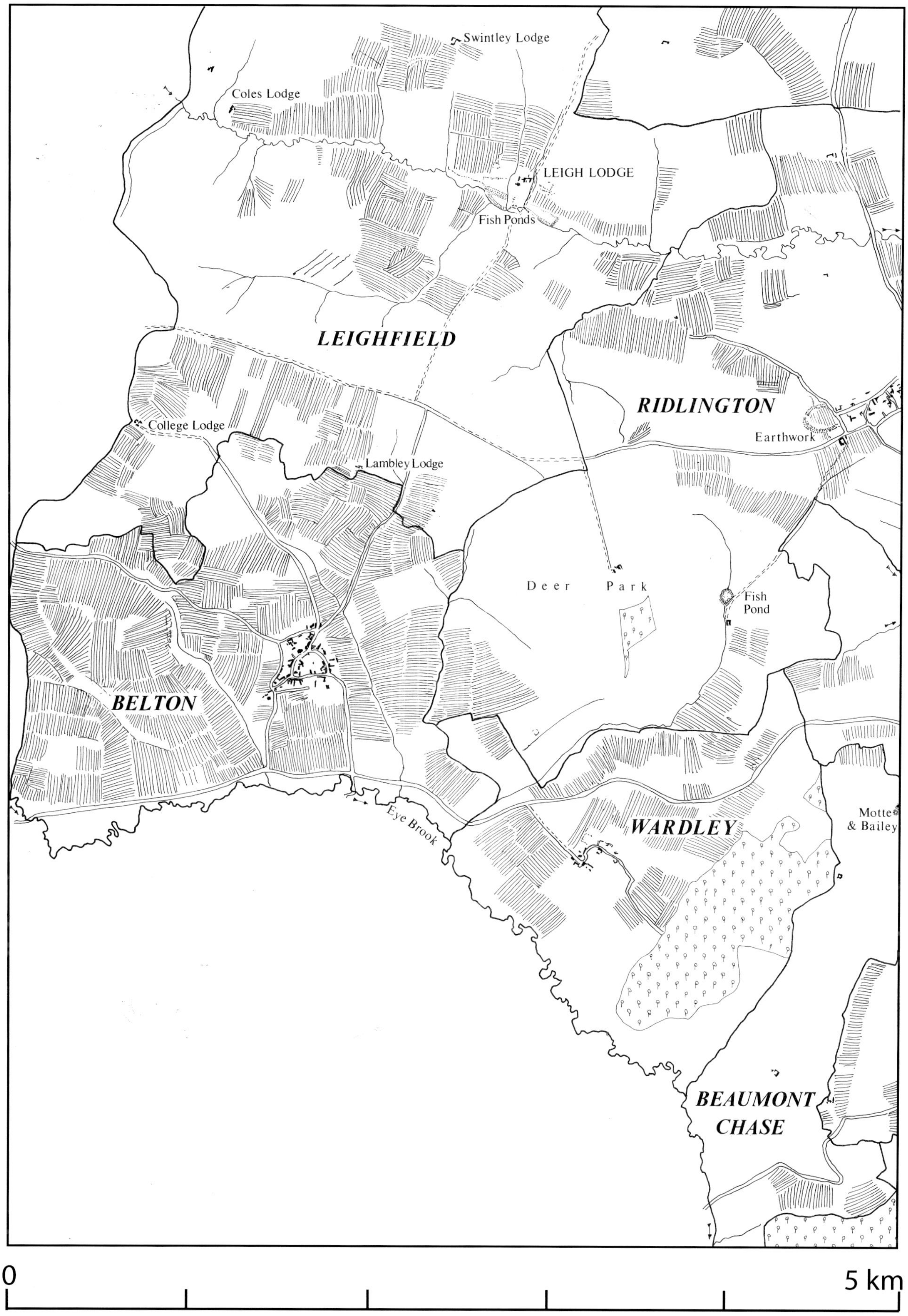

Landscape Map 12: Leighfield, Ridlington, Belton

Landscape Map 13: Uppingham

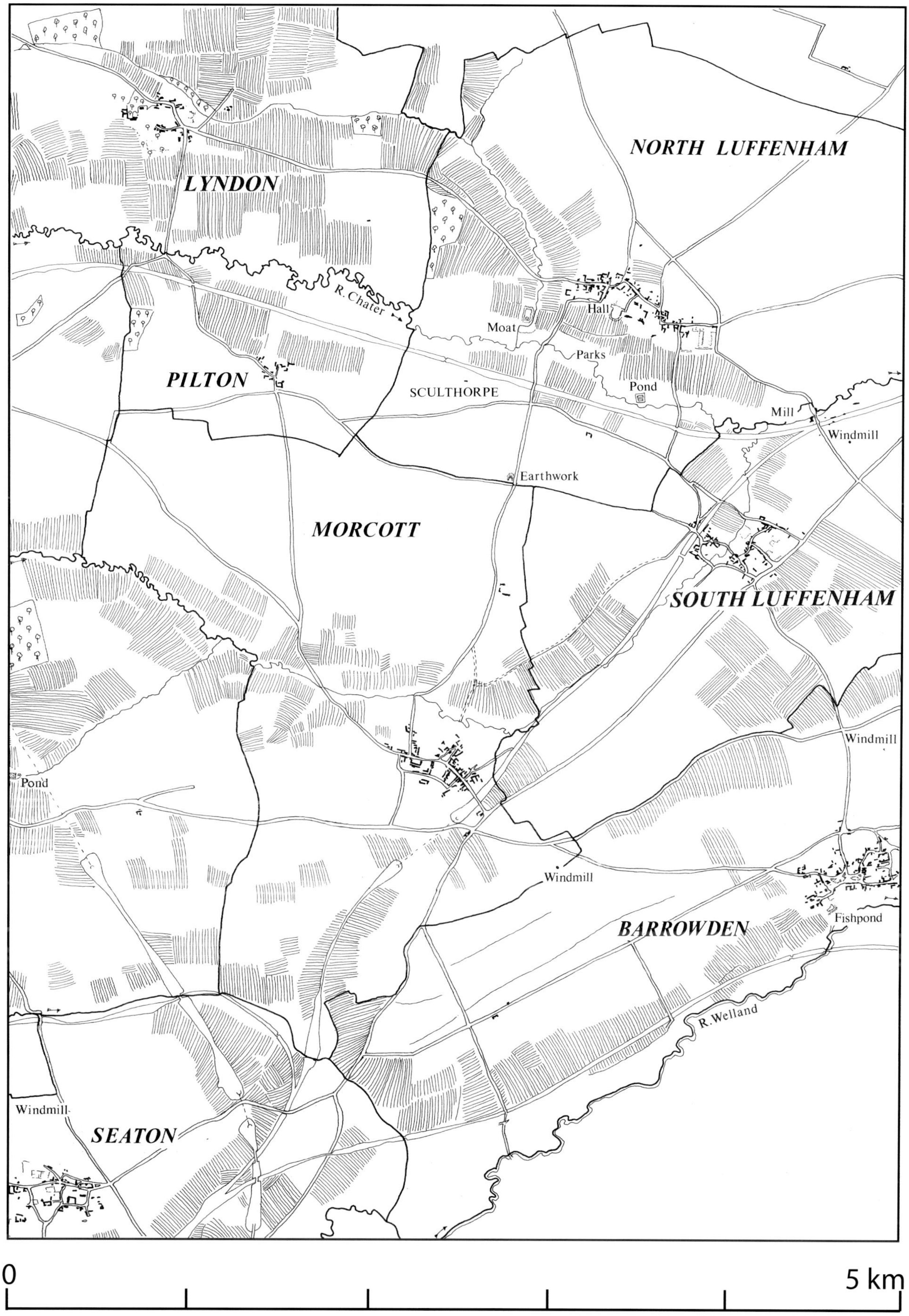

Landscape Map 14: Seaton, Morcott, Luffenham

Landscape Map 15: Tixover, Ketton

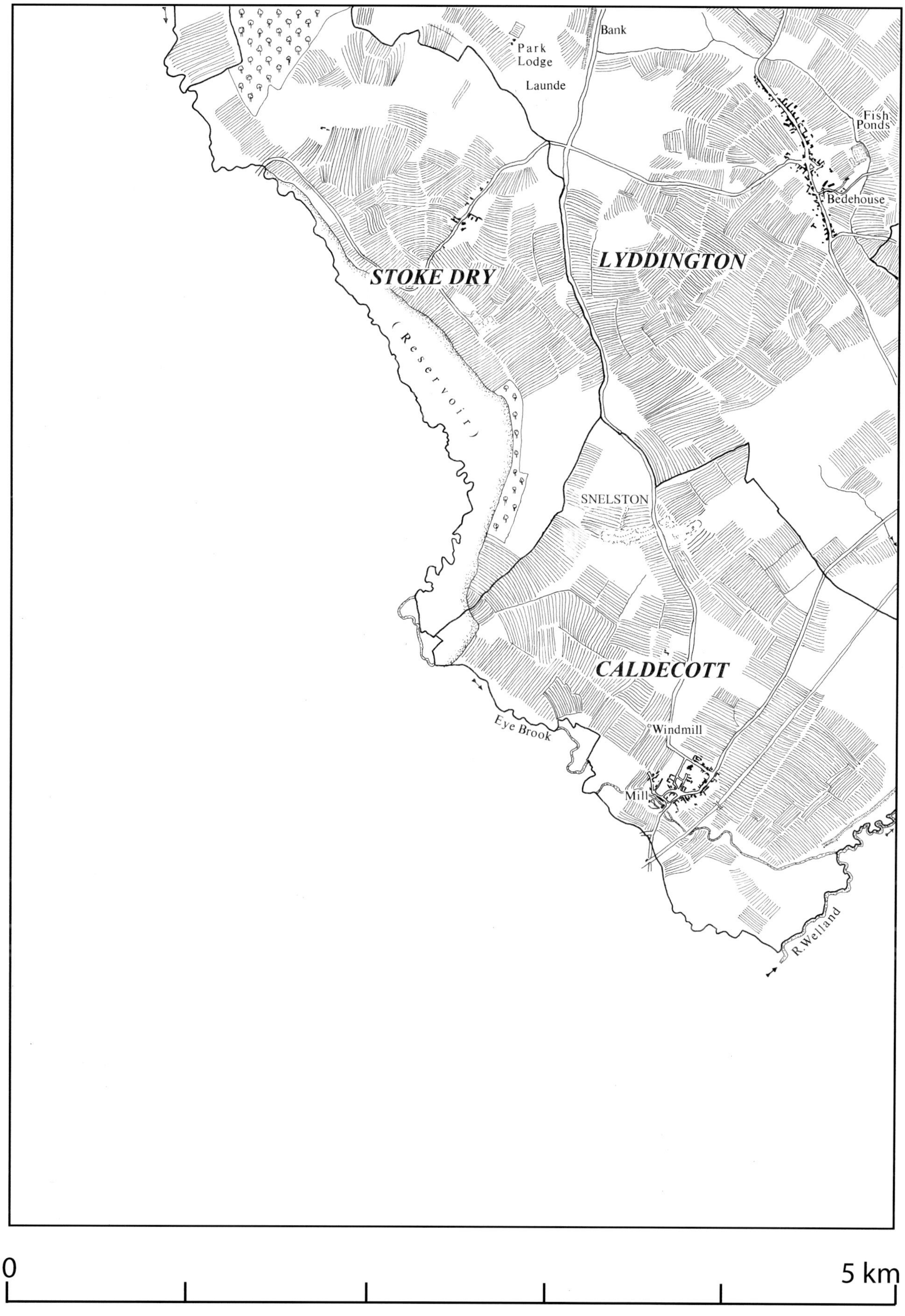

Landscape Map 16: Caldecott, Lyddington

Landscape Map 17: Thorpe by Water

REFERENCES

Bonser, R., 2001. *Aviation in Leicestershire and Rutland.* Midland Publishing: Hinckley.

Blore, T., 1811. *The History and Antiquities of the County of Rutland. Vol 1, Part 2, The East Hundred.* The Author: Stamford.

Brown, A., 1975. *Archaeological Sites and Finds in Rutland – A Preliminary List.* The Author: Department of Adult Education, Leicester University (typed and duplicated).

Brown, A., 2015. 'Ridge and Furrow in Southern Leicestershire' in: Elkin, K., (ed.). *Medieval Leicestershire.* Leicestershire Fieldworkers, monograph No 3, Leicester, 195-204.

Cantor L. M., 1980. 'The Medieval Hunting Grounds of Rutland'. *Rutland Record* 1, 13-18.

Cantor, L. M., 1976-7. 'The Medieval Parks of Leicestershire, II', *Transactions Leicestershire Archaeological & Historical Society*, 52, 73-76.

Cantor, L. M. & Squires, A., 1997. *The Historic Gardens of Leicestershire and Rutland.* Kairos Press, Newtown Linford.

Capp, B. 2010. Vincent Wing and Political Astrology, *Rutland Record* 30, 386-396..

Clough, T., 2007. 'Medieval Settlements at Nether Hambleton and Whitwell', in: Ovens, R., & Sleath, S., (eds). *The Heritage of Rutland Water.* Rutland Local History & Record Society, Rutland Record Series No 5, 421-443.

Clough, T. H. McK., 2016. *Oakham Lordshold in 1787: a map and survey of Lord Winchilsea's Oakham estate.* Rutland Local History & Record Society Occasional Publication No 12.

Creighton, O. H., 1999. 'Early castles in the medieval landscape of Rutland', *Transactions Leicestershire Archaeological & Historical Society* 74, 19-33.

Creighton, O. H., 2000. 'The medieval castles of Rutland: Field archaeology and landscape history'. *Rutland Record* 20, 415-424.

Crocker, John, (ed) 1981. *Charnwood Forest: A changing landscape.* Loughborough Naturalists Club, Sycamore Press, Leicester.

Crosby, A. G., 2017. 'The Lowthers at Cottesmore and Barleythorpe', in: *Rutland Record* 37, 302-314.

Dunning, G. C., Issue 4, October 1936. 'Alstoe Mount, Burley, Rutland'. *Antiquaries Journal* 16, 396-411.

Exton Papers. Ridlington Map DE3214/4606. Estate records: 'A Survey and Mapp of the Whole Manour of Ridlington in the county of Rutland belonging to the Right Hon the Earl of Gainsborough as it was taken in the year 1759 by Edmund Dipper'. In: DE3214 *Records of the Noel Family, Earls of Gainsborough and Viscounts Campden, of Exton, Rutland and Chipping Campden, Glos. 12th to 20th Century.* Record Office for Leicestershire, Leicester and Rutland.

Fox, L., & Russell, P., 1948. *Leicester Forest.* Edgar Backus, Leicester.

Gray, H. V., 1915. *English Field Systems.* Cambridge, Mass.

Hall, D., 1995. 'The Open Fields of Northamptonshire', *Northampton Record Society*, XXXVIII.

Hartley, R. F., 1983. *The Medieval Earthworks of Rutland: a survey*. Leicestershire Museums, Art Galleries & Records Service, Archaeological Report No 7.

Hartley, R. F., 1984. *The Medieval Earthworks of North-west Leicestershire*. Leicestershire Museums, Arts and Records Service, Leicester.

Hartley, R. F., 1987. *The Medieval Earthworks of North-east Leicestershire*. Leicestershire Museums, Arts and Records Service, Leicester.

Hartley, R. F., 1989. *The Medieval Earthworks of Central Leicestershire*. Leicestershire Museums, Arts and Records Service, Leicester.

Hartley, R. F., 2008, *The Medieval Earthworks of South-West Leicestershire*. Elkin, K (ed). Leicestershire Fieldworkers, monograph No 2, Leicester.

Hartley, R. F., 2015. 'Coalmining in medieval Leicestershire' in: Elkin, K., (ed.) *Medieval Leicestershire*. Leicestershire Fieldworkers, monograph No 3, Leicester, 195-204.

Hartley, R. F., 2018, *The Medieval Earthworks of South & South-east Leicestershire*. Elkin, K (ed). Leicestershire Fieldworkers, monograph No 4, Leicester.

Howlett, S., 2007a. 'Barnsdale', in: Ovens, R., & Sleath, S., (eds.), *The Heritage of Rutland Water*. Rutland Local History & Record Society, Rutland Record Series No 5, 45-54.

Howlett, S., 2007b. 'Hambleton: the Settlement on the Crooked Hill', in: Ovens, R., & Sleath, S., (eds.), *The Heritage of Rutland Water*. Rutland Local History & Record Society, Rutland Record Series No 5, 149-191.

Jones, R., 2010. 'Contrasting patterns of village and hamlet desertion in England', in Dyer, C., & Jones, R., (eds.), *Deserted Villages Revisited*. in: Explorations in Local and Regional History, vol. 3, University of Hertfordshire Press, 8-27.

Honeybone, D., & Honeybone, M., 2022. 'William Stukeley and Rutland: antiquities, science and sociability'. *Rutland Record* 42, 70–88.

Knox, R, 2015. 'The Medieval Fortified Sites of Leicesteshire and Rutland'. in: Elkin, K., (ed) *Medieval Leicestershire*. Leicestershire Fieldworkers, Leicester, 123-142.

Mills Archive. https://catalogue.millsarchive.org/ This website is dedicated to research about wind and water mills in the UK.

Pevsner, N. & Williamson, E., 2003. *The Buildings of England - Leicestershire & Rutland*. Yale University Press: New Haven & London.

Pythian-Adams, C., 1980. 'The Emergence of Rutland and the Making of the Realm'. *Rutland Record*, 1, 5-12.

Ryder, I. E., 2006. *Common right and private interest: Rutland's common fields and their enclosure*. Rutland Local History and Record Society, Occasional Publication No 8.

Squires, A., 1992. 'Flitteris and Cold Overton: Two medieval deer parks'. *Rutland Record* 12, 47-52.

Squires, A., 2003. 'The Medieval Park of Ridlington'. *Rutland Record* 23, 105-113.

Squires, A., 2014. 'Leighfield Forest: Woodlands and Landscape in the Sixteenth and early Seventeenth Centuries'. *Rutland Record*, 34, 155-179.

Squires, A., 2015. Leicester forest, it's woodlands and parks, in: Elkin, K., (ed.), *Medieval Leicestershire.* Leicestershire Fieldworkers, monograph No 3, Leicester, 161-193.

Squires, A., & Peat, C., 2020. 'Market Bosworth in Domesday Book: a cautionary approach'. *Leicestershire Historian* 56, 32-36.

Sterndale Bennett, R., 1943 (compiler). *The Field Names of Rutland.* Ordnance Survey Maps of Rutland annotated with field names. Copies in the ROLLR and Rutland County Museum.

Trollope, Rev. E., 1858. 'Notices of Ancient and Medieval Labyrinths'. *Archaeological Journal*, 15, 217-235.

Wacher, J., 1963-4. 'Excavations at Martinsthorpe, Rutland, 1960'. *Transactions of the Leicestershire Archaeological and Historical Society*, 39, 1 -19.

Wing, John. 1710. . Northamptonshire Record Office, Map/4372. Photostat copy of an Exact Map of Pickworth Lordship in the County of Rutland. Surveyed by John Wing, Surveyor. Cartouche of the lands belonging to the Earl of Exeter. (Orig. in MSS of Marquis of Exeter)

Wright, J., 1684. *The History and Antiquities of the County of Rutland.* Bennet Griffin, London. (download available from Google Books).

ABBREVIATIONS

ROLLR - Record Office for Leicestershire, Leicester and Rutland, 38 Long Street, Wigston, LE18 2AH

NRO - Northamptonshire Record Office, Wootton Hall Park, Mereway, Northampton, NN4 8BQ

VCHR - Victoria County History of the County of Rutland: Vol I, 1908. ed Page, William. Constable & Co, . Vol II, 1935, ed Page, William, Constable & Co. Index, 1936. ed Salzman, L. F. Oxford University Press.
Vols I & II are available for download at the internet archive via https://archive.org/ and an online version of Vol II is available at https://www.british history.ac.uk/vch/rutland/vol2

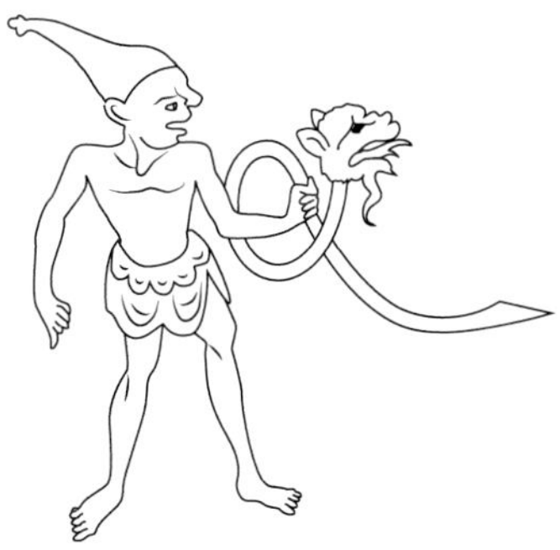